Critical Theory at a Crossroads

Critical Theory at a Crossroads

Conversations on Resistance in Times of Crisis

EDITED BY

STIJN DE CAUWER

COLUMBIA UNIVERSITY PRESS

New York

Columbia University Press
Publishers Since 1893
New York   Chichester, West Sussex
cup.columbia.edu
Copyright © 2018 Columbia University Press
All rights reserved

Library of Congress Cataloging-in-Publication Data
Names: Cauwer, Stijn De, author.
Title: Critical theory at a crossroads : conversations on resistance in times of crisis /
edited by Stijn De Cauwer.
Description: New York : Columbia University Press, 2018. | Includes bibliographical
references and index.
Identifiers: LCCN 2018014924| ISBN 9780231186780 (cloth : alk. paper) |
ISBN 9780231186797 (pbk. : alk. paper) | ISBN 9780231546836
Subjects: LCSH: Critical theory. | Power (Social sciences)—Europe. |
Political participation—Europe.
Classification: LCC HM480 .C743 2018 | DDC 303.3094—dc23
LC record available at https://lccn.loc.gov/2018014924

Columbia University Press books are printed on permanent and durable acid-free paper.

Printed in the United States of America

Cover design: Milenda Nan Ok Lee

Cover photo: Leon Neal / © Getty Images

Contents

Acknowledgments

This book has come out of the activities of the interdisciplinary IdeaLab on the topic of biopolitics formed at the University of Leuven in Belgium in 2014 and funded by the Academische Stichting Leuven. Funding for this book and conducting the interviews has come from the Academische Stichting Leuven, the Department of Literary Studies and the Faculty of Philosophy of the University of Leuven, and the Research Foundation Flanders (FWO). I would like to thank the different interviewers and translators, Joost de Bloois, Tim Christiaens, Sven Fabré, Erik Meganck, Gert-Jan Meyntjens, Jolien Paeleman, Heidi Peeters, Massimiliano Simons, Evelien Van Beeck, and Arne Vanraes, as well as the different interviewees and other contributors, Tariq Ali, Zygmunt Bauman, Rosi Braidotti, Wendy Brown, Roberto Esposito, Maurizio Lazzarato, Angela McRobbie, Jean-Luc Nancy, Antonio Negri, Jacques Rancière, Saskia Sassen, and Joseph Vogl, for generously lending us their time and insights.

I also would like to thank Lydia Azadpour for correcting the first draft of this book and Sarah Warren for correcting later drafts of the book.

Furthermore, I would like to thank all the following people, in no particular order, who in one way or another were helpful in the making of this book: Bart Philipsen, Anneleen Masschelein, Judith Butler, Mia Hamels, Clarissa Colangelo, Mateusz Burzyk, Jonathan Sholl, Kim

Hendrickx, Gert Meyers, Rudi Laermans, Daniel Blanga-Gubbay, Angela Mengoni, Jeroen Verbeeck, Jens De Vleminck, Michiel Rys, Sonja Lavaert, Juliana Barbi Almeida, Jeremy Bell, George Bruseker, Michael Jaworzyn, Nataliya Nesterova, Ena Gojak, Una Blagojevic, Matthias Somers, Jonas Rutgeerts, Laura Smith, Sjoerd van Tuinen, and Michele Fiorillo.

Finally, I would like to thank the editors of Columbia University Press, especially Wendy Lochner, Caroline Wazer, Lowell Frye, Marisa Lastres, and Robert Demke, for their assistance with the publication of this book, as well as the anonymous reviewers of the book for their suggestions.

This book is dedicated to the memory of my father, Boudewijn De Cauwer, who passed away on April 17, 2017.

Introduction

Resistance in Times of Crisis

STIJN DE CAUWER

In the past years, we have seen one crisis situation following another at a fast pace. Especially since the global financial crisis of 2008, the term "crisis" has never really disappeared from the headlines. We have seen the financial crisis, with housing bubbles and investment banks ruining themselves with toxic speculative mechanisms, requiring bailouts from the state. We have seen the ongoing crises of sovereign debt in different European countries accompanied by austerity regimes. In countries such as Greece, the standard of living has been reduced in a catastrophic way, shattering the idea that the European project is one of steadily growing prosperity. We have seen a never-ending and almost farcical series of summits and crisis meetings with hapless European leaders and diplomats, unable to make sound decisions or to overcome the lack of mutual solidarity between EU member states. We have seen the arrival of hundreds of thousands of refugees fleeing atrocious wars in Syria and elsewhere, causing identitarian anxieties and nationalist reflexes. A series of events, from the debt crisis to the Brexit referendum, has brought the European Union as a construction into an increasingly deepening crisis, to the point that its future is now questioned. The populations of different countries feel increasingly alienated and disenfranchised by the present political structures, expressing their disenchantment in an occasional referendum or by voting for grotesque, opportunist politicians. Terrorist attacks have been followed by the imposition of far-reaching security measures, lockdowns of cities, and poorly planned military actions. In the United States, the continuing police violence toward black citizens has caused widespread anger and indignation, with parts of the population expressing that the situation is insufferable and that they "cannot breathe." As one crisis situation follows the next, the governing structures are often too indecisive, incompetent, or dysfunctional to cope with the magnitude of the problems they are facing, but nevertheless a series of "exceptional measures"—cutbacks, border closures, travel restrictions, expanding the use of surveillance techniques, etc.—is being imposed.

At the same time, the past years have seen the rise of a diverse series of new protest movements, as well as experiments in how to conceive political resistance. The havoc wreaked by the financial markets and investment banks caused people to occupy public squares and experiment with assemblies as a form of democracy in practice, which became the trademark of the Occupy movement. The disenfranchised youth of Spain gathered in 2011 on the Puerta del Sol in Madrid and other city squares to express their indignation about austerity measures, enormously high youth unemployment figures, and the extent to which the political structures in Spain were an extension of the banking and financial system that caused the crisis. The Indignados movement in Spain gradually changed from having an emphasis on practices of direct democracy and collective decision-making in assemblies into the political party Podemos, winning important political positions. In Greece, SYRIZA, an amalgam of smaller left-wing parties, was able to channel the anger about the austerity measures imposed on Greece by the European Union and the PASOK and New Democracy governments. Partly due to popular figures such as Alexis Tsipras or Iannis Varoufakis, SYRIZA was able to form a government and organize the much-discussed referendum in which the Greek population voted a resounding *oxi* to the austerity deal proposed by the delegates of the European Union. However, in an almost Shakespearian twist, the SYRIZA government decided to implement the proposed austerity measures anyway, causing a rift in the party and a decline in their popularity.

Starting in Tunisia, protestors took to the streets or gathered on squares in Tunisia, Egypt, Bahrain, Libya, Yemen, Syria, Turkey, and other countries to stand up to the dictators or authoritarian structures ruling their countries. The initial demand for political change that marked the Arab Spring, however, found its demise in shameless repression, the retaking of power by the old power blocks such as the Egyptian army, and full-blown wars in Syria and Libya—with Western countries playing a particularly unsavory role, seemingly backing the calls for change while actually arming repressive regimes (Saudi Arabia, Egypt, Turkey, Bahrain) or rebel groups in stalemated armed conflicts (Libya, Syria). We have also seen strong protests against austerity measures and drastic tuition fee hikes in certain countries. Students in Québec and, especially, in Chile have shown the importance of persistence when pursuing one's demands. The combination of cutbacks in the educational system, tuition fee hikes, and the continuing transformation of the organization of the university system according to the model of private companies, with increased administration, dependency on external funding, and constant evaluations, has led to the birth of inspiring initiatives by students and professors in different countries, from the demands for another kind of university in the Netherlands, with student occupations of university buildings, to large student protests in the United Kingdom, Canada, and Chile. Tired of political indecision and constant stereotyping in the public media, refugees have started to organize themselves, for example, in Germany, where groups such as Refugee Movement Berlin, Refugee Protest Camp Hannover, and Lampedusa in Hamburg organized a meeting in Hamburg in 2016 to provide other refugees legal aid and information and to foster cross-national solidarity. When Tunisian refugees protested their lamentable detainment conditions in Italy in 2011, shortly after the Arab Spring had broken out in Tunisia, they used the same slogans as during the protests against Ben Ali (shouting "*Huryia*," or "freedom").[1] In so doing, they emphasized the continuation between their struggle for more freedoms in Tunisia and their demands in Italy, thus challenging the policing of which demands can be made, when and where demands can be made, and who is permitted to make them.

While the past years were clearly an inspirational time for protest movements, with diverse experiments with new forms of political resistance, many of the protest movements have also come to a tragic ending. If they didn't fizzle out due to the waning of momentum, or because the nature of their demands and their organizational form drastically changed, they were often met with brutal repression. If we can derive inspiration from the different experiments with creating resistance movements or political organizations, we have also seen plenty of unromantic examples of how political movements come to their demise. Both these aspects, however, can be equally instructive.

Many of the contributors to this book challenge the function of the term "crisis" in public discourse and in the media. It is remarkable how ubiquitous the use of this term is, while at the same time its use is largely unquestioned. Etymologically, "crisis" derives from the Greek *krisis*, which refers to a turning point in a disease: the moment when a disease can turn either toward a recovery or toward death. *Krisis* is related to the verb *krinein*, which could be translated as "to make a judgment," "to discriminate," or "to make a decision." Over the course of centuries, the term "crisis" has been used in many other contexts besides the original medical one, gathering diverse connotations along the way. Such connotations include legal connotations (judgment in a trial), the use of the term in a military context, and the use of the term in social, economic, or cultural contexts, such as in late-nineteenth-century economic crisis theories or early-twentieth-century theories about the crisis of cultures. In English, the term "crisis" was adopted in nonmedical domains from the seventeenth century onward. Giorgio Agamben has also pointed out the theological use of the term, such as in the Last Judgment. It is precisely because of the ambiguous combination of different connotations, such as medical, legal, and social ones, and the implicit slippage between them that the term "crisis" has been able to become such a powerful trope, gaining traction in the most diverse domains and discourses. The different connotations also provide the term with specific rhetorical effects, such as suggesting an organic or processual character. In the interview with him in this book, Joseph Vogl, for example, finds the use of the term refugee "crisis" a misleading term to use to refer to the catastrophic situation of the refugees. It falsely suggests an organic, wave-like process, while the situation is completely man-made.

Some of the scholars in this book claim that, in recent years, the use of the term "crisis" has become inflationary, meaning everything and nothing. Rosi Braidotti points out that, in the theoretical humanities, one crisis after the next has been pronounced. Crisis has always played a central role in Western philosophy and she agrees with Gayatri Chakravorti Spivak, who claimed that crisis has always been the modus operandi of Western reason. However, Jean-Luc Nancy suggests that something has changed in recent years in our use of the term "crisis." According to him, the very idea of crisis itself has entered into a crisis (*la mise en crise de l'idée de crise*). Jacques Rancière remarks that, in the past decades, economically, there has always been one form of crisis or another, so "crisis" simply refers to the "regular" mode of operation of capitalism. Though its use has become inflationary, the term "crisis" plays a crucial role in contemporary modes of governance.

When the term "crisis" is evoked, it is generally to set up the conditions to impose different kinds of exceptional measures, often on a semipermanent basis "justified" by the urgency, for which different rights and freedoms, as well as the general functioning of the democratic institutions and practices, are suspended. By emphasizing that a situation is a crisis, measures can be installed that under normal conditions would not be accepted by the general public or that, at least, would be met with much resistance. A crisis situation is often an "opportunity" to introduce far-reaching mechanisms of control, cutbacks, or practices of large-scale extraction of resources, such as in the kinds of "crisis management" following natural disasters like earthquakes. The "crisis situation" allows for the bypassing of the usual protocols of democratic control, decision-making, or public debate. In a public lecture given in Athens in 2013—in what is considered to be the birthplace of democracy, at a time when the elementary principles of democracy had to make way for the crisis measures imposed by the European Union and the IMF—Agamben points out the role of crisis in a new form of governance: "Not only in economics and in politics, but in every aspect of social life, the crisis coincides with normality and becomes, in this way, just a tool of government."[2] A society ruled by this kind of governance is, according to Agamben, not only not democratic but also no longer political. By continuously creating a state of exception, government, Agamben claims, has taken the form of a constant coup d'état. The term "crisis" plays a crucial role in what some have described as postpolitical or postdemocratic forms of governance. Similarly, in an online collective publication by the New Keywords

Collective, the authors remark that evoking a "refugee crisis" has always been part of the way the European Union manages its borders.[3] Furthermore, if "crisis" designates a state of "sickness" that requires a "doctor" to make a sound "diagnosis" or "judgment" and to prescribe the right "medicine," then it becomes immediately clear that the evocation of the term "crisis" goes along with the attempt to claim and designate authority. Whoever proclaims a crisis often implies that he or she also knows the right "recipe" to get out of the crisis, if only their advice is followed swiftly and without hesitation. In the interview with Jacques Rancière, he remarks that the ones proclaiming to be the "best experts" to manage a crisis caused by capitalism often will prescribe more of the same measures that caused the crisis in the first place—creating a vicious circle. Thus, crisis becomes a tool to continue the exploitative and destructive process of shameless accumulation of capital.

Does all this mean that the term "crisis" is at best a hollow term ubiquitously used in meaningless ways and at worst a trope to justify questionable forms of governance? Do years of acquiring medical, legal, military, theological, social, cultural, philosophical, and economic connotations make the term suspect to use? Or can the term "crisis" still be used to evoke a situation of great urgency requiring people to get together, organize themselves, and use the momentum to build a movement with specific demands for change? Can the term "crisis" be used to, for example, point out the urgency of certain situations that our political leaders largely seem to ignore, such as global warming and other environmental crises, or humanitarian crises largely ignored by the media? Or is framing certain catastrophes in terms of a "crisis" already playing into the hands of those who want to gain control of the situation, often with the help of certain NGOs, many of which have always relied on an alarmist discourse?

Whether we see the term "crisis" as a tool in a mode of governance, as the modus operandi of a certain kind of reason or as a trope with specific connotations used to frame a certain situation, it would be a big mistake to merely shrug one's shoulders every time the term is used. The term "crisis" has always been linked with the capacity to make judgments, to assess a situation, to "read the signs," or to diagnose the symptoms. It is linked with the capacity to discern, to name, or to distinguish. Nancy clarifies that during a crisis, something is revealed.

Symptoms are revealed that should not be condemned or repressed, but interpreted. As Joseph Vogl points out, "crisis" and "critique" have always been complementary. Every time the term "crisis" is evoked, there is a struggle about how to "read" a problematic situation. What parameters and concepts are used? How is the problem formulated and which questions are raised? Which causes of the problem are discerned and which solutions are proposed? Though certain people deploy the term "crisis" to frame a situation and to close off different possible assessments of the situation and the diversity of solutions—as in the notorious phrase so popular in neoliberal political discourse, "there is no alternative"—these descriptions of the crisis situation always invite contestation. The rhetoric about crisis, used to impose dubious "exceptional measures," should be met with alternative assessments, concepts, and presentations of the situation. Other questions should be formulated and different projections of the future should be proposed. Not only is "another future possible," but so are other assessments of a "crisis situation" and this is an important struggle if the Left wants to regain the traction it seems to have lost. A "crisis situation" is an invitation to sharpen our capacity for judging a situation, to propose different concepts, theories, and narratives, and to invent alternative solutions to the attempts to manipulate the anxieties, uncertainty, and suffering of the people by different political fractions. However, in the past years, academic "critique" has been under attack from many sides. Not only has it been under threat because of the cutbacks in the funding of academic programs, but academic critique has also been declared redundant—it has allegedly "run out of steam," to borrow Bruno Latour's expression,[4] or, even worse, it has been accused of providing the current "postfactual" Right with powerful rhetorical tools, or of being unknowingly congruent with the ideological operations of neoliberalism. Our times have been called "postcritical"—a time in which there is no more place for the lofty or utopian aspirations of critical theory. Though a debate on the current state of critical theory is of course always welcome and even necessary—and I hope this book will contribute to that—it is not surprising that the same people who claim that "there is no alternative" in times of crisis also hope to bury academic critique, especially when we recall that Edward Said described "critical consciousness" as "an unstoppable predilection for alternatives."[5]

In the past decades, as Jacques Rancière says in this book, there has been a victorious hegemony of the Right in the public discourse in terms of the concepts, theories, and analytical frameworks adopted to assess the political-economic situation. Much speculation has already been provided about the possible reasons for the inability of the Left to formulate credible narratives and alternatives for the larger public. The transformation of European social democracy into "third way" Blairites and the labor reforms they introduced in countries such as the United Kingdom, Germany, and France, as well as their role in the most neoliberal policies of the European Union or the IMF, has done great damage to the credibility of the Left in proposing alternative analyses of the current state of society. The entire social-democratic project has never been able to overcome the fact that it is now associated with people such as Tony Blair, Dominique Strauss-Kahn, Jeroen Dijsselbloem, or Gerhard Schröder, though with the election of Jeremy Corbyn as leader of the Labour party, the British Labour members at least gave a sign they have had enough of the Third Way transformation of the party. As the financial crisis was raging, as the European project was crumbling, and as the European Union was imposing the harshest social destruction Europe has experienced in decades in Greece, there was no social-democrat politician to be found who spoke out on the situation in a clear and credible manner. The socialist parties were far too implicated in the current national and supranational political structures, the banking world, and the governments whose policies had paved the way for the financial and European crisis to be able to offer a credible critique of the situation. The capitulation of the European social democracy to a more (neo)liberal and entrepreneurial rhetoric about society and the economy has been instrumental in the gradual installment of a hegemony of the Right in the political debates in the public media. At the same time there has been fatigue about the strategies adopted by the unions—with increased demonizing and stigmatizing campaigns targeting strikes or people receiving unemployment benefits—and large NGOs. It is partly because the power of the traditional Left has waned and because the Left has lost a lot of its prominence in public debates that, every time there is a "crisis situation," people turn to critical thinkers and critical academics as a source of counterarguments to the hegemonic framing of the "crisis." As opposed to the iterations of the "there is no alternative" mantra, certain critical thinkers still manage to get other opinions, questions, concepts, and analyses out to the public, whether by means of opinion pieces, texts circulating online, interviews in the media, speaking at public events, books that sometimes are unexpectedly widely discussed, or the classroom. If the use of the term "crisis" invites "critique," then it is often critical academics who take up this task of critique.

There is the risk that we expect too much from "public intellectuals"—that we treat them as oracles who have to provide us with clear suggestions and directions for what to do. In the interviews in this book, the limits of what a critical academic can offer are also clear. They are not in a position to provide grand sweeping answers and solutions or to provide recipes for a political course to follow that would be guaranteed to be successful. Moreover, this position of an "oracle" who has to provide clear answers and solutions also goes against the political and theoretical standpoint of some of the critical academics, sometimes putting them in a paradoxical situation. Politically, certain critical thinkers would find it unsound to tell people what they should do from their specific position as an academic. They want to provide their views and analyses of a situation, but, ultimately, what kind of politics and organizations certain groups of people want is something they have to decide for themselves. Theoretically, many critical thinkers would be skeptical of providing a theoretical framework that "fits all situations." Their concepts and analyses change over time, and political ideas will have to be tried and tested in concrete situations, and, if necessary, be adjusted or discarded, no matter how important persistence or a certain kind of "fidelity" to ideas and principles might be.

At the same time, we should be wary of a phrase that has become commonplace, namely that academics "do not give answers, but formulate the right questions." This seems to be a cop-out when it comes to clearly speaking out, and "formulating the right questions" once and for all would be equally as dubious and deluded as "providing the right answers" once and for all. What critical thinkers can do is to expose and to question the framing of a problem. In doing so, they open up once again the possibility of formulating other questions, interpretations, hypotheses, and projections of desirable outcomes. One of the premises of this book was to ask, point-blank, the opinion of the interviewees on certain contemporary issues, and especially on the different protest movements we have seen coming and going the past years. What do they think of the strategies that were chosen? Were they well conceived or did they have a problematic approach from the start? Which new possibilities did the protest movements reveal? What inspiration could be drawn from them for future political action, or which mistakes made should be avoided in the future? To avoid the fact that interviews with academics sometimes remain too abstract or theoretical, the interviewers in this book all chose to ask these questions bluntly. Of course, most critical academics would be skeptical of becoming just mere fodder in the daily stream of easy opinions that keep the infotainment mill turning. Reducing the complexity of a certain phenomenon to a simple judgment about whether one is for or against something is anathema to the very idea of critical thinking. Yet, all the scholars interviewed in this book do have outspoken opinions, and we aimed to find a good balance between careful reflection and unambiguous, clear opinions. The opinion pages of newspapers and the social media are rife with middle-of-the-road opinions and the originality and sharpness of the scholars in this book should not be reduced to that.

Most of the interviews in this book were conducted in early 2016. That means they were conducted before important political events such as the Brexit referendum in the United Kingdom and the election of Trump, though some of the interviewees have continued to revise the transcript of the interview months after the interview took place, which explains why some of them do refer to events that took place more recently. The world has been quite accustomed to unsavory antics of important politicians, from the drunken ramblings of Boris Yeltsin to the shameless pompousness of Silvio Berlusconi. For eight years, we heard George W. Bush struggle with the English language. But this was before *the Donald* entered the presidential scene. Presidential statements are now tweeted, spelling errors and blatant lies included. American foreign policy is now whatever Trump feels like blurting out this week. After the eloquence of Obama, Trump has won the elections with a campaign fueled by hate speech, crude misogyny, demonizing and targeting minorities, "alt-right" conspiracy theories, and declaring the mainstream press to be "fake news." Many have wondered whether the election of Trump has caused a huge shift in the political coordinates, from the relations of the United States with Europe, Russia, and other parts of the world to Trump's "economic nationalism." Or was Trump merely the result of dynamics that have been going on for a long time, gradually undermining the American democracy, such as commercialized news stations that are only interested in what gives them high viewer ratings?

Events such as the Trump presidency and Brexit have certainly marked political debates. The people who voted for the United Kingdom to leave the European Union or for Trump to become president were allegedly motivated by a deep distrust and resentment toward the existing political structures and "liberal elites." The people who have been left disenfranchised by globalization and the increased marketization of every aspect of society expressed their hatred for "Washington" or "Brussels" in their vote. The rude way of speaking of Trump is perceived as a license for the people to no longer feel "silenced" by the "politically correct elites," who "condescendingly" say that the views of some people are racist or amount to hate speech. In the United Kingdom, politicians systematically repeat that "the people have spoken." When those who lament Brexit point out how questionable and misleading the information was that was disseminated during the campaign, they are called "bad losers" and "saboteurs." Any attempt to hold the people accountable who voted for Trump, UKIP, Front National, Alternative für Deutschland, the Partij voor de Vrijheid (PVV), or any other right-wing party campaigning with openly xenophobic discourse is now immediately accused of not respecting the concerns of "the people," such as when Hillary Clinton referred to a part of the Trump voters as "deplorables." Evoking "the people" is once again a powerful tool in the rhetoric of both government and opposition parties, which has brought once again to the fore the debates about the meaning of notions such as "the people," "populism," or "democracy." As Wendy Brown points out in the interview with her in this book, if democracy means the self-rule of the people, then populist movements can also be at odds with democracy. Some populist movements do not want more self-rule of the people or a more inclusive politics, but, on the contrary, to increase the power and sovereignty of the leaders of the country, not of the people. Moreover, as Judith Butler has described in her recent works, any evocation of "the people" amounts to a speech act that also excludes certain groups of people from belonging to "the people."[6] Just like the European debt crisis or the arrival of Syrian refugees, the election of Trump has once again manifested the importance of asking the question of what a democracy is, who "the people" are, and which excluding effects evocations of "the people" entail.

For this book, we have consciously tried to interview critical thinkers who come from different disciplines, who focus on different aspects of the present, and who propose diverse concepts. As the reader will notice, some of the interviewees defend opinions that are in disagreement with the views of other interviewees in this book. These disagreements are productive for reflection. The different approaches, focuses, and backgrounds allow for a sufficiently diverse picture of the massive problems caused by the current stage of global capitalism. In all the interviews in this book, one question figures prominently: What political action should be undertaken to counter the huge problems that some try to frame by calling them a "crisis"? What kind of organization or form should political action have in our present situation to be most effective? In the remainder of this introduction, I will explore some issues or contradictions that frequently recur in the debates about political action, including in these interviews, and I will provide some general suggestions to move beyond these contradictions.

Of course, we expect critical thinkers to provide strong opinions. We expect them to clearly speak out about certain issues and to take an unambiguous stance about a certain issue. We expect them to be squarely for or against something. We expect them not to waver about taking a position—if necessary, a controversial position. We appreciate it when someone dares to advocate a point of view that will evoke a lot of public derision, even from the Left, such as when Tariq Ali states that he no longer can see any value in the European Union in its current shape and defended voting against staying in the European Union in the referendum about Brexit. Going against what seems to be the common opinion, also the progressive and leftist public opinion, is a part of "critical thinking." However, complex problems are often framed and reduced in the media and public debates to a choice between two options, and the complexity of the issue is narrowed down to a false binary choice. In fact, the best way to manage and control a complex situation is by reducing it to a choice between two, often two undesirable, options. Sometimes, the choice is formulated such that one option has to be chosen to avoid an even worse outcome. Philippe Pignarre and Isabelle Stengers have astutely named this "infernal alternatives."[7] Make your labor and environmental laws less strict or companies will relocate to another country. Impose heavy cutbacks in social spending or everything will collapse in chaos. A striking example of this was the cynical slogan "vote for the crook, not the fascist" ("Votez escroc, pas fasho"), used in 2002 when the two French presidential candidates were François Chirac and Jean-Marie Le Pen. This is of course an attempt to shut down all political reflection by presenting something as a nonchoice.

This often-impossible binary choice becomes an apparent problem with referenda or elections. The complexity of the issues the European Union is facing, not to mention the question of national sovereignty in times of globalized capitalism, cannot be reduced to a question like the one asked to the British citizens: Do you want to remain in the European Union or not? Some people who voted to stay in the European Union also find the European Union in its current state dysfunctional and problematic and would be of the opinion that it needs to be significantly reformed. Some people who voted to leave the European Union do not want their vote to play into the hands of xenophobic politicians or a small group of conservatives who want to rekindle a sense of English nationalist pride. The bigger issues at stake in such a vote—for example, the feeling of the decreased global significance of the United Kingdom after the decline of the British Empire, or the reasons why a large segment of the population feels disenfranchised—are left undiscussed, while political parties receive a budget to campaign with blatantly false information. A similar issue occurs in the debates about a president or a government perceived to be "on the left," such as the diverse governments in South America in the past decade. Many people identifying themselves as leftist feel the obligation to back certain politicians or governments in the same way one backs a team in a football game. Pointing out their mistakes and questionable policies is perceived as playing into the hands of the opposition, all too ready to denounce and oust the current government. Reducing the complexity of a situation to a questionable choice between two options is a much-adopted tool for those who want to call something a crisis to impose dubious exceptional measures. It plays into the hands of those who want to claim that "we have no other choice," and that "there is no alternative." It will be the task of critical thinkers to question the conditions and the framework in which a certain problem is posed, including the reduction to a choice between two nonalternatives. Finding the right balance between questioning the frame in which a problem is posed and taking a clear stance on specific issues or in specific situations (such as elections or referenda) is a challenge any critical thinker who wants to speak out publicly will have to face.

This brings us to another recurring issue, namely, at what level should we seek to form an effective countermovement? Political effectiveness is often solely located at the level of governments or the state. But a politics of the Left has increasingly been concerned with finding a genuine way of being democratic or "horizontal" in its manner of organization and decision-making. Here we can see maybe the most divergent opinions among the interviewees in this book. How to combine a form of political organization that is sufficiently effective and powerful, not restricted to a small-scale, local situation, with a sufficiently horizontal, inclusive form of political organization will be one of the biggest challenges for future leftist political movements. More and more countermovements locate their democratic and egalitarian ideals in their practices of organization and decision-making, such as in the famous assemblies. As techniques of horizontal and inclusive decision-making, they were already adopted for the organization of activist networks (for example, Peoples' Global Action) and protest camps by the antiglobalization movement (such as the big "protestors' village" in Annemasse during the G8 summit in Evian in 2003), but they became truly a central principle for movements such as Occupy, the Indignados in Spain, or the Nuit Debout gatherings. The political ideals are directly put to work in the very practices of organizing and forming the protest movement. This view often goes hand in hand with a lot of skepticism of politics at a state level, or of the hierarchical organization of many NGOs, unions, and political parties. Several prominent critical thinkers such as Alain Badiou regard the state as nothing else but a mechanism to facilitate market mechanisms and big capital. Presidential elections, or elections in general, are false choices between candidates with slight differences, but none of them would fundamentally alter the system.

In this view, state politics, with all its media display, spin, and personality cult, distracts citizens from the spheres where political agency is actually located, namely, in daily practices and the practical organization of social movements.

However, though horizontality remains an ideal, or the point of departure, in the view of Jacques Rancière, in the past years, we have seen more and more the limits of the assembly approach. There is a danger that techniques intended to organize other, more effective forms of protest in a horizontal manner become fetishized for their own sake. It is also often forgotten that assemblies might *seem* like the most inclusive form of organization, but this may not necessarily be the case. Not every segment of the population feels equally compelled to join an assembly, and the outreach of gatherings with assemblies is rather limited. There is also the problem that the transition from very localized forms of organization to one bigger, national or transnational, more powerful movement is not easy to achieve. Mostly, one is confronted with the problem of how to remain faithful to the horizontal principles when switching to another organizational structure, such as a political party. This issue was clearly visible in the transition from the gatherings of Indignados, who were maybe the most successful and inspirational in their use of decision-making via assemblies, to Podemos, but also in the organization of the huge World Social Fora.[8] This is also the problem faced by the movement that Iannis Varoufakis is trying to form to democratize the European Union.[9] Several interviewees in this book clearly express their disenchantment with the tendency of action groups to remain too local, not being able to form a much bigger, transnational movement with clear demands and with much greater capacity to make an impact. Different action groups remain too concerned with their own local issue or situation and do not manage to form a transnational movement with the power to reach out to a larger part of the population, and thus to become a much stronger force to be reckoned with. At the same time, several scholars, such as Angela McRobbie, warn against giving up the state too quickly, since many forms of solidarity mechanisms are still organized at a state level, and giving up on that level altogether might amount to giving up the level at which the organization and defense of many important solidarity mechanisms take place, as well as other social mechanisms.

This problem of horizontality and how to construct a bigger movement in a sufficiently horizontal way is connected to a series of related
concerns. One of them is the question of timing. There is often a conflict between action groups who believe that one should seize the
moment, make use of the feeling of urgency that is sometimes present
after a critical event, and those who believe that one should not allow
oneself to be rushed into forms of political organization that will disappear again shortly after being formed, that one should take the time
and effort to slowly build a movement for the long term. The momentum when the anger and indignation are high after a critical event is a
very powerful thing that no protest movement can afford to ignore.
However, one has been able to witness that, over and over again, the
momentum of protest movements fades out after some time, after
which the movement basically disappears. The choice to make horizontality a priority often implies that one opts for the slow construction of
a movement.[10]

A second issue that is connected to the problem of horizontality is
what one considers to be the "political" factor in a protest movement.
Does one want to scream out indignation about a situation, attract
media attention, disrupt a summit, or put pressure on a government or
a head of state, or does one seek the political effectiveness of one's movement in the concrete practices of collective organization, decision-
making, and setting up spaces where ideas can be shared and expressed,
and forms of solidarity organized? Especially the thinkers who locate
political agency either in the sphere of affects or in the domain of the
aesthetic place the locus of political struggle in common daily practices.
For example, Lauren Berlant has described the contemporary forms of
neoanarchist political organization as practices in which the "political"
is redefined.[11] Politics is not regarded here in terms of a future ideal, but
it is achieved in concrete practices of community-building and setting
up solidarity practices. Here, politics is located in the affective construction of a community by means of modest gestures and practices.
Politics is what one *does* and the goal is in the concrete practices one
sets up on a daily basis. At the same time, she is aware of the fact that
locating politics on this level of affective daily practices might mirror
the "neoliberal orchestration" of our political emotions, "producing dis-
tractions that inflate the relative importance of the *sense* of belonging

in relation to dealing with the hard questions of distributing resources, risk, and vulnerability in the polis."[12] Locating politics on the level of affective gestures might be too negligent of the bigger national and transnational political structures in which hugely important decisions are being made.

Of course, these same neoanarchist groups, in all their diversity, do not limit themselves to only local, small-scale community-building practices; they have also been largely responsible for raising the awareness of, and active resistance against, large global organizations such as the WTO, the IMF, the World Bank, the European Central Bank, Wall Street, the World Economic Forum in Davos, the diverse meetings of world leaders such as the G8 summits, and large lobbying meetings, as well as trade agreements from NAFTA to TTIP. From Seattle to Blockuppy in Frankfurt, neoanarchist groups have sometimes managed to confront large, powerful transnational organizations more effectively than more "traditional" political fractions, such as political parties, unions, or NGOs (though, of course, certain NGOs and unions were seminal in offering their resources and mobilizing power to the large protests of the antiglobalization movement in Seattle, Genoa, and elsewhere). Slavoj Žižek has rejected the attempts to seek political agency in the sphere of affects—claiming that they confuse forms of sensational self-absorption with effective political struggle—as well as the attempts to locate politics in the sensible as a desire for "pure politics."[13] Both could be regarded as ways to avoid doing the hard struggle to concretely change political structures and policies, which often involves getting implicated with difficult choices and the unromantic wheeling and dealing of the existing political structures. This question often arises when a horizontal movement, or a part thereof, wants to take part in parliamentary politics and potentially join the government. In this case, the horizontal structure is often replaced with a more or less standard party structure, with party leaders, coalitions, compromises that have to be made, forms of corruption, and political intrigues. The question then arises whether a political movement has lost its defining principles, a question that arose with the transition from the Indignados to Podemos in Spain, with the formation of the SYRIZA government in Greece, and with the Lula-led government in Brazil, which could not avoid the existing levels of corruption.

A third issue that is related to the problem of horizontality is that of the extent to which one considers certain existing structures, from global capital to the European Union, as structures that are simply unavoidable or unchangeable and that one can never escape. The feeling that certain existing structures simply cannot be escaped from, changed, or abolished—such as capitalism itself or the current form of the global economy with its rules of competition—has caused many critical thinkers to seek political effectiveness not in the common political structures and struggles, but in increasingly abstract and ephemeral suggestions: calls for negative acts such as forms of withdrawal or Bartleby-style refusals, concepts so abstract that they amount to wishful thinking or messianistic hopefulness, and thinkers turning to an obscure past—such as monastic rules in the case of Agamben—to find possible acts of resistance. The level of abstraction of some of the suggestions put forth by certain critical thinkers or the calls for very defensive gestures as the rare remaining locus of resistance come out of the fact that one has given up on the very idea that big political structures or global capitalism itself could ever be changed through political struggle. While increasing abstraction or purely negative gestures are one consequence of giving up on traditional political struggle, another effect is the overly optimistic belief in certain affective gestures to be effective. To give one example, Brian Massumi writes, playing with the image of global capitalism as a bull: "Add a Frisbee to the bull. We can be the wind. We can throw the bull a curve. I mean, we can throw it a gesture that inflects its course, just as a gust inflects the path of the Frisbee. Make the bull gaseous. Wind it onto another path."[14] Though these kinds of statements about affective politics are attempts to bring people out of a feeling of impotence and despondency in the face of massive global structures and powers, and Massumi adds that, "politically, things are never as simple as a bull in a ring,"[15] they might go too far in the direction of wishful thinking about the effectiveness of small gestures. Locating political agency *primarily* in art or in performance is another symptom of giving up on confronting large powerful structures through direct political struggle, however valuable art and performance may be for political action.

Several interviewees in this book adopt the view that an effective political struggle will have to be a combination of a struggle at two (or more) levels: one level is the formation of social movements, and the second level is the level of the existing political institutions, such as governments, the state, or transnational structures such as the European Union. One could call this, as Negri does in this book, a horizontal and a more vertical movement. These two movements have to reinforce each other. Though the social movements will always be the main driving force of political organization, it would be too much of a loss not to try to have one's demands implemented at the level of the governing institutions, even if this implies adapting one's principles to the often-questionable rules and practices of institutional politics. Conversely, attempting to win political struggles only at an institutional level, as political parties try to do, will never succeed without having a sufficiently large social movement creating the pressure and the demand for changes. One should also not make the mistake that, after transforming a protest movement into a more institutional political structure, such as a party, the entire dynamic of the protest movement fades away and everybody just looks to what will happen (or not) at the institutional level. We have seen all too often that the strange shenanigans of a progressive political party that won elections on the hope of a lot of people end up disappointing the people so greatly that they become disillusioned about any form of political struggle. SYRIZA has been a painful example of this process. When strategically endorsing a certain presidential candidate or a political party, one should never forget to continue the struggle after the election has been won. Social movements and action groups have to keep up the pressure on those with a mandate, and, reversely, social movements can help politicians to push through certain policy changes.

One final issue I would like to address is the problem that any critical thinker or protest movement should be aware of: the fact that one's theories, concepts, or chosen strategies can unwillingly and unknowingly play into the hands of the forces one is trying to fight. We are all familiar with the critical analyses that regularly appear such as Luc Boltanski and Eve Chiapello's *The New Spirit of Capitalism* or Nancy Fraser's *The Fortunes of Feminism: From Women's Liberation to Identity Politics to Anti-Capitalism*, in which the authors show that certain concepts or theoretical approaches adopted by critical theorists at a certain point in time end up being recuperated or playing into the hands of the flexible and changing strategies adopted by neoliberal politics.[16] One of the most debated topics in activist circles is what one now calls in a derisive manner "identity politics." After the New Left gradually discovered the importance of the struggle of diverse minority groups that were previously not so much on the agenda of traditional leftist politics, the strategies adopted by certain advocacy groups has sometimes unwillingly played into the hands of the governing principles of neoliberalism, and caused heated debate within the Left because of the sometimes overly high-strung political correctness, amounting to a form of self-censorship. The current forms of neoliberal politics gladly appeal to the different minority groups asking for recognition as long as they drop the demand for fundamental societal and economic changes. Politicians from left to right will endorse gay movements and call themselves feminist as long as the groups they are trying to please do not demand a more just form of social, political, and economic organization, and as long as their demands and aspirations fall within a standard consumerist and entrepreneurial economic model. Angela McRobbie has formulated a poignant critique of this consumerist, postfeminist rebranding of feminist demands for social change and justice.[17] She has also sharply analyzed the rhetoric about creativity taken from the artistic world as a form of labor reform by stealth, forcing people to become entrepreneurs of themselves while the social security network and different forms of social programs are being cut.[18] The current protests in the United States against extreme police violence and the way the responses to different terrorist attacks reveal that some victims are deemed more worthy of mourning than others—not to mention the openly racist and misogynist rhetoric of Trump and the rise of various white supremacist groups in the United States and elsewhere—clearly show how important it is to struggle against racism and systematic discrimination. Nevertheless, one should remain aware of how certain political tactics such as certain forms of identity politics can be recuperated.

The same problem arises in many situations of mass popular protest. Sometimes a well-meaning large protest movement can accidentally play into the hands of the imperialist and geopolitical interests of large global powers, who will overtly or covertly back, fund, and arm those factions that will most likely lead to an outcome that is in their favor. We have seen recent examples of this in Syria, Egypt, and Ukraine, where the popular protests trigger responses from very powerful countries, power blocks, or oligarchs, who try to thwart the outcome of the situation in a direction that is most opportune for them, if necessary by bringing in foreign armed fighters and stirring up an armed conflict with devastating consequences. A similar concern for large protest movements is the way they are presented in the mainstream media. Sometimes protests become a sensational media spectacle like any other. Images of protests dominate the news while, a few weeks later, the same media (along with the general public) is no longer interested in the political situation in the country where the protests took place. The hype that the media creates around, for example, the diverse protests that made up the Arab Spring is followed by a complete lack of coverage of the situation in countries such as Tunisia, Libya, or Egypt after the protests are over. In this sense, like anything else, protests become sensationalist media fodder: partly hyped up one day, completely forgotten shortly thereafter. The media will of course also strongly frame certain protests. They will enlarge "spectacular" elements such as scenes of violence, enigmatic spokespersons, or photogenic situations that lend themselves to becoming iconic. Some protests are presented as positive while others will be derided for being nothing more than violent, chaotic, or lacking a clear goal. There is a danger that protesters themselves believe the hype, followed by the disappointment and the deflation of the hype at a later stage. Thus the sheer enigmatic momentum of a movement glosses over the actual demands of the protests and "falling in love" with certain characteristic features and slogans of a movement buries the constant reflection required on the tactics being used.

There is also the danger that we are allowing our focus and our enthusiasm to be framed too much by the popular media, which chooses to sensationalize certain protest movements for a period of time, especially when they match the liberal phantasms of what popular protests should be, and largely ignore the diverse movements that operate in different parts of the world, but that generally remain out of media attention and public awareness, for example, indigenous struggles for the common governance of land and resources, protesting the policies of extraction even by presumed left-wing governments (such as in Bolivia, Ecuador, and Peru), the self-organizing of landless farmers (such as in

Brazil), the struggles for food sovereignty or communal forms of farming (such as in Mexico or India), the struggle for common forms of education or open access to information, and so on. The alternative practices and new subjectivities produced in these struggles remain mostly out of the media spotlight, creating a false impression that a "wave" of protests appeared and faded out again. All this should, of course, not lead to resignation, but we should all document and learn very well the different strategies adopted in public discourse and in the media to frame, thwart, and recuperate a situation. Learning to recognize these strategies, being able to anticipate them, and having enough savviness to adapt one's chosen tactics and interventions are crucial skills for the formation of future protest movements and a task for critical thinkers. Judith Butler has pointed out "that 'the people' are not just produced by their vocalized claims, but also by the conditions of possibility of their appearance, and so within the visual field."[19] Who counts among "the people" and who does not also depends on the capacity to be "recognized" and appear in the media. If this is the case, "then 'media' is not just reporting who the people claim to be, but media has entered into the very definition of the people."[20] The struggle over media framing and representation is also a struggle one can never avoid, however tiresome and frustrating this may be, and setting up good alternative forums for sharing information will remain very important in this struggle.

To conclude, I would like to derive from this discussion a few general suggestions:

1. We should always confront the terms in which a situation is framed, especially when the term "crisis" is evoked. We should not let others dictate the terms and analytical framework of a situation. The terms of the debate have to be questioned and other concepts, analyses, and presentations have to be put forward.

2. A political struggle should be conducted on different levels, without fetishizing one level only (such as a presidential race or a very localized action group). There should be a strong interaction between the construction of local struggles, broader social movements, and attempts to influence governing structures, however frustrating that might be. We should not completely neglect certain levels because it might seem

hopeless to change them. At the same time, the bigger a social movement making certain demands is, the more leverage there is for those attempting to change things at the level of governing, national and transnational, institutions. There are plenty of historical examples of large powerful structures that were forced to cave in and implement certain policy changes or change their own structure due to popular pressure.

3. We must remain aware of the problems with certain forms of identity politics and the way they can be recuperated. But, at the same time, we should always remain aware of the specific sociological context of a protest movement and which demographics it appeals to. We must remain cautious of the fact that any protest movement is a situated practice that can appeal more to certain segments of society than to others. Sometimes it is too easily presumed that one's organization form is inclusive.

4. We must always keep on reflecting about our chosen tactics, concepts, and public interventions and not turn a certain tactic into a fetish, valuable for the sake of itself. Sometimes the context can change and certain tactics and concepts end up playing into the hands of the powers we are trying to fight. We should always remain critical and reflective about our chosen tactics and evaluate whether they are still appropriate and effective for the current context.

5. We must remain savvy about the way media frames the protest movement and its demands, and the way it can turn a protest into a spectacle. We must never cease to counter these framings and must present our own forms of information and presentations of a situation. For this, the development of alternative media and information forums remains important.

6. Any future leftist movement will always aspire to be as "horizontally" organized as possible. Though this will be best achieved by having protest groups that are embedded in local communities and that are set up by the people through collective decision-making, we must also try to transcend this local situation and try to form bigger, transnational alliances. Only a sufficiently large movement will have enough weight to change things. We can take inspiration from the ways the antiglobalization movement and the Occupy movement have tried to form transnational alliances and solidarity (as well as learn from their

failures). The prime challenge for the Left will be in finding a way to combine local organization, decision-making, and embeddedness with the formation of transnational alliances into a more global movement with clear demands shared by heterogeneous local groups.

7. Nothing will ever change unless we have enough persistence in our struggles and demands. Only when we persist in keeping up the pressure can a change be achieved. Without persistent pressure, nothing will ever be won.

Notes

1. See Martina Tazzioli, "Discordant Practices of Freedom and Power of/Over Lives: Three Snapshots on the Bank Effects of the Arab Uprisings," in *Biopower: Foucault and Beyond*, ed. Vernon W. Cisney and Nicolae Morar (Chicago: University of Chicago Press, 2016).
2. The title of this lecture was *For a Theory of Destituent Power* and it was delivered in Athens on November 16, 2013. The full transcript of the lecture can be read on the website of ΧΡΟΝΟΣ: www.chronosmag.eu/index.php/g-agamben-for-a-theory-of-destituent-power.html.
3. http://nearfuturesonline.org/europecrisis-new-keywords-of-crisis-in-and-of-europe/.
4. Bruno Latour, "Why Has Critique Run Out of Steam? From Matters of Fact to Matters of Concern," *Critical Inquiry* 30 (Winter 2004): 225–48.
5. Edward W. Said, "Traveling Theory," in *The World, the Text, and the Critic* (London: Faber and Faber, 1983), 247.
6. Judith Butler, *Notes Toward a Performative Theory of Assembly* (Cambridge, MA: Harvard University Press, 2015).
7. Philippe Pignarre and Isabelle Stengers, *Capitalist Sorcery: Breaking the Spell*, trans. Andrew Goffey (Basingstoke, UK: Palgrave Macmillan, 2011), 23–30.
8. In a conversation with Chantal Mouffe, Iñigo Errejón of Podemos explains that he does not agree with the view that first social movements have to be built before one can build political parties. He also finds that it is wrong to claim that the various left-wing governments in South America came out of the gradual accumulation of power by social movements. In his view, the social movements were often in decline when there was an electoral success. Errejón is of the opinion that the social is always built by the political and that electoral processes can be a strong force in mobilizing and unifying people. As he writes: "As I think is the case with us, it was electoral competition which started to produce a bond and a new political identity, around new leaders and symbols." Iñigo Errejón and Chantal Mouffe, *Podemos: In the*

Name of the People, trans. Sirio Canós Donnay (London: Lawrence and Wishart, 2016), 51.

9. DiEM25: https://diem25.org.

10. Michael Hardt and Antonio Negri point out that though the constructing of a "constituent" movement is a slow process, this does not exclude the construction of what they call "counterpowers" to act up against issues that are very urgent. Michael Hardt and Anontio Negri, *Declaration*, self-published, distributed by Argo Navis Press, 51–54.

11. Lauren Berlant, *Cruel Optimism* (Durham: Duke University Press, 2011), 260–62.

12. Berlant, 262.

13. Slavoj Žižek, *The Parallax View* (Cambridge, MA: MIT Press, 2006), 55, 320.

14. Brian Massumi, *The Power at the End of the Economy* (Durham: Duke University Press, 2015), 53.

15. Massumi, 57.

16. Luc Boltanski and Eve Chiapello, *The New Spirit of Capitalism*, trans. Gregory Elliott (London: Verso, 2005); Nancy Fraser, *The Fortunes of Feminism: From Women's Liberation to Identity Politics to Anti-Capitalism* (London: Verso, 2013).

17. Angela McRobbie, *The Aftermath of Feminism: Gender, Culture and Social Change* (Los Angeles: Sage, 2009).

18. Angela McRobbie, *Be Creative: Making a Living in the New Culture Industries* (Cambridge: Polity, 2016).

19. Butler, *Notes Toward a Performative Theory of Assembly*, 19.

20. Butler, 20.

Critical Theory at a Crossroads

A Critical Europe Can Do It!

Interview with Rosi Braidotti

Let's start with the notion of "crisis" itself. It seems that for you, coming from a Spinozist and feminist perspective, the very notion of "crisis" is already problematic. From a Spinozist perspective, it's all about creation and affirmation, and from a feminist perspective, there are many reasons to be very skeptical about the very idea of "crisis." Those who are supposedly "in crisis," whether from a sociopolitical or economic perspective, are clearly gendered: it is usually the Western male subject that is "in crisis." Would you even endorse a notion like crisis?

Well, a crisis is not always critical, and chaos is not necessarily chaotic. However, "crisis" has been a constant in philosophical discourse, from the early days of poststructuralism and antihumanism, through various attempts to reconstruct whatever we were deconstructing: crisis of "Man," crisis of "Woman," crisis of European hegemony, crisis of colonialism, of the concept of equality, etc. Of course the same people who are involved in the crisis are also saying: "But it's not really a crisis, it's also an opportunity." Gayatri Spivak said it very sharply in the middle of the "Edward Said–Michel Foucault" controversy of the late 1970s: "crisis" is the modus operandi of Western reason, which continues to be hegemonic even in its weak, "postmodern" way. It really starts with Socrates, if we follow Derrida's analysis of the *pharmarkon*.[1] There is a sense therefore in which "crisis" is both ubiquitous and meaningless, and what is genuine and productive about the state of crisis is the processes of transformation and change it entails. I have not been alive at any other point in time, so I can't generalize, but having reached the age of sixty now, I feel that I've lived through multiple historical eras and time zones,[2] spanning from the late nineteenth century, through the "short" twentieth[3] into the twenty-first century. I remember a world without television, a world without mobile telephones, and it is by now a sociological truism to say that the speed of technological transformations is breathtaking. I think a lot about these enormous social and also symbolic disruptions because I see thinking as taking place in the world, not (only) in classrooms. So, many discourses about the "crisis" of the traditional cultural and intellectual categories and values—take European humanism, for instance—are simply a set of adjustments to real-life upheavals. They may be genuinely disruptive for some, but totally generative for others. I remember a conversation with my dear friend Matthew Fuller, in which I was outlining the state of exhaustion of philosophical thought throughout the 1990s, only to have him point out that new media studies, cyberculture, cyberfeminism, and artistic practices associated with technology in music, art, and antiart exploded with incredible theoretical vitality in the exact same period. The critique of humanism was a comparable explosion for my teachers, way back after May '68. The entire generation of the poststructuralists lived through and took to heart the crisis of humanism, and—by the way—they all paid a heavy professional price for it. These intellectual giants are still criticized or even dismissed for being anarchical, relativistic, and even amoral. The academic and social establishment, safely ensconced at the heart of the panopticon, does not take kindly to people who proclaim the crisis as a productive state, take accountability for world-historical events, and offer a theoretical translation of them. It is one thing to be "socially responsible" according to the neoliberal ethos, but quite another to think critically about the present. The two positions are often opposites.

The poststructuralist generations responded ethically and conceptually to the convulsive political transformations following the end of the Second World War, then of the Cold War and decolonization. They took stock of the consequences of the end of European hegemony and of the American century, next to the irresistible rise of media and technology. I think this accountability for the present is the key to the poststructuralists' vision of philosophy as the cartography or diagrams of power. Why do you think they emphasize so much notions like biopower, immanence, *amor fati*, etc.? Paradoxically enough, however (and this is true especially for Deleuze), the conceptual depth of their philosophical response ends up obliterating the very concept of "crisis." Isn't that typical of critical thinking? Two other discourses unfold from the "crisis" but then go their own way. On the one hand, an increased sense of vulnerability and melancholia. On the other hand, the euphoria of willful transformation and quasi-evolutionary optimism. For me, they are equally inadequate, being mirror images of each other. Somewhere in between those two poles, Deleuzian ideas of becoming and my own nomadic variations attempt to find a way of assembling something that would make it possible for us to think critically and creatively. When I reflect back upon this, I often feel we are in the seventeenth century, and maybe I've been in the seventeenth century all my life! I remain positive about our times, not only because I'm a pathological optimist, but also because dealing with the side effects of this ongoing situation, namely, crisis management, basically defines our jobs! As academics, crisis management is what we do all the time, at the institutional level, where we seem to go from one badly thought through university reform—usually just a series of mergers based on standard corporate templates—to the next. And guess what? Every new wave of austerity measures and budget cuts mostly targets the humanities. This type of institutional governance has accelerated as capitalism reinvents itself as a knowledge-based system, gobbling up everything along its way. There's much more to say about this, so we must pick it up again later.

Rhetorically the discourse of crisis is also a leftover from the Marxist vision from the 1970s of history as a succession of socioeconomic breaks, which are expected to result in the overthrowing of dominant ideological and social relations, to pave the way for the new. I speak about this in the past tense, but I know that this hope is still very much alive, in both neo-Leninist and "accelerationist" versions. And yet, the loss of credibility of this vision—as well as its world-historical failings—is also one of the sources of contemporary melancholia. Why else did the generation of my teachers—notably, Foucault and Deleuze—support the switch from Hegel to Spinoza, that is to say, from dialectical binaries to a monistic political ontology? Critical Spinozism was developed in the 1970s precisely as an alternative to the contradictions of Marxism.[4] Deleuze's vital neomaterialism is trying to find a position in between these two post-Marxist poles: the vulnerability/melancholia option and the shallow optimism of neoliberal capitalism ("Just do it!"). Somewhere in between and beyond them lies the monistic and neomaterialist project of constructing transformative change. Sustainability for me is praxis, not a given. And we should not expect philosophical systems of thought to contain all the answers ready to go. Both Foucault and Deleuze defend a practical and active kind of philosophy: you have to actually work to construct possibilities of regeneration and affirmative transformation. For instance, Deleuze emphasizes time and again that the whole point of a complex notion such as "the virtual" is that it has to be actualized—that is to say, activated as praxis. Let us not hide behind discourses of the crisis as a pretext for inaction.

We are having this conversation literally "the day after" the so-called Brexit: the issue of Europe seems to impose itself. In fact, one of the things I was genuinely struck by when rereading your work is the emphasis on "Europe" and "European-ness."[5] What I found remarkable is that there seems to be a kind of double bind. On the one hand, you strongly critique what you call the "sense of entitlement" that comes with the notion of Europe, both on an epistemological level and on a political level. Our thinking, our philosophies remain profoundly Eurocentric. On the other hand, you do continue to plea in favor of a certain idea of Europe, a "post-Eurocentric Europe." In the context of the recent Brexit, it seems that what we see today is a relapse of sorts, not into even a "Eurocentric Europe," but into European nationalisms. It is as if we are witnessing a return to a sense of entitlement that is not even European but national entitlement, or perhaps European entitlement disguised as national entitlement. I was wondering how you envision Europe, in this context of emerging populism and neonationalism?

It's a great question and you're completely right, it's central to my work. Very sensitive of you to pick it up. Europe is a knot of contradictions— Where should I start? A certain idea of Europe as being able to criticize itself lies at the core of critical theory. I do think, however, that the

European roots of critical theory have been in trouble since colonialism and then the Second World War. All the roads lead back to fascism, the unexplored institutional but also theoretical long-term implications of the Second World War, the Holocaust, the genocidal aspects of our culture. In philosophy, the historical and intellectual event of fascism was particularly devastating, and I believe we haven't yet worked out the full implications of what it meant then and the long shadow it casts over our practice even now. Just think of what it meant for European science, philosophy, and the arts—not to speak of cinema—to destroy the European Jewish community.

There are so many questions here: Why was Nietzsche put on a black list after the end of the Second World War, and Heidegger—who never repented for his Nazi collaboration—wasn't? Let's look again at what happens to European, French, and German philosophy after the war. France has Sartre and Beauvoir as the moral conscience of the nation and the critical leading lights for the entire European continent. The moral and theoretical status of French philosophy throughout the postwar years is enormous, also because the rest of the European intellectual landscape was devastated, our ranks depleted by the war and the Holocaust. Think of the lucid pages that Zygmunt Bauman writes on the moral bankruptcy of fascist Europe and of course Levinas with his analysis of the "Kantian" dog! The Frankfurt School, led by Jürgen Habermas, attempts a sort of rescue and revival operation: the revival of new-Kantian universalist premises, coupled with the importation of American social and moral theory. The point is to support the efforts to de-Nazify not only his country, but the whole of Europe. How to disinfect the European psyche, trying to return philosophical thinking to some human dignity after Auschwitz, that was the question! This has been essentially the project of this great wise man who simply had to hold on to humanism because he wanted to hold on to the hope of Europe's spiritual and philosophical survival—as do I, by the way, but not through humanism. And that is also what the Allied forces and the Americans wanted Europe to hold on to in the context of the Cold War. Our value systems embraced humanism in opposition to Soviet barbarism. This oppositional Cold War context prevented, however, a serious analysis of the fallout of European fascism. My students today do not even know that the Berlin Wall on the Eastern side was called the "antifascist barrier." We have erased all that from our collective memory, as part of the "end of history"[6] phase after 1989, and that is a pity.

This is not the case with the French, however, and this is where French philosophy plays a unique and crucial role. Foucault's attack on humanism in the announcement in 1966 of the "death of Man"[7] is a moral and political condemnation of the hypocrisy and equivocation that dominated the debate on the intellectual roots of European power—both material and discursive power. Power that had a lot to do with a supremacist, nationalist approach best expressed in fascism and colonial domination. The critique of reason and scientific rationality emerges from this moral indignation about European deeds—as opposed to our ideals. It comes down to the profoundly anti-Kantian notion that reason and horror are perfectly compatible, that "vigilant and insomniac rationality"[8] breeds monsters and that the constitutive link between reason and violence needs to be acknowledged and exposed. Michel Serres adds to this insight the disenchantment he experienced after the events of Hiroshima and Nagasaki.[9]

Thus, the "moment" of French theory grows from this in-depth critique of a self-congratulatory idea of Europe as the "home" of "human" rights. But what is the notion of the human implied in this humanism? It is a masculine, white, Eurocentric, heteronormative, urbanized, able-bodied, "legal residents–only" vision of the human. The critique starts right there! And this has nothing to do with relativism and all to do with situated perspectives. But paradoxically, as you rightly point out, this is also how the European critical spirit, for better or for worse, is kept alive. It gets expressed through the double critique the poststructuralists produced of liberal individualism and Western democracies—in terms of their democratic deficit—but also of Soviet communism and its despotic and genocidal character. They look to anticolonial struggles and national liberation movements, notably in Algeria. For the left-leaning Cold War youth of Western Europe, "Neither with the USA nor with the USSR!" was our slogan. Foucault, Deleuze, Derrida, and the rest of Althusser's students of the 1970s were advocating and in many ways preparing the post–Cold War worldviews in a philosophical effort to go beyond binary thinking. This is where the turn to Spinoza's monism or antidualism originates. I'm not saying that out of a superficial sense of European authenticity, but because those critical tendencies, which have been and still are of vital importance, are also in terrible trouble: we are always on the verge of losing them. The erasure of a critical notion of Europe starts with fascism—let us never forget that the Nazis burned the books of Marx, Freud, and Darwin as enemies of European civilization, before they proceeded to kill and burn millions of humans. But the process continues throughout the 1970s, as we sort of lost sight of Europe as a point of theoretical or genealogical reference and, after 1989, practically turned our backs to it.

It is well known but often forgotten that the de-Nazification of Europe, coupled with our de-militarization, is the historical and intellectual root of the European Union. It channeled much of the energy of those who aspired to a "third way" between the two geopolitical blocks. Without forgetting, of course, the economic aspects. During the Cold War that meant we had to showcase the West. After 1989 the European Union showcased the largest and allegedly most free democratic economic block in the world. Mindful of this history and its consequences, I want to build a self-critical European space and I think critical theory is the perfect tool for it.

From very early on in my youth, I have been a European federalist and embraced the European Union as the antidote to Eurocentrism and nationalism. I read the whole project of the European Union with the texts of the founding fathers, notably the first European commissioner, Altiero Spinelli, and his wife and intellectual partner, Ursula Hirschmann. I hope to see a revival of interest in these pioneering figures today. The vision has always been necessary to construct the European Union as the place that is capable of reelaborating its own history and thus will be antifascist, social-democratic, and open to all kinds of freedoms of movement. I know, I know . . . I can feel your skepticism from afar, but do consider for a moment the advantages of the political project of a postnationalist Europe[10] and contrast it with the return to hypernationalist "sovereigntism"[11] at both national and regional levels across this continent. Which one would you rather have? Just to make it clear, this is how I would put the case for the European Union: as a site of criticism, as a critique of Europe's hegemonic past and mind-set. Against shallow triumphalism, I fear that we're forgetting our history. Foucault said it: Europe has to be the place that is historically condemned to reflect on its history. I am in dialogue with Étienne Balibar

on this point: Europe is the place that has elaborated on the consequences of its worldly actions.[12] We can't afford to be amnesiac, and
that tendency is very strong right now.

But the critique of Eurocentrism from within Europe has many different genealogies: sure, there is the philosophical antihumanism and
the political critique of fascism, but fundamental for my work are feminism and anticolonialism. "We" don't believe in the old imperial Europe
that, let's face it, left the center stage of history a long time ago! Anti-
and postcolonial thinkers, like Fanon, Said, Césaire, Glissant, stress this
point with breathtaking lucidity. They dream of a cosmopolitan Europe
where diversity rules and humanism does not equate domination, "statist realism," or supremacism. Think of Stuart Hall's vehement critiques
of the rise of the Right in the European Union, combined with the swell-
ing of racism and xenophobia.

The problem of forgetting the roots of European critical theory has
been particularly acute in political movements like feminism and
LBGTQ+, especially after 1989. I have always pushed for the European
tradition in issues of emancipation and sexual liberation, also in the
making of European women's studies.[13] We have a long tradition in this
continent of explicit discussions about the body, embodiment, and sexuality that have nothing to do with the puritanism of American culture.
Foucault rightly says it: We have never been Victorians! We have other
problems, but not this particular one. And here again, historical events
like colonialism and fascism have created different forms of state feminism, linked to advanced bio- and necropolitical mechanisms of sexualized, racialized, and naturalized domination.[14] We need to study them
as complex phenomena, not dismiss them a priori.

Besides, European culture, notably France, has an established tradition of libertine thought not only in literature, with Sade and others,
but also in critical theory, with towering figures like Bataille and Pasolini. We should not forget them. In 1989 these critical roots come under
renewed attack, as the United States declares it has won the Cold War
and human history has reached its peak. As Eastern Europe has to be
hastily liberated from the communist mind-set, university curricula
and established canons change swiftly. We need to look more closely at
what goes on then. After 1989, the canonical texts of the American
feminist tradition are spread throughout Eastern Europe as a sort of

antidote to the old stuff. It is a case of democratization, but also of enforced amnesia—a real erasure of the collective memory. Of course, those strong traditions of state feminism in Eastern Europe, for instance, in nonaligned Yugoslavia under Tito and in the Soviet satellite states, were integrated into major forms of authoritarian regimes. I don't mean to forget or condone those aspects, but to try to reach a more balanced view after communism fell apart.

It is dangerous to forget one's political traditions. There is a whole genealogy that needs to be rediscovered. If younger scholars come to me for advice or supervision today, I'm sending them back to the archives, to research a history-genealogy that has yet to be situated, respected, embedded, and embodied without obligatory references to any canonized American scholarship. This is crucial in the present, where everything has to pass through the U.S. filter in order to exist in English.

The Spanish-speaking worlds are freer of this linguistic domination than the Anglophone ones. And they are producing amazing critical theory, as well as new social movements. I am aware, of course, that all theory today circulates and has become traveling theory, not only for those of us living in the opulent periphery that is Europe. Yes, but critical theory cannot be just this flowing exchange of dominant models. We must not allow this political economy to ruin the radical potential of local movements. You see this so clearly in the South of the world today: so much critical thought and political energy!

The French-speaking worlds are also less integrated in the transatlantic axis. What I appreciate about the French philosophical archives is that they do continue to refer to a tradition, say, the phenomenology of the body and discourses about sexuality, but also their history and philosophy of science, their mathematics and epistemology. Too bad that this attachment to their own genealogies takes them occasionally into loops of destructive self-referentiality, as in the laïcité and burkini debate . . . What a letdown that is! But a critical Europe can do it! It is as simple as this: anti-Eurocentric, situated European perspectives are the way ahead. And why? Because we are condemned historically to our history, of success with both old democracies (the Netherlands, the Nordic States) and new democracies (Italy, Spain) that have been democratized in major experiments. And we are all in this, including the Eastern Europeans who are the objects of virulent racist attacks themselves and yet are encouraged by their political leaders to be very aggressively nationalistic against others. We are all developing countries now, we are all struggling to become members of the global international community. And we all have to learn to think differently about what we're in the process of becoming. How many times have I said that?

For me, in spite of its failings, the European Union is an incredible experiment in trying to become post-national, and falling short because nationalism still gets our hearts beating faster . . . The European Union does not make us dream,[15] because nationalism is in our social, political, and psychic system. We need to be detoxed big time. And one of the ways to do this is to learn more from the South, to join in global forces that help us to decolonize our minds, to open up and acknowledge also our partial irrelevance, as well as our great contributions. As a feminist and antiracist, I feel I've been trying to strike that balance all my life.

A federalist European Union is a glorious idea, which became a very flawed project, compromised through the different enlargements and adjustments. Many of these compromises, by the way, were due to the ambivalence of Great Britain, which never shared any of the post–World War II ethical and political premises on which the European Union was built. You could see that very clearly in the Brexit campaign: the dominant social imaginary was the Battle of Britain and the defeat of the Europeans during that war. The other prominent issue was the unwillingness—or is it inability?—of the United Kingdom to let go of a delusional vision of its former imperial self. Since Thatcher, the British have made Euroskepticism into a permanent feature of their work. Their record is appalling: they have sabotaged the project of the *political* union, which I was hoping might start up again after the shock waves of Brexit have settled. (I don't give up easily, do I?) The political union is the answer, so that we can construct a system that works efficiently and comprehensively, not these endless compromises with greedy and profoundly opportunistic nation-states that support and reward micronationalism at all scales. I would like to say to the neonationalist leaders of Poland, Slovakia, Czech Republic, and Hungary today—the Visegrad group—and to the opposition leaders in France, Italy, and Austria: "Come on, read the EU founding fathers' documents: we need more political union, fiscal cohesion, and solidarity!" The situation is far from simple, with, on the one hand, the internal tensions between the European Commission and the nation-states and, on the other, the mixed effects of globalization and the devastation of war. It is very difficult to explain to the former working classes who are still losing their jobs because factories and plants are closing down and moving elsewhere that the problem is China and the BRICS, not only Brussels. If you look at the situation this morning, the morning after the Brexit, it is almost flagrant: 75 percent of the former industrial North of England voted against the European Union, as did plenty of the middle classes in the South of England, while 75 percent of Central London for remaining. It's a class system: the UK establishment is scapegoating by blaming the European Union for their own ruthless neoliberal economics and the ravages of their austerity policies. But what about their youth, my students? They voted massively to remain in the European Union, but their future was jeopardized in a reckless political gamble. In a global world, you can't seriously offer to the young ones a return to parochial protectionism and xenophobic nationalism: How attractive a country would that make?

The question however is, how do we cope with globalization? I think the reality principle has to be straightforward. I'm an educator and a teacher, my problem is my students' prospects and opportunities and Europe protects their jobs! Am I in favor of capitalism? No. Am I a professor looking after her students? Yes! Power is a two-faced structure: one face is repressive, the other is empowering. *Potestas* and *potentia*, as Foucault teaches us, work in tandem. Of course, left-wing Euroskeptics like Paul Mason would say: "The European Union is a neoliberal project, so we must fight against it!" And I would retort: "But the City of London isn't? And Theresa May and before her David Cameron aren't?" This kind of leftist rhetoric is as irritating as it is ineffectual. At least Žižek and Varoufakis have stopped just performing their successful public intellectual shows and have now joined forces to create a radically democratic alternative for Europe.[16] As I grow older, I have become more careful in criticizing so cynically the people who dare to try to govern at times like this. I am not sure that I could be in Angela Merkel's or Christine Lagarde's shoes, and although I do not share their political views, I sometimes admire them for their endurance and skills in governance. And let's not even open the Hillary Clinton chapter!

A great deal of my sense of European-ness has to do with working in a public university, a state institution, where I am a professorial civil servant. On top of that, I belong to the generation that took up "the long march through the institutions" in the 1980s, in an attempt to change them from within. And, of course, the institutions also changed us in the process! All responsible radicals try to strike a balance between the management of what we have (*potestas*) and the pursuit of alternatives (*potentia*). In these days of both right- and left-wing populism, we need to reinvent critical theory with a bit of critical distance from the rhetoric of self-appointed radicals, who always assume they are in charge of the course of history or of the next revolution. We need to invent a different image of thought and of the critical thinker. One has to be a bit more tactical these days: look at SYRIZA in Greece—the moment they went to power, they had to become hard-nosed pragmatists. Podemos in Spain and especially in the municipality of Barcelona is also tracing a complex and careful path. What's the point of reading sophisticated theories if then you fall into political oversimplifications?

I do not know how many hours I have spent going through the two volumes of Deleuze and Guattari's *Capitalism and Schizophrenia*. Their analysis of fascism is of the greatest relevance. So how about we get smarter about this issue and much more savvy. Let us be consistent with this argument and state that the problem is capitalism, not the market economy as such. We need a different market economy; it just doesn't have to be a capitalist one, because capitalism is structurally unjust for people, unsustainable for the planet and actually bad for business, and disastrous for higher education! Even the IMF has recently abandoned the neoliberal model.[17] Obviously the IMF is not saying that out of concern for social justice, but because they are afraid of social unrest and insurrections, but at least they're admitting that it doesn't work. I'd like to add that antagonistic violent political action doesn't work, either. In response to the return of Marxist theories and practices today, I would bring the model of dialectical antagonism much closer to lived experience and daily practice, like the feminist I will always be at heart. We need to embed our protest, make it embodied, situated, and accountable. But, first of all, we must constitute the assemblage, the "we" that is carrying out the project. This capitalist system works because "we" make it work, because we love the technological powers it gives us—and very few of us are prepared to go without our "smart" objects. It actually profits to the detriment of the multiple forms of exclusion that are being implemented. There are other models of market economies available, however. Think of the commons, both digital and others, the alternative globalization movement, the land rights and First Nation peoples' struggle for clean water and land ownership, etc., etc. Some of the alternative models have already been picked up as social experiments: take, for instance, the idea of a universal minimum wage. Several countries have adopted it and are currently experimenting with it, in Finland, the Netherlands, Switzerland. Of course, these are all small and prosperous countries. Great model, though—let's work with it. Suppose we talk to all the people involved in the Panama Papers and bring them to some form of accountability, let us say to them: "Universal minimum wage, how about it? Everyone is taxed, offshore is taxed and we give everybody eight hundred euros a month the world over!" Financially it may be feasible, as Amartya Sen points out, but where is the political will to make it happen? Why not discuss such a different system of wealth distribution, on the road to experiment with alternative models of the market economy. Why go into the repetition of leftist slogans? I can hear skeptical moans, but I will stick to this affirmative mode of thinking.

Having said that, populisms on the right and of the left are the key phenomena of today. And one of the things we need to hold our ground against is the populist Right's vehement anti-intellectualism. Those populist movements are made, like all social movements, of a mixture of idealists, desperados, and opportunists. I am struck and excited about the resurgence of students' movements across the European Union and the United States, but also in South Africa and India. I taught at Columbia University in the early days of the Sanders campaign and all my students were active supporting "Uncle Bernie." Kids living in Brooklyn, hipsters, not all of them poor and all in love with the idea of a socialist revolution, of solidarity. I think some of them equated socialism with caring for others and it was a real epiphany. They shared a sense that the social horizon was closing, because neoliberalism means, in their case, building enormous financial debt, so it is understandable. I just wished they gave Hillary Clinton some credit for her enormous work over the years, though, but the generation gap, plus sizable doses of—often-unprocessed—sexism, separates them. It saddened me a bit, I must admit. On the other hand, the right-wing populism of the likes of Donald Trump and Boris Johnson is such a blatant form of manipulation, it is nauseating. I can't help wanting to approach this with Nietzsche, reread with Deleuze: we have a regime of "posttruth politics" fueled by *negative passions* like resentment, hatred, and cynicism, and they are getting enhanced, constructed, rewarded by a class of manipulators bent on consolidating their own egotistic interests. It is like Derrida says: beware of the suicidal character of democracy![18] It makes me shudder and I am determined to analyze it as a critic, fight it in the classrooms as a teacher, and try to assert a minimum amount of accountability as a citizen. Simple antagonism is not enough, why do you think I wrote so much about the politics of affirmation? We need to come back to this point, because it is crucial for my work.

Populisms for me, whether on the left or from the right, are the same. In the 1930s free citizens democratically voted for the wrong people, leaders who went on to deprive them of basic freedoms and commit atrocities. Now we seem bent on doing it again! There are days when many of us are afflicted by a sense of impending doom: Are we in the Weimar Republic, or what? A lot of commentators are writing on the uses and abuses of the referendum as a tool of government: Isn't representative democracy about allowing our democratically elected representatives to research and pass the suitable legislation to confront the complex issues of the day? Why call a referendum on intricate constitutional issues? I think it would be far more useful to set up a serious educational program, backed by a full-scale information campaign, talking to people and fellow citizens. The dialogical model of the South African "Truth and Reconciliation" commissions should be adopted in the European Union as well. What to make of the fact that the so-called advanced economies fall for "posttruth," while the emerging economies opt for "truth and reconciliation"?

Now, if we look at the economics on a macro scale, at the metadiscourse, Thomas Piketty and Joseph Stiglitz are right: the current (non) distribution of wealth is unjust and unsustainable—we need a new economic model. And higher education is right in the middle of it! I have been watching what has happened to the international research university model—the pattern is clear: let's increase the enrollment fees for the kids from the emerging economies and our problems will be over. So much for the famous "pursuit of excellence"! So how about a university instead that is actually serving a nonprofit, nonexploitative world? Why are the tenured radicals not fighting for that? As a feminist I practice the politics of location—think and act from where you are at, don't do the "God's trick" of speaking from nowhere. As a Deleuzian I think through radical immanence: compose materialist grounds of encounter for ideas and projects that can be shared, avoid generalizations such as the fall of capitalism, and fight instead for its concrete demise through the micropolitics of disassembling its codifying power. This is what Deleuze and Guattari invite us do, by targeting our collective desire for strong leaders and their alleged power. Think also of Maurizio Lazzarato's extraordinary work on debt![19] The point about capitalism is that it doesn't break, it bends. Why? because it's made by "us"—here we go with the constitution of the "we" again—by our labor and intelligence. Unless you have been under a rock for the past thirty years, you will know that it's called *cognitive* capitalism.[20] Of course "we" are not a homogeneous class, but an internally fractured one, with those enormous disparities in access and distribution that many critics rightly denounce.

There are many questions at stake here: the role of what used to be the intellectuals, the end of their sense of estrangement, which has been growing over the years. The much-beloved Gramscian model of the organic intellectual I grew up with cannot be directly adapted to the reality of today. An organic intellectual works alongside a social and political movement, providing intellectual insights, methodological tools, and historical perspectives to the people's struggle. That model doesn't work today, when intellectuals have been redefined as "ideas brokers," after having been declassed to "content providers" throughout the 1990s. And now that the Internet provides all the content, what are we to do? Cognitive capitalism changes the rules of the game, and I firmly believe feminists, antiracists, and post- as well as decolonial thinkers have developed amazing ways of being radical intellectuals. It is just that the relationship with the neo-Marxist Left has never been easy, though all of "us" would claim the Left as our political affiliation. The deletion of feminist scholarship from the agenda and references of contemporary critical thought—Badiou, Žižek, Morton, Harman, etc.—is as frustrating as it is self-defeating. Mason writing in the *Guardian*—about the Clinton–Sanders divide—that the only category that really matters is class and all others—gender, age, ethnicity, sexual preference, and able-bodiedness—are just cultural issues and identity politics![21] How can you seriously write that in 2016? And then, to add insult to injury, go on to proclaim a grandiose left-wing Euroskepticism! This is the triumph of Nietzschean negatives! I protest against the deletion of feminism, the deletion of postcolonial theory, the deletion of race from their great curriculum, from their canons of critical theory and their great sense of entitlement. I oppose to this a philosophical approach based on the politics of location, the dialogical and collective production of theoretical cartographies as diagrams of power. And as Europeans who are accountable for their history, most of all, we need to aspire to the creation of new concepts, combining philosophical critiques with feminist, postcolonial, and antiracist reconstructions of both knowledge and social relations. We must come back to this.

Since you asked about Brexit and populism: I think what you have in Britain and what we have less of in other countries, such as the Netherlands—but Philomena Essed and Gloria Wekker[22] may disagree—is *postcolonial melancholia*. Paul Gilroy has a wonderful book on this.[23] If you look at the Brexit campaign: people were singing "Rule Britannia" and were actively making references to the empire, as well as disparaging foreigners. Now, that disjunction of reality is postcolonial melancholia. People can't accept the loss of prestige. Significantly it's not just the elites and the UKIP neonationalists who promote these views; the socially underprivileged classes can't accept this. Nationalism is the boost of pride: when everything else is going, you're still British, white, local—you belong here! There is a serious identity crisis (again, that word!), of having to readjust your perception of yourself. I don't see the Netherlands or the rest of the European Union, notably Italy and Spain, doing this, partly because they are in denial of their colonial past. Denial produces a virulent form of right-wing populism disguised as civic pride. And it is in that fog of disavowal that manipulative politicians can do a lot of harm. But melancholia eats away at your political soul. Look at the post-Brexit United Kingdom. In the end, it is the poorer sections of society that are going to pay the bills when the international companies pull out and the pound continues to plunge, while the Tories—who after this right-wing coup by UKIP may be in power for decades—will deregulate every aspect of UK society. Do I sound bitter about Brexit? I'm more like heartbroken! Like the end of an affair that was never self-evident to begin with.

All in all, I believe we need much more detailed studies of the different kinds of European populisms and how they relate to different representations of our nationalistic past. Of course, there is a correlation between postcolonial loss of prestige, identity, indeed vulnerability, and access to the resources and advantages of the global economy. The process is painful, in that it generates negative passions among those who are worst hit by the economic disparities. They are encouraged by manipulative politicians to scapegoat migrants, foreigners, asylum seekers, and other figures of "otherness." The appeal to strong nationalist leaders who basically promise to build more walls around every single constituency produces what Deleuze and Guattari call *microfascism*.[24] Whether they are on the left or on the right, they are microfascists. How many new walls have gone up since the Berlin wall came down?[25] Fortress Europe is one of them, and that's our responsibility.

Perhaps we could delve into that idea of microfascism and melancholia a little deeper. What is truly remarkable in the populist, right-wing discourse of today—of Geert Wilders in Holland, but also of Marine Le Pen in France (Donald Trump seems to be far more regressive in this respect . . .)— is an attempt to incorporate what used to be called "progressive" themes, such as gay marriage, women's rights, secularism, etc. They are now being incorporated into what is an aggressively melancholic, even microfascist, or even outright fascist discourse. That is obviously an interesting development, but also one that is unsettling for radical academics, or people who think of themselves as progressive generally. I wonder, again, how would you respond to what seems to be an almost-irresolvable issue?

How to deal with proliferating microfascisms and their tendency to incorporate sexual nationalism and "pink-washing," enlisting them in a crusade against Islam, that is one of the great battle-lines of today! It is so Spinozist, you know, this confrontation with a toxic—Spinoza would say "poisonous"—social context. Spinoza lived through the end of the Dutch Republic, and could see an entire social and political system collapse! The lynching of the De Witt brothers, for example; he lived through terrible, terrible times. And he wrote *The Ethics*[26] as an antidote—Deleuze calls this a "clinical" as well as critical text—against the negativity of the times.

Microfascism in the critical Spinozism defended by Deleuze and Guattari rests on their monistic political ontology. It has been at the heart of many controversial debates with the Marxist Left, precisely about the question of the political. Basically, monism rejects the dialectical method and insists that all subjects—human and nonhuman, manufactured and generated—are part of a common matter, which means a common world. They are interrelated, coconstructed, and symbiotic, moving radically in and out of each other. The key term for me is "relational." By extension this means that political subjectivity is not postulated along the dialectical axes of negativity and opposition. So the obvious objection is, is radical immanence not just a form of passivity? Is there not a danger of acquiescence with the conditions of the present? This is Hegel's classical objection to Spinoza and, today, Badiou's objection to Deleuze.[27] The short answer is no, but things are not as simple as that.

This idea that politics has to be antagonistic in a negative mode needs to be reviewed.[28] Are we to assume that all modes of relation are intrinsically positive? What are we to make of destructive, negative relations? What about violence, dispossession, rape, and murder? I think, you know, that so many contemporary philosophical debates on neomaterialism, the affective turn, and the object-oriented ontology rotate around this question. In response to these objections, I think that both Deleuze and before him Spinoza are perfectly aware of the dangers of a sort of semimystical harmonization of all conflicts. This is why both insist on the need for a structure of *differentiation*, which, however, and this is the key point, need not be dialectical or antagonistic in a violent mode. My entire project started by thinking about the positivity of difference, as opposed to its antagonistic structure. A monistic worldview, guided by the ethics of affirmation, is the perfect way to proceed on this line. To this purpose, Deleuze and Guattari devise a praxis based on the actualization of the virtual. What a mouthful, right?

To explain, I need to take a step back. Basically, I do philosophy by drawing critical cartographies of the present. The critical thinker can and should account for the power relations at work in the present conditions and for how they have an impact on the ways subjects are constructed. Accounting for a set of conditions, however, does not mean endorsing them—this is the whole point. Producing an adequate anatomy of advanced capitalism—the way Deleuze and Guattari do—is not a form of acceptance, but rather the first step in the opposite direction: providing the building blocks of an alternative system.

Cartographies are theoretically infused readings of the present, and in order to navigate in the tumultuous water of contemporary complexities, we need navigational tools. Another name for them is "figurations"— but Deleuze calls them *conceptual personae*. They actualize a virtual position, illuminating aspects of the present that may not be directly accessible through established academic conventions of thought. My favorite navigational tools or figurations are the feminist philosopher (the subject of my first book, *Patterns of Dissonance*), the nomadic subject (the subject of my trilogy), and now the posthuman. By traveling across the fields of contemporary scholarship with these navigational tools, I am empowered to draw cartographies of discursive formations that express alternative ways of knowing by creating unexpected locations for the thinker herself. Instead of the biopolitical, I produce the corporeal neomaterialism of relational subjects capable of accounting for one's multiple—and potentially contradictory—locations in terms of space and time.

The collective efforts at cartographic accounts compose the different planes of an "assemblage," that is to say, a transindividual form of subjectivity, which includes nonhuman factors as well as technological mediation. This is a plane of relational encounters, which composes a community that was virtual till it got materialized through this epistemological and ethical effort of understanding together the conditions of our bondage. Subjectivity is not linked to liberal individualism, but neither is it "collectivized" as a synthetic conjunction—like a class, or a multitude that is supposed to drive the progress of world history. What we get is processes of becoming in transversal assemblages that flow across and displace the binaries. Are you still with me? Although they allow an analytic function to be negative, they reject negativity and aim at the production of joyful or affirmative values and projects. A new alliance of critique with creation is put to the task of actualizing alternatives to the dominant vision of the subject, resisting the hegemony of reason and the pull of transcendentalism.

The first step is always the formation of a collective subject—a "we." Without the collective assemblage that is this missing "we," which needs to be composed and sustained, we can't even start the process. And what the process is supposed to do is to actualize virtual alternatives. What this monistic, neomaterialist approach does assume, however, is that we are part and parcel of what we are trying to fight, not external to it. This is why the feminist politics of locations, or situated knowledge, is so important: it is radical empiricism, immanence at work. Foucault's work on power as both restrictive and productive—entrapment and empowerment—is also inspirational here. Let us remember that Foucault did not believe in liberation *through*, but only *from*, sexuality. And the Xenofeminists have picked up this point in their rock-opera conceptual style: "It is through, and not despite, our alienated condition that we can free ourselves from the muck of immediacy."[29]

I've never given up on the question of political subjectivity: it is too important to the ethical-political praxis. And of course, as the philosophers taught us back in the 1970s, this "we" as nomadic assemblage— the missing people, as Deleuze calls it—is supposed to be a critique of both liberal individualism and Marxist-Leninism. The alternative is the composition of transversal subjects that aim at releasing transversal alternative lines. The aim is not to assert affirmative differences in happy coexistence, but to bring about together productive subversions of the status quo by actualizing virtual possibilities. In my later work, I have stressed the extent to which this subjectivity is a compound of human and nonhuman factors, including technological mediation.

For me it goes like this: critical theory is both critical/clinical and creative. It starts with the composition of a transversal subject through the making of discursive and material cartographies of the power relations that are at work in the specific locations one is starting from. My cartographic approach is spiced with heavy doses of feminist politics of locations, which then sneaks in my favorite concepts: the body, embodiment, lived experience, transversal nomadic subjectivities. Feminism is the original historical and theoretical manifestation of embodied and embedded, affective and relational immanence. The early Irigaray is so right when she defines it as a form of corporeal or sensible empiricism.[30]

I know, I mustn't digress too much, but after so many years, my intellect has become rhizomatic and I have to keep multiple ideas in my mind at once. Whereas Marxism would argue for ideological rupture, Deleuze and Guattari emphasize that to actualize this rupture requires subjects who actively desire otherwise and in an otherworldly way and thus break with the *doxa*, the regime of common sense. The function of the virtual is to actualize the real issues, which means precisely the effort to interrupt the acquiescent application of established norm and values, to deterritorialize them by introducing alternative ethical flows. The virtual is the laboratory of the new.

To accomplish this political ethics, we need to engender together a qualitative leap that engages with but also breaks productively with the present, by understanding how it engenders the conditions of our bondage. That's pure Spinoza.[31] The affirmative politics of becoming mobilizes a subject's ontological desire—the vital *potentia* of the subject—and collectively reframes it in disruptive directions capable of resisting codes and powers. This ethical transformation of negative critique into creative affirmation is the key to Deleuze's idea of revolutionary subjectivity, as being activated by the shared desire to create new conditions that break with the replication of the same and the reiteration of the obvious, which are supported and marketed by the current system. The virtual or affirmative force—backed by a Bergsonian philosophy of a time[32]—is the motor of political change, and not oppositional dialectics.

Thus, living the antifascist life—which is how Foucault[33] explains the neo-Spinozist ethics proposed by Deleuze—implies the transcendence of negativity. What that means concretely is that we need to work hard because the conditions for renewed political and ethical agency cannot be drawn from the immediate context or the current state of the terrain. They have to be generated affirmatively and creatively by composing an "elsewhere," a different "people," or another "we." They need efforts geared to creating possible worlds, alternative futures, by mobilizing resources and visions that have been left untapped and by actualizing them in daily practices of interconnection with others. We need more visionary energy.

So how does this work on the analysis of microfascism? Let us assume the working definition of microfascism as the love for a strong leader—the Man of destiny—who promises to solve the sources of collectively shared resentment by scapegoating mostly on racist grounds. For some, despots are just attractive, think of Putin and his good friends Berlusconi and Trump, who admire him so much! So what do we have here? First, serious social and economic distress. In the 1920s and 1930s, it was palpable: a big economic crisis, an interbellum period, war debts, huge unemployment figures, the financial crisis in 1929. For us today all this resonates with the Lehman Brothers crisis in 2008 (again!). And there is always a sense of that melancholia, a sense of loss and decline. Spengler's *Decline of the West* was *the* textbook of fascism, and this theme is a favorite of the Trump administration, courtesy of Steve Bannon.[34] Second, microfascism indicates the abdication of responsibilities to a leader who is going to make your decisions for you, promising a happy ending to a sad tale. In my monistic neo-Spinozist language: the triumph of the negative. What there also is, however, is a strong affective and—I may add—libidinal attachment to that strong leader. Remember that Mussolini and Hitler were democratically elected. And look at Leni Riefenstahl's films about the Nazi rallies and Hitler: people love them. Third, there is redemption: "Cometh the hour, cometh the man!" belies a Messianic sense of historical inevitability. There's a link between a sense of decline, vulnerability, and a desire to transcend it through a powerful man.

It all sort of rotates around a *wound*. I think that is how I would analyze this with feminism and critical theory: the wound of the white male body. When another woman is raped or black man shot dead again, when the refugees drown or another LBGTQ+ is violated, not much changes, though often indignation is expressed. But if the dominant white male is hurt, then all hell breaks loose and then we do have an official crisis. This fundamental lack of symmetry in power relations defines a hierarchical relation of bodies to the public space. Supposing we go with the postcolonial definition of fascism as "colonialism come home," how do things look then? Achille Mbembe's work on this is of great inspiration.[35] Once such violence hits the dominant body, that's a different kind of pain. You have the wounded white male, who gets enraged and cannot cope, also because his political leaders do not offer any outlets other than xenophobia.[36] But the white woman in this narrative is not innocent. Right-wing women are right in there: they were massively for Brexit in the United Kingdom and they are very active in most neonationalist movements in Europe, not only in France. So we have the dominant bodies, male, female, the whiteness of it, and then we have their "crisis." All of a sudden, the center asks: Why am I out of a job and I'm British, or French, or Dutch?

Instead of offering a balanced analysis, for instance, of global economics and the technological divide, it is so much easier for the political class to blame the Polish workers, the EU free movement of people, the war refugees. There is always a manipulation of the negative passions by a discourse that justifies scapegoating through racism and xenophobia. Whatever it is: the refugees, the Jews, the Muslims, you pin your pain on the others and you make them pay for it. It is René Girard's logic of the sacrifice.[37] It is so primitive and it works so effectively.

There is a correlation between this violence and the negative passions and affects that both feed and are fed by it, that are exploited by the opportunistic classes of politicians. They're scapegoating. If you look at the racist pro-Brexit poster that Nigel Farage paraded, showing the "invading hordes" of refugees pouring into the United Kingdom, you just want to cry. Is Great Britain truly xenophobic, or just unable to detect these clear signs of fascistic scapegoating because of their postcolonial melancholia? Maybe the United Kingdom needs to learn how to lead the antifascist life right now, too.

If I can repeat what I said earlier, namely, Europe is the place that *has* to remember its history, then I feel that the European Union *has* created a space where it is possible to say: "We can't repeat this." We have to detox the neonationalists, especially now that they seem to gather momentum in Europe. This is where I want to come with a Spinozist prescription, which is a form of disintoxication from a poisoned body politic. So let us collectively detox it. How? By socially constructing affirmative ethical relations. In other words, we need antidotes, we need to actualize virtual alternatives, we need the *pharmakon*! Roberto

Esposito's work on the biopolitics of immunity and especially autommunity is also a relevant way to deal with the rise of microfascism.[38] I would plea for unfolding doses of relational ethics, made of external/internal, that is to say, transversal interventions and ethical vaccinations against such hatred. Coming from feminism, I am very interventionist in this respect.

All the more so, as it's sad but striking to see how power just repeats itself. For instance, in the wake of the austerity measures and the socioeconomic crisis, we witness the persistency of violence against women and LBGTQ+. Reports from Spain and Italy (with its highly contested "Fertility Day"!)[39] are especially alarming: women and LBGTQ+ are being beaten up, killed. So much so that there is a new law now on *feminicide*. And yet, in another perverse twist, these populist movements are enlisting emancipation to their own racist causes I mentioned before. The organizers of Gay Pride marches have to deal with the enthusiastic support for gay causes by people like Wilders and others. Their argument is that the West treats minorities decently, whereas the Muslim world oppresses and destroys them. This manipulation of feminist and queer causes and issues by the nationalist right-wing movements in Europe right now is objectionable. The cooption is so bad that in France, even a feminist who campaigns against the veil and calls for the boycott of the burkini and Islamic fashion—Elisabeth Badinter—has taken a firm position against these political manipulations of the issue. She does not want *laïcité* to become *lepeniste*. When I read sentences like that I think: What would the Xenofeminists think of something like that? And what do the burkini-clad Islamic feminists say? What would Pussy Riot say? I think we need to listen to the younger generations on these issues. Contemporary populists in the European Union are pro–Israel and against anti-Semitism, pro–white feminism, pro–gay rights, and pro–trans rights, proemancipation within narrowly confined and ethicized boundaries. They rewrite their own infamous history of sexism, homo- and transphobia—and thus disguise their virulent xenophobia—through this putative support of human rights for categories they have historically persecuted and marginalized. Dressing up racism in the unmistakable colors of sexual nationalism, they add a new nefarious chapter to cultural racism.

All this is connected to the major axis of masculinity, of whiteness, of urbanism: it's the problem of the center. When centers in globalization get multiplied, and when they get dispersed—Grewal and Kaplan coined the term "scattered hegemonies"[40]—and they become regional, they go down in flames. In Italy we are now down to town against town. The Lega Nord is by now a classic form of populism, the Five Star Movement is up and going, promoting even more capillary and endless fragmentation until the reterritorialization is down to your genes![41] Then there is nothing left, there is no possible assemblage. There is no possible plane of composition of a people. That would be another sort of working definition of microfascism, as despotic fragmentation where you can't compose a people. Then you are exposed, incredibly vulnerable to the very political forces that are offering you false solutions based on violent negation of otherness, under the leadership of ruthless politicians who profit from unhappiness, frustration, and injustice. So much for pretending to care for feminism and LBGTQ+ issues!

This unethical behavior rests on self-implemented ignorance, that is to say, a misreading of one's location and practice. Spinoza is really great on this point: living the ethical life means acquiring an adequate understanding of one's position. Adequate to what, you may ask? To what bodies are capable of becoming. This is where the ethical differentiation occurs in the form of an ethology of forces. And please remember that in monistic philosophes bodies are embrained and brains are embodied—it is all one matter. We need to find out what the self-organizing and intelligent slice of matter that we are can actually do. That is to say, what it can actualize. We do this by embracing an ethics of experiment with virtual forces, which Deleuze also calls intensities. I have written a trilogy on nomadism[42] to argue for a sustainable ethics for nonunitary subjects that rests on an enlarged sense of interconnection between self and others, including the nonhuman or "earth" others and technological artifacts, by removing the obstacle of self-centered individualism on the one hand and the barriers of negativity on the other. This is really the core of my philosophical project. Epistemology joining forces with ethics to detox us from fundamental errors, which are not errors of judgment in a Kantian sense, but rather "mis"-takes, or inadequate forms of understanding one's own location. Xenophobia does not only affect the object of our hatred; it also betrays a relational deficit on our part. (But who is "we" in this plane of composition of a transversal subject?) It is the transversal assemblage that needs to be composed and actualized against negative passions. The big battle today is against microfascism and we need to give priority to an ethics of affirmation. Why do we delegate authority, why do we love strong leaders, why do we believe those lies, why do we think that killing others is a solution?

Here I need to open a parenthesis. This return of "posttruth," that is to say, delusional public discourses, coupled with the apology of violence, worries me. I have been strongly influenced by psychoanalysis in my work, but also in my life, as I did an analysis in Paris for many years. Best thing I ever did! The only disadvantage of the current Deleuzian fashion, by the way, is that, at least as far as my students go, nobody seems to read or refer to psychoanalysis anymore. But psychoanalysis is the last great conceptualization of the politics of desire produced by Western culture and it casts a crucial light upon the politics of passions, the mechanisms of fantastic projection. Basically, psychoanalysis explains the role of negativity: why we are all attracted to "posttruths" and even delusional nontruths about ourselves. Narcissism and paranoia are the fundamental psychic, but also social, structures. Where the analytic approach is at its strongest is in proposing an ethics based on learning to recognize or read one's patterns of projections and mystifications. This is totally compatible with Spinoza's point about reaching an adequate understanding of the conditions of our bondage or unfreedom. You can't read Deleuze and Guattari without at least some understanding of psychoanalysis.

In fact, it would be really useful to have a public discussion here about the sort of projections populism is encouraging in the public sphere today, from feminicide ("Be my body—so I can kill you") to xenophobia ("Blame the foreigners for what your government is doing to you, to save myself!"). To argue, against all historical and political evidence, that right-wing populists are proud of the fact that "our" women and LBGTQ+ are free, whereas "theirs" are not—and that the West, of course, is the best. This is pseudofreedom predicated on xenophobic negativity. Again, the idea of critical theory as detoxing us from stupidity and untruths, clinical and critical, is crucial. Why is complexity in public discourse such an issue? Why can't we have complex arguments at the center of the discussions? Why do they leave complexity to us in the universities when it should be the operating principle of the government of reality?

You could perhaps also argue that recent political movements such as Nuit Debout in France, and Occupy being the most emblematic example, are attempts at finding a new plane of composition, at incorporating complexity. In spite of the fact that their means often are not very effective, as they appear to prefer the tools of nineteenth- and twentieth-century "direct" democracy.

Why would "direct action" be reduced to protests in the open spaces? Affirmative activism can take place in a multitude of other places and spaces, though I agree that these are important new movements. For me, composing a community around the shared affects and concepts of becoming-minoritarian is the key to transformative politics. As I said before, it all starts with putting together a situated "we: a missing people" that can labor together to create alternatives. It expresses the affirmative, ethical dimension of politics as a gesture of collective self-styling. A community of this kind gravitates around the same issues or projects, so there is a strong affective element, and it is held together by a shared praxis. At the heart of it all I would place the acknowledgment of interdependence or mutual specification.

A microfascist plane of composition does not incorporate complexity, but rather paralyzes it. This is molar segmentarity. Social movements like Occupy, on the other hand, operationalize complexity. Central to the political today is the issue of mediation: if any project today doesn't have technology written into it, it simply doesn't apply. Media ontology is fundamental. Guattari[43] takes the lead here, even above Deleuze: the whole concept of general ecology and media ontologies. Look at the work of Matthew Fuller and Mark Hansen:[44] it's all about media philosophy, that is to say, about embodied but also virtual ways of relating, in a nonlinear manner, to a global technosphere that is both most public and totally intimate. General media theory, in the post-Snowden era, touches upon the logic of algorithms, but also on deeply material issues— I am thinking of the work of Jussi Parikka on media geology and Jen Gabrys[45] on digital rubbish—with all the security issues, the privacy and copyrights laws attached to them, and, of course, the perennial question of access to these technologies in the first place. How could we possibly do without these perspectives? For me, a vital materialist philosophy for today has to start from there, from how intelligent and alive our machines have become (while we, as Donna Haraway so wittily puts it, are becoming more and more inert!).[46]

If we start from mediation, however, supposing "we" accept that academics today are operators of cognitive capitalism, a whole series of new questions come up: What are the qualitative shifts introduced by these new technologies in our practice? How do we take accountability for them? And how do we react to the state of confusion and underfunding that has hit the standard humanities today, while everybody is getting excited about the so-called digital humanities? We need to have some sort of formula, we can't just say: "Down with cognitive capitalism, so destroy the university, because it is an integral part of it!" No, I'm sorry—we are the university! And this is a centuries-old institution, venerable, dignified, important, we need to have a project to counteract what is happening to us today. It is absolutely true that I am part of a radical generation that went into the university to reform it, but that does not mean we ever wanted to get rid of it. On the contrary, the humanities have been the breeding ground for critical theory and other experiments in democratic criticism, which are very important to me.

The momentum for a different university is growing within the antiglobalization movement. I work closely with Vivienne Bozalek in South Africa and also with Achille Mbembe and Sarah Nuttall, following the "Rhodes Must Fall" and "Fees Must Fall" movements from the angle of the radical pedagogies that I have always been involved in. That movement is part of a worldwide move for the decolonization of the university, which is terribly important. I also care about the Rhodes Scholarship scheme, however, which has brought generations of students to the best universities in the world. Again, I need to think several things at once here, and even my nomadic mind cracks under the strain. First, it is crucial that the decolonization movement takes off here in Europe, to undo that denial, disavowal, or nostalgia for the colonial past we were talking about before. Next, but at the same time, we need to have plans and blueprints for how to bring the humanities into a global arena in the third millennium, learning from the South. We cannot just destroy and make them fall, because advanced capitalism is doing that already! I think a little bit of complexity in the enunciation of your critical position is vital. And the politics of radical immanence is the way to embody and embed our practice.

My philosophical teachers were very careful on this issue. Foucault, for instance, taking a chair at the Collège de France in 1970—which, in the French system, is like ascending to Mount Olympus—but out of that position, he actually critiqued the power of the chair, the figure of the professor, both respectfully and ruthlessly.[47] I believe that that level of accuracy in the political analysis of one's location is crucial and cannot get lost. And yet, carefully grounded political analyses are more necessary than ever, because neoliberal economics have created very disadvantageous class relations within the university staff structure. Our students are teaching up to twenty hours a week on temporary contracts that give them no research opportunities, no pension rights, and no professional future unless they can raise their own salary through grant submissions—they are the academic "precariat."[48] So nobody in my age group today can afford the indignity of saying that they are tenured radicals fighting for the revolution, unless they are prepared to resign and give the young ones their job. We need a collective reality check here. I prefer, to continue what I said before, to work on an *alternative* economic system, *alternative* market economies, noncapitalist *alternative* universities with fair labor relations and intergenerational accountability. I tend to agree with Martha Nussbaum on the importance of nonprofit as an academic ideal, though I disagree with her uncritical support of U.S. liberal humanism![49] How about some posthumanist idealism instead? The politics of radical immanence means you fight on the grounds of your own locations: in the classrooms, in the university, in print. There is not only *one* public space nowadays, but many. This is due to globalization, the new emerging economies, the generational divide, and the huge impact of media and technology. We need a multilayered, nomadic, and situated approach.

Let me pursue further the argument I made before: that the market is not our enemy—capitalism is. Today we can work with, which means trying to imagine and realize, alternative economic schemes. Suppose we aim at constructing other market economies against the capitalist axiom of profit at all costs. The struggle for the commons is a huge, worldwide movement. A new class of digital artisans creates start-ups for the most unexpected things and sells them two years later for millions: well done! I think this new economy—fully mediated and running on the advanced technologies—deserves a little more thinking on the part of people emerging from the left. We have to denounce the extreme polarizations, but also acknowledge that the mutation of the economy is deep and fast. There's a generation of really clever creative people, many trained by us, who are redesigning the frontiers of what is possible. Sure, many of the technological developments will result in suppressing the jobs that were central to the old economic order, but does this make the new economy into our enemy? Are we going to fight to bring it down? I object to the Bolshevik imaginary that pops up every time we on the left think about politics. Could we not update our imaginary a bit and dream in multilayered transformative ways instead? And get over the legacy of left-wing technophobia?

At heart, I repeat, we need much more careful cartographies of power relations here, within cognitive capitalism. Maybe we are watching the end of a *certain* chapter of capitalism: the neoliberal chapter, even before the Brexit, which will paradoxically introduce much higher degrees of state control and intervention. The question is, what are the alternatives? There are significant discussions at present about the future of the university in a posthumanist framework of reference and the question of what structure we should give to the contemporary humanities is being discussed at the highest levels. For instance, UNESCO, together with the International Council for Philosophy and the Humanities, is launching the first world conference for the humanities in 2017.[50] I work with them as well. I feel very strongly that, if we could come up with a prototype, with a new mode of relation of the academic humanities to the issues of decolonization—and the critique of nationalisms—and of the new economy, then we would have done our share of both critical and clinical detoxing and of creative transformation. My line would be to send out countercodes and alternative projects that start from the plane of negativity and pause reflexively, but do not stop there, at the issue of vulnerability-precarity; these projects would instead rework the plane of negativity in an affirmative framework that goes to the core of the system. What is that then? Invent new institutional configurations of power within a mutating economy. An economy defined by immense doses of technological mediation and polarized accumulation of wealth—with a strong illegal underbelly. Then rethink all this through again in the light of the Anthropocene and use philosophy to detox ourselves and reflect on what the contemporary university can offer.

I believe indeed this ties in with the issue of pedagogy, on both the institutional level and the level of the formats available for pedagogy today. What should today's university look like and how do we teach in it? In your book on the posthuman,[51] you refer to the "global multiversity," which I think is a really interesting notion. From the perspective of current critiques of neoliberalism, for certain strands of the Left, something like a "global multiversity" sounds like a nightmare. At the same time, you also speak of the level of pedagogy itself: you advocate the "posthumanities," news forms of interdisciplinary, etc.—but also you are concerned with the forms and formats pedagogy may take today. In your work, you have introduced notions such as "cartographies" and "transpositions" that could offer such new formats. I wonder how you see the interconnections between those two levels: the infrastructural level of the "global multiversity" and the level of the form itself of pedagogy.

My recent work is exactly on this: the critical posthumanities.[52] That is to say, what can the humanities become in the era of the decolonization of the university—which is to say, the decline of the Eurocentric parameter of universalist "Man"—but also of the end of anthropocentrism and of the supremacist Anthropos? The era of mediation, global flows of information, and perpetual surveillance? Of course, it's a long story and there is an ongoing debate about this, which for me goes back to the modern–postmodern controversy of the 1980s and then, after poststructuralism became popular in the United States, the violent theory wars of the 1990s.[53] The very idea of "theory" was at the core of a debate that actually has more to do with institutional politics,[54] so in a rather puzzling way, in the American debate, a correlation was established between the institutional attack on the humanities and the attack on theory itself, with "theory" meaning mostly critical thought, including French philosophy.[55] Theoretical radicalism, especially in gender and postcolonial studies, was savaged by the opposition—these are precisely the places where the ideas of Occupy and "Rhodes Must Fall" are being developed. Coetzee has even suggested that the aim of these campaigns was to depoliticize the university campuses and stop all dissent by marginalizing the critical thinkers as dangerous anarchists or rabid lefties.[56] The scholarship on this aspect of the contemporary humanities is huge, and it makes for some depressing reading at times.[57] But things are not much better here in the European Union, where the populist right-wing politicians especially after 9/11 developed very hostile platforms against the fields of culture and the arts, both in society and as an academic curriculum. In the Netherlands Geert Wilders, for instance, dismissed them as "left-wing hobbies" and targeted them for large government cutbacks in funding. The question of the public value of the humanities has been reduced to a merely economic budget-balancing issue.

I share your concern about a neoliberal version of "the global multiversity," but so many universities now have campuses and franchises abroad, mostly in China and the Arab states, that the bad dream has already become reality. The hope therefore lies with the radical pedagogics. My argument is that today we see the emergence of the critical posthumanities, as a new transversal field that reflects creatively both the transformations and the conflicts of today. I have proposed a cartography of the critical posthumanities and connect them to the interdisciplinary fields of inquiry that have been growing in the last thirty years around the edges and in the interstices of the disciplinary humanities and that simply call themselves "studies." My prototype of these transformative discourses are gender, feminist, queer, race, and postcolonial, but also, of course, cultural studies, and then film, television, and media studies, but there are more. I see these "studies" as proliferations of alternatives within the conservative landscape of the humanities. They are young, hip, and chronically underfunded radical epistemologies that have highlighted the importance of pedagogics and therefore call for methodological innovations. The contemporary humanities would be dead without the input of these "studies" areas. I should know, as I have spent the entirety of my career in their midst: I have never had a disciplinary institutional affiliation.[58]

What I find fascinating as you look at the phenomenon more closely is how these "studies" areas intermarry, crossbreed, and continue to grow rhizomatically. They are the "minor science" Deleuze and Guattari write about. The first generation was big on posthumanism and the critique of methodological sexism and nationalism. A second generation of "studies" areas has now become quite visible, and it centers on my beloved posthuman perspectives: we have mediation, on the one hand, and the critique of anthropocentrism, on the other. Just think of the explosion of interest in animal studies and ecocriticism, religion and postsecular studies, disability studies, fat studies, success studies, globalization studies, and celebrity studies. New media has become its own galaxy, generating whole series of software studies, Internet studies, game studies, algorithmic studies, and more. But it flips over into security studies, conflict studies, human rights studies, death studies, suicide studies, queer inhuman studies, extinction studies, etc., etc.

So here is my thought: the Critical Posthumanities are new transdisciplinary assemblages that are currently being composed across the multiple generations of "studies" areas, at times with some support from the disciplines themselves. I am thinking especially of the environmental and the digital humanities, which are so popular at the moment. But also the neural, biogenetic, and medical humanities—very strong institutionally, and capable of combining human with postanthropocentric premises, issues of social construction with attention to technological mediation. I see them as rising to the challenge of our historicity without losing sight of ideals of social justice and fair redistribution of resources. I am currently analyzing this phenomenon in the light of my nomadic subjectivity work, proposing monistic neomaterialism, as the most suitable ontological grounding for the practice of the critical posthumanities.

The next phase of my work will try to assess these developments in a nondialectical logic. That is to say, it is not a case of "either-or," but of "and . . . and." The posthumanities are both contiguous with cognitive capitalism and potentially transformative practices. The task of the critical theorists is to generate the margins of affirmative intervention in these new fields, which are coextensive with the contemporary university structure and mission. They consequently define our daily practice. So it is for me a question not just of quantitative growth of discourses, but also of qualitative changes in pedagogical approach and especially in ethical purpose.

In other words, I do think that cognitive capitalism has done its best to reterritorialize the institution of the university. Noam Chomsky is completely right: they did it to health care, and now they've landed in the university. This has happened partly because the technological knowledge we are producing—particularly in the two leading areas: IT and biotech—are coextensive with corporate interests. The university lost the control of research on cancer already years ago, and we never had the digital technologies, which are being invented in the private laboratories of corporate groups like Microsoft, Google, and Skype. This is why I'm skeptical about the concept of a research university—it is actually a misnomer and I'm not sure about the purpose of it. I think that it is a mistake to make it the core mission, because most research today is geared to and coextensive with cognitive capitalism. If, on the other hand, we can train people to think critically, we can actually do something new that nobody else is doing. Maybe with the younger generation we can have this discussion, including acknowledging the economic consequences of these technological advances. So back we go to the discussion about universal minimum wages!

The technologically driven changes that excite our starting researchers and define their scholarly and social roles also produce unmanageable amounts of anger and frustration in those who get marginalized by them. You can see that in Donald Trump's campaign, but in the European Union as well. So we need to give outlets, possibilities, both to the former working class of an economy that no longer exists and to the non-profit-minded youth of today.

We need a new framework for these internally contradictory developments—and I am thinking of the critical posthumanities. For example, let's go back to the genesis of the digital humanities and the environmental humanities, which didn't exist until eight years ago and at one particular moment . . . *woosh*—just do it and up they go! Now they are in many ways the core of a new university, with strong ties to the corporate sector, millennial youth culture, and the security apparatus. Why don't our university governors just say that their model is basically STEM education and they all want to be MIT? Japan shut down twenty-eight humanities faculties last year!

It's as if teaching people how to think were neither profitable nor desirable anymore. I never thought that we would end up at this level again, that we would need to say that if research is reduced to financial profit-making, then research is not enough to define the university today. We need the university as critical training for democratic criticism: Edward Said meets Microsoft, meets Gloria Anzaldúa, meets Deleuze, meets Facebook, meets the Anthropocene, meets Black Lives Matter, meets Xenofeminism, and this goes on more rhizomically than ever. I would bring these concerns back to the core of our training for teaching and research, but the exclusive focus on research is a hybrid that doesn't work, because it's neither fish nor fowl, neither fundamental research nor a real corporate form of research.

Look at it pragmatically: if the IMF is saying that neoliberalism is over, then cognitive capitalism is going to need generalists, dreamers, people who can read and interpret the world freely. If we could accept that, we would support, and not cut back, the humanities and consider them as a double capital. First, because their creativity is generating waves of critical "studies" discourses, which are currently coalescing in the critical posthumanities. But second also in themselves: it's so short-sighted to close down the fields that are actually the true and unique capital. China is not going to send only its engineers here. Chinese and Korean students will come here to study art history and philosophy, our humanism and the democratic critiques of that tradition by gender and postcolonial studies. What we are capable of teaching—humbled and instructed by our mistakes as well as by our achievements—is democracy through civil academic criticism. I see it in my Chinese students all the time, the interest in questions like "How does a big society like ours allow radical feminists and 'out lesbians'—as we used to call ourselves—to teach and research?" Ultimately, the mystery question is, how do you do democracy? That's what the world needs to know! We have done this over hundreds of years of wisdom, reflection, scholarship, dialogues, killing one another and then learning not to kill one another, using the arts of rhetoric, etc. Now we are pretty sophisticated in self-reflection and metadiscourse, but also all the more apt to disavow them and scapegoat instead.

Four hundred years of democratic criticism—it's a capital, and the humanities are written into that capital. How not to understand that? It is a missed opportunity, because you can't reconstruct a scholarly community after having destroyed it. To throw away this capital is to be myopic. There is only one way to teach democracy, that is, to actually teach it historically and enacted in a community of scholars who can disagree with arguments and not just respond with opinionated gestures such as "I like, I don't like," which is Facebook thinking! It is fun, but it is hardly an argument. We need arguments, disagreements, negotiations, and a civic responsibility. We are part of a community, we're not on a campus in a bubble, answering only to a committee who wants to know how many publications you've done this year. By the way, the recent wave of real-estate deals made by universities in the European Union is really significant: they're selling off the historical university buildings in the heart of the old cities. They did it in Bologna, and also in Amsterdam: they're selling out this ancient civic core of the university. All universities in our world were city-based—historically, town and gown were the same thing. How can you take the heart out of this institution? The European university stands for constructing a certain type of critical citizen, inhabiting the city space in a literate and responsible manner. What we all need to learn, the world over, is how to become a functioning and inclusive democracy. If they let us do our job instead of having to create a flawed monster called the research university, we would be fine. The model of the critical posthumanities that I'm working on rests on the idea of the clinical and the critical. It's linked to Spinozist depoisoning as the running figuration or conceptual persona for critical thinking nowadays. This is all the more important because of the growth of xenophobia and protofascism in the European Union at present. Shame! I am thinking of Deleuze on the shame of being human. A posthumanist university needs to take this shame very seriously.

Perhaps we could ask ourselves what lies beyond these variations of humanism. I am intrigued by your notion of "zoé-egalitarianism".[59] it seems to be an attempt to move beyond the now ubiquitous concept of "biopolitics." Does it, for you, signify a move away from the dominant Foucauldian frame? Also, I believe it can be read as an attempt to break with what you could call political modernism, or simply political modernity—that is to say, of another idea, the anthropocentric notion of egalitarianism or equality, as embodied today by the thought of Alain Badiou or Slavoj Žižek.

That's a trigger question! Yes indeed, for me the politics of radical immanence is the way to move out of the circular discourses of the biopolitical—Thomas Lemke[60] is so right in saying that the concept of biopolitics is by now a sort of buzzword that shoots in all directions. One really needs to supplement Foucault with Deleuze in order to get a convincing politics, but that's hardly a dominant line in biopolitical research.

First, we need to work harder at comparing the transatlantic readings of Foucault with other approaches to the same question. A dominant social constructivist, legalist, Rawlsian approach goes hand in hand with residual Kantianism. I am thinking of Nick Rose, Bernard Harcourt, and other very brilliant scholars. Butler introduces queer Foucault. But then compare them to the Italian interpretations: Roberto Esposito, with his careful philological approach and a concrete political horizon, next to Agamben, who mixes and matches to produce a powerful cocktail of otherwise incompatible thinkers: Schmitt with Arendt and Foucault! Compare it then to the Australian school, highly politicized and extremely well read. It runs brilliantly from Paul Patton to Melinda Cooper.[61] An articulated cartography of these different schools of thought would make a terrific contribution, based on a global approach and not only on the United States.

I think we need to reread the unfinished project of Foucault with Deleuze's rigorous corpus, accepting the notion of complexity that Deleuze works through in his Foucault book.[62] If we do this, we will see how Deleuze takes Foucault across the big divide, *out* of modernism. The biopolitical raises the question of the appropriation of the embodied human flesh by a coding mechanism that disciplines and punishes, which is pretty primitive but highly effective. Deleuze replaces it with a system of coding that differentiates the despotic lines of segmentation from the monistic, neovital forces. A monistic political ontology foregrounds the coding processes and flows of forces, relying on the ethics of affirmation as its compass. What is crucial for me is the focus on technological mediation. This works through the Internet, but is also mediated through massive biogenetic interventions. In synthetic biology, artificial meat has been produced. In fact, gene editing is now producing human genome 3.0, which is, in terms of Esposito, an immunized system, where we've edited out imperfections. We need to stop the panic and have a serious political discussion, for instance, about the pharmaceutical consequences of gene editing. Who will have access to the practice? The question of access and equal participation is crucial. This connects, of course, to issues of disciplining, but not in a dualistic system. In "Societies of Control,"[63] Deleuze already goes in the monistic direction. We should go with Deleuze's Foucault book and move into what really matters, which is monistic, neovital, highly mediated systems of coding and recoding. By the way—if I may be rhizomic again—that book by Deleuze on Foucault is such a love letter! I find it a gesture of great generosity to do that to Foucault, who didn't manage to finish his work: he died in 1984! This unfinished aspect of his thought generates supplementary readings, which I call the "imaginary Foucaults," and there are so many of them.

Where the biopolitical is strong is that it unfolds into the necropolitical.[64] With Foucault we should be thinking of bodies and death. All this emphasis on vulnerability is fine, so many fine scholars are working on it, but actual death? There's even a new field of death studies, but it is disconnected from the critical theory debates. I do not do much with mourning, but as an affirmative thinker I have written on death.[65] Affirmation is not a denial of pain, or indifference to vulnerability, absolutely not: it is just another way of reworking it into praxis. It's another way of extracting knowledge from pain! It's just that we shouldn't want mourning as an endless process that runs the risk of resulting in paralysis. The negativity of negative passions—remember Spinoza on this?—is not a political disposition, but an ontological factor. The negative is what disempowers us to act and relate to others, whereas the affirmative is what empowers us to act. Of course, melancholia is profoundly relational and deeply engaged with others, so the critical effect of melancholia and affirmation is very analogous. They just have different genealogical roots and theoretical frameworks. And they generate different political praxes and different views on the role of the humanities.

I respect the politics of vulnerability, as developed by my friends Butler and Gilroy.[66] But why not open up to possible assemblages? It also affects the idea of the critical intellectual as a sort of lonely figure that supports and escorts the masses in their revolt. Not that that's the way Butler actually does her remarkable political work—she is a very affirmative critical thinker,[67] but the emphasis on vulnerability often flips onto the politics of complaint. And more importantly for me, there's no media! Occupy's "human mic" is picturesque, but we need to take mediation far more seriously as a structural political issue. The great assembler today is the Web.

I uphold a different model of intellectuality. Intellectuals are not there to interpret what the masses are doing and give it theoretical significance. That is not even a Gramscian model; it's a Hegelian model: reading the course of history. I come from feminism, from radical situatedness: politics hurts the most when it is really close to where you live. We need a politics of location, radical immanence, we need to be looking at our role as educators. Now there we can make a difference.

Let's listen to the younger generations: the Xenofeminists:

Melancholy—so endemic to the left—teaches us that emancipation is an extinct species to be wept over and that blips of negation are the best we can hope for. At its worst, such an attitude generates nothing but political lassitude, and at its best, installs an atmosphere of pervasive despair which too often degenerates into factionalism and petty moralizing. The malady of melancholia only compounds political inertia, and—under the guise of being realistic—relinquishes all hope of calibrating the world otherwise. It is against such maladies that XF inoculates.[68]

Left-wing melancholia versus right-wing nihilism? As I said before, neofascist movements manipulate negative emotions for the sake of racist scapegoating. That alone makes me repudiate negativity in any form. We—critical Spinozists—should be saying: "Empower us to relate and unfold upon the world with others." Others—both human and nonhuman—whom we encounter on the plane of immanence of a shared praxis or political passion. That impetus—ethics as living energy—is Spinoza again. I do not see that coming out of biopolitical scholarship, as it always goes either into mild forms of neonormativity or into self-styling techniques of the self, which invites reflection on critical legal theory, with disputes over sovereignty, the limits of the Law, and its inherent violence. There is a lot of Levinas in these accounts of biopower, actually! But we must beware of terrible pessimism. We can't do this to people. Let's stay upbeat—remember Emma Goldman: "If I can't dance, I don't want to be part of your revolution!"

This is made all the more relevant by the urgency of the Anthropocene condition, which, read in the light of Félix Guattari's three ecologies, combines the analysis of technological mediation with the psychic and affective effects of extreme economic and social inequalities. It sets the frame for my understanding of the posthuman condition. Monism is a zoé-centered form of egalitarianism, which assumes that all matter is one, that it is intelligent and self-organizing (autopoietic); it takes "living matter" as zoé-centered process,[69] which is geophysical but also psychic and nowadays interacts productively with the technosphere. This complex transversal subjectivity proposes an affirmative ethics of relations. Zoé-centered egalitarianism, the nonhuman, the vital force of life are the transversal entity that allows us to think across previously segregated species, categories, and domains. Neomaterialist immanence requires ethical accountability for the sustainability of these assemblages or transversal compositions.

The respect for zoé/geobound diversity lies at the core of this system: zoé celebrates all life-forms in a nonhierarchical manner, which recognizes the respective degrees of intelligence and creativity of all organisms. Stacy Alaimo puts it beautifully: thinking is the stuff of the world. If vital-materialist monism unfolds into a form of relational ecosophical ethics, it also supports the idea of ecological cocreation and mutual interdependence, while recognizing the specificities of humans. This is the politics of radical immanence: the awareness that thinking is the expression of ontological relationality, that is to say, of the power (*potentia*) to affect and be affected. Critical thinking assesses and amends our relational deficit. Built within this picture there is indeed a critique of modernist politics and of the reliance of the Left on a Hegelian philosophy of history. The conflict of opinions between Hegel and Spinoza lies at the core of this debate, as I said before.

You can see, I hope, how this radical relocation of difference outside dialectics would speak to my feminist and antiracist intellectual passions? We are used to criticizing "difference" as a term that indexes exclusion from the entitlements to subjectivity. The equation of difference with pejoration results in the disqualification, marginalization, and exclusion of entire sections of living beings. I call them the sexualized, racialized, and naturalized others who carry difference as a negative tattoo on their backs. Vital materialism—*zoé*-egalitarianism—delinks these "others" from oppositional dialectics, resulting in different forms of political resistance. This is the nomadic politics of "becoming-minoritarian," or the politics of radical immanence, which is concerned with human vulnerability, but reworks it nondialectically, in a multilayered and multidirectional relational manner. This is the "ecosophical" approach that grows out of monism.

What I'd like to stress in response to your question is that posthuman monism, or *zoé*-egalitarianism—by stressing the unity of all living matter—introduces a methodological kind of naturalism that does displace anthropocentrism, but does not solve all of our problems. We actually need to do some extra work ourselves. Deleuze is very keen to stress the proactive nature of critical thought by redefining thinking as the invention of new concepts, methods, and conceptual personae. This challenge enlists the resources of the imagination, as well as the tools of critical intelligence, but it throws multiple challenges our way: from the defamiliarization of cognitive habits I mentioned earlier to the necessity of nuturing more conceptual creativity. The collapse of the nature–culture divide, for instance, requires that we need to devise a new vocabulary, with new figurations to refer to the kind of subjects we are in the process of becoming.

The Left historically hated monism and historically rejected anything that is ecological. Red politics was never green politics. That partition is still playing a role today. As if we could separate the environment from the Internet, and the Internet from wealth and well-being. This level of complexity we're in requires very different types of alliances. With my idea of *zoé*-egalitarianism, I disagree with Agamben[70] that *zoé* should be the horizon of death. It is the generative force of so much! Indeed, Elizabeth Povinelli does it very well with body parts and technological reconnaissance of them. Anthropologists do it very well.

That is why I identify so much with the vital neomaterialism of Spinoza. The world is changing and we're not up to it. As the intellectual classes, as teachers, we really need to build up our ammunitions to make it possible to think of forms of saving *zoé*, in order to be able to live with it in an equitable manner. Our ignorance of our *zoé*-based conditions is unhelpful, to say the least. I would argue again that this is a job for us as critical humanities scholars, and I think we try to do it to the best of our ability, but it is not what "royal science" rewards. Royal science invests in cognitive capitalism. But "minor science," if, again, we use a Deleuzian distinction, is what is really transformative. Minor— or nomadic—science is to do the sort of interconnection and assemblage that is fundamental to the composition of a new people. If that is not considered fundable, there is something really wrong in our sociopolitical thinking. We can do minor sciences and make these different from the cognitive capitalist ones. Imagination is not something that you can clone. This active concept of monism is also activist, in that it labors to express our virtual force (*potentia*) and our innermost freedom (*conatus*). For me it produces a kind of ontological pacifism central to the critical or nomadic posthumanities.[71]

INTERVIEW CONDUCTED AND TRANSCRIBED BY JOOST DE BLOOIS

Notes

1. Jacques Derrida, "Plato's Pharmacy," in *Dissemination*, trans. Barbara Johnson (Chicago: University of Chicago Press, 1983).
2. See Rosi Braidotti, "The Untimely," in *The Subject of Rosi Braidotti*, ed. Bolette Blaagaard and Iris van der Tuin (London: Bloomsbury Academic, 2014).
3. Eric Hobsbawn, *The Short Twentieth Century* (London: Penguin, 1994).
4. See Pierre Macherey, *Hegel or Spinoza*, trans. Susan M. Ruddick (Minneapolis: University of Minnesota Press, 2011).
5. See Rosi Braidotti, "Nomadic European Citizenship," in *Nomadic Theory: The Portable Rosi Braidotti* (New York: Columbia University Press, 2011).
6. Francis Fukuyama, *The End of History and the Last Man* (London: Penguin, 2012).
7. Michel Foucault, *The Order of Things: Archaeology of the Human Sciences* (London: Routledge, 2001).
8. Gilles Deleuze and Félix Guattari, *Anti-Oedipus*, trans. Robert Hurley, Mark Seem, and Helen R. Lane (Minneapolis: University of Minnesota Press, 1983).
9. Michel Serres and Bruno Latour, *Conversations on Science, Culture, and Time*, trans. Roxanne Lapidus (Ann Arbor: University of Michigan Press, 1995).
10. Jürgen Habermas, *The Postnational Constellation: Political Essays*, trans. Evald Ojaveer (Cambridge: Polity, 2001).

11. Seyla Benhabib, "The New Sovereigntism and Transnational Law: Legal Utopianism, Democratic Scepticism and Statist Realism," *Global Constitutionalism* 5, no. 1 (2016): 109–44.

12. Étienne Balibar, *We the People of Europe: Reflections on Transnational Citizenship*, trans. James Swenson (Princeton: Princeton University Press, 2003).

13. From 1996 to 2005 Rosi Braidotti was the founding scientific director of the Thematic Network of Women's Studies in Europe—ATHENA—for the Socrates program of the European Commission, which had 120 institutional members throughout the European Union. In 2010, ATHENA was awarded the Erasmus Prize in recognition of its outstanding contribution to education and training.

14. Braidotti, *Nomadic Theory*.

15. See "Europe Does Not Make Us Dream: An Interview with Rosi Braidotti by Rutvica Andrijaševic," http://translate.eipcp.net/strands/02/andrijasevic braidotti-strands01en#redir.

16. This is the DiEM25 Organization: https://diem25.org.

17. IMF, "Neo-Liberalism: Oversold?," www.imf.org/external/pubs/ft/fandd /2016/06/ostry.htm.

18. Jacques Derrida, *Rogues: Two Essays on Reason*, trans. Pascale-Anne Brault (Stanford: Stanford University Press, 2015).

19. Maurizio Lazzarato, *The Making of the Indebted Man*, trans. Joshua David Jordan (Cambridge, MA: Semiotext[e], 2012). See also "Indebted Citizenship—an Interview with Rosi Braidotti," interview with Andrea Mura, *Open Democracy*, February 26, 2014, www.opendemocracy.net/can-europe-make-it/rosi -braidotti-andrea-mura/indebted-citizenship-interview-with-rosi -braidotti.

20. Yann Moulier Boutang, *Cognitive Capitalism* (Cambridge: Polity, 2012).

21. Paul Mason, "Only Bernie Sanders Can Break the Power of Capitalism in the US," *Guardian*, April 18, 2016, www.theguardian.com/commentisfree/2016/ apr/18/bernie-sanders-break-power-capitalism-us-democratic-presidential -race-hillary-clinton.

22. Philomena Essed, *Understanding Everyday Racism: An Interdisciplinary Theory* (London: Sage, 1991); and Gloria Wekker, *White Innocence: Paradoxes of Colonialism and Race* (Durham: Duke University Press, 2016).

23. Paul Gilroy, *Postcolonial Melancholia* (New York: Columbia University Press, 2006).

24. Deleuze and Guattari, *Anti-Oedipus*.

25. See Wendy Brown, *Walled States, Waning Sovereignty* (New York: Zone, 2014). See also the interview with Wendy Brown in this volume.

26. Spinoza, *Ethics* (London: Penguin, 2005).

27. Alain Badiou, *Deleuze: The Clamor of Being*, trans. Louise Burchill (Mineapolis: University of Minnesota Press, 1999).

28. Benjamin Noys, *The Persistence of the Negative: A Critique of Contemporary Continental Theory* (Edinburgh: Edinburgh University Press, 2012).
29. Laboria Cuboniks, "Xenofeminism: A Politics for Alienation," www .laboriacuboniks.net.
30. Luce Irigaray, *This Sex Which Is Not One*, trans. Catherine Porter (Ithaca: Cornell University Press, 1977), 31–33.
31. Genevieve Lloyd, *Routledge Philosophy Guidebook to Spinoza and the Ethics* (Abingdon: Routledge, 1996).
32. Suzanne Guerlac, *Thinking in Time: An Introduction to Henri Bergson* (Ithaca: Cornell University Press, 2006).
33. Michel Foucault, "Preface," in Deleuze and Guattari, *Anti-Oedipus*.
34. Spengler's work continues to be widely read by the "alt-right."
35. Achille Mbembe, *On the Postcolony* (Berkeley: University of California Press, 2001).
36. Klaus Theweleit, *Male Fantasies*, trans. Jessica Benjamin (Cambridge: Polity, 1987).
37. René Girard, *The Scapegoat*, trans. Yvonne Freccero (Baltimore: Johns Hopkins University Press, 1989).
38. Roberto Esposito, *Bios: Biopolitics and Philosophy*, trans. Timothy Campbell (Minneapolis: University of Minnesota Press, 2008).
39. Annalisa Coppolaro-Nowell, "Italy's Fertility Day Posters Aren't Just Sexist— They're Echoes of a Fascist Past," *Guardian*, September 5, 2016, www.the guardian.com/commentisfree/2016/sep/05/italys-fertility-day-posters-sexist -echoes-of-fascist-past.
40. Inderpal Grewal and Caren Kaplan, eds., *Scattered Hegemonies: Postmodernity and Transnational Feminist Practices* (Minneapolis: University of Minnesota Press, 1994).
41. Lega Nord is a right-wing political party, founded by Umberto Bossi, that advocates more autonomy for the regions in Italy. In the past, it has advocated the separation of the North of Italy from the South. The Five Star Movement (Movimento 5 Stelle) is a more recent party founded by comedian Beppe Grillo.
42. Rosi Braidotti, *Nomadic Subjects: Embodiment and Sexual Difference in Contemporary Feminist Theory* (New York: Columbia University Press, 2011); Braidotti, *Metamorphoses: Towards a Materialist Theory of Becoming* (Malden, MA: Polity, 2002); Braidotti, *Transpositions: On Nomadic Ethics* (Malden, MA: Polity, 2006).
43. Félix Guattari, *The Three Ecologies* (London: Continuum, 2008); Chaosmosis, *An Ethico-Aesthetic Paradigm* (Bloomington: Indiana University Press, 1995).
44. Matthew Fuller, *Media Ecologies: Materialist Energies in Art and Technoculture* (Cambridge, MA: MIT Press, 2005); Mark Hansen, *Bodies in Code: Interfaces with Digital Media* (New York: Routledge, 2006).

45. Jussi Parikka, *A Geology of Media* (Minneapolis: University of Minnesota Press, 2015); Jennifer Gabrys, *Digital Rubbish: A Natural History of Electronics* (Ann Arbor: University of Michigan Press, 2011).

46. Donna Haraway, "A Cyborg Manifesto: Science, Technology and Socialist-Feminism in the Late Twentieth Century," in *Simians, Cyborgs, and Women: The Reinvention of Nature* (New York: Routledge, 1991), 149–81.

47. Michel Foucault, *L'ordre du discours* (Paris: Gallimard, 1970).

48. A term obtained by merging precarious with proletariat. It designates the bottom social class in advanced capitalism with low levels of economic, cultural, and social capital. See Guy Standing, *The Precariat: The New Dangerous Class* (London: Bloomsbury Academic, 2011).

49. Martha Nussbaum, *Not for Profit: Why Democracy Needs the Humanities* (Princeton: Princeton University Press, 2010).

50. For more information, see www.humanities2017.org.

51. Rosi Braidotti, *The Posthuman* (Malden, MA: Polity, 2013).

52. Rosi Braidotti, "The Contested Posthumanities," in *Contesting Humanities*, ed. Rosi Braidotti and Paul Gilroy (London: Bloomsbury Academic, 2016).

53. Lisa Duggan, "The Theory Wars, or, Who's Afraid of Judith Butler?," *Journal of Women's History* 10, no. 1 (Spring 1998): 9–19.

54. Michael Berubé and Cary Nelson, eds., *Higher Education Under Fire: Politics, Economics and the Crisis of the Humanities* (New York: Routledge, 1995).

55. Jeffrey Williams, *How To Be an Intellectual: Essays on Criticism, Culture, and the University* (New York: Fordham University Press, 2014).

56. John M. Coetzee, "Take a Stand On Academic Freedom," *University World News* 298 (2013), www.universityworldnews.com/article.php?story=2013112 6223127382.

57. See, for instance, Bill Readings, *The University in Ruins* (Cambridge, MA: Harvard University Press, 1996).

58. Rosi Braidotti and Judith Butler, "Out of Bounds: Philosophy in an Age of Transition," in *The History of Continental Philosophy*, vol. 7, ed. Rosi Braidotti (Durham: Acumen, 2010), 307–35.

59. Braidotti, *The Posthuman*.

60. Thomas Lemke, *Biopolitics*, trans. Monica J. Casper (New York: New York University Press, 2011).

61. Paul Patton, *Deleuze and the Political* (London: Routledge, 2000); Melinda Cooper, *Life as Surplus: Biotechnology and Capitalism in the Neoliberal Era* (Seattle: University of Washington Press, 2008); Cooper, *Clinical Labor: Tissue Donors and Research Subjects in the Global Bioeconomy* (Durham: Duke University Press, 2014).

62. Gilles Deleuze, *Foucault* (Minneapolis: University of Minnesota Press, 1988).

63. Gilles Deleuze, "Postscript on the Societies of Control," *October* 59 (Winter 1992): 3–7.

64. Achille Mbembe, "Necropolitics," *Public Culture* 15, no. 1 (2003): 11–40.

65. Braidotti, *Transpositions*.

66. Judith Butler, *Precarious Life: The Powers of Mourning and Violence* (London: Verso, 2006); Paul Gilroy, "The Black Atlantic and the Re-Enchantment of Humanism," Tanner Lectures, Yale University, February 2014.

67. Judith Butler, *Notes Towards a Performative Theory of Assembly* (Cambridge, MA: Harvard University Press, 2015).

68. Cuboniks, "Xenofeminism."

69. Braidotti, *Transpositions*.

70. Giorgio Agamben, *Homo Sacer: Sovereign Power and Bare Life*, trans. Daniel Heller-Roazen (Stanford: Stanford University Press, 1998).

71. Catherine Stimpson, "The Nomadic Posthumanities," *LA Review of Books*, July 12, 2016, https://lareviewofbooks.org/article/the-nomadic-humanities/.

2

We Should be Modest, When It Comes to the Designation of the Possible Subjects of a New Politics

Interview with Jacques Rancière

In a recent interview you made a connection between the rise of the Front National in France and the current discourse about secularism (laïcité*) and freedom of expression. You have remarked that such values, which are being defended by both the Left and the Right, are used as a way to repress certain social groups because they allow one to distinguish between "those who know" and "those who don't know." Could you explain this? In which way does the defense of so-called universal values contribute to the repression of certain groups of people?*

The main target of that intervention was a phenomenon that is typically—though not exclusively—French, namely, the ideology of the republic (*l'ideologie republicaine*). During the 1980s, this ideology was transformed into a defense of the so-called universal values of the republic. Originally, this defense provided a substitute for lost socialist and revolutionary aspirations. However, over time, it took on a more specific character; it allowed one to distinguish those who possess these universal values from those who are perceived as communitarian. As a matter of fact, for a long time, the notion of communitarianism didn't exist in France. It was imported to indicate parts of the population that did not obey the law of the universal. Particularly important in this regard was the instrumentalization of the concept of secularism (*laïcité*).

Initially, "secularism" was a term indicating the relationship between two powers: the Church and the State. When secularism was imposed in France at the end of the nineteenth century, it was mainly to exclude the Church from the schools. Prior to that period, the Church had a strong grip on the education system, for instance, on the hiring process of teachers. In this respect, the introduction of secularism was a way of keeping the Church outside of the school gates and of stripping it of some of its prerogatives, for example, by introducing the possibility of civil marriages and civil funerals alongside the religious rites. In this way, secularism was used to liberate the people's lives from the grip of the Church, and especially to liberate the school system from this grip. The essential point here is, of course, that for a long time secularism was a matter of the relationship between institutions. In contrast, in the new ideology of secularism, secularism has been transformed into a moral obligation of the individuals themselves. Before, making schools secular meant that schools did not concern themselves with religion, that they did not teach religions, and that they did not ask their students what religion they adhered to. This has changed completely, as the discussions about wearing a headscarf in schools notably showed. Instead of the school being secular and not asking the students what religion they adhere to, it is now the students who have to hide the fact that they adhere to a certain religion.

What is important is not only that entire groups of the population are being targeted for not being secular, for example, the Muslim population, but also that the question of religion has been focused on the issue of the headscarf, that is to say, on a physical feature. One interprets a piece of clothing as a form of religious propaganda. Obviously, this type of reasoning does not hold. It is not because one wears a certain piece of clothing that one wants to impose the ideas of a religion on others. What is crucial, I believe, is that by reducing the question of secularism to a discussion about a piece of clothing, one has truly adopted a prominent trait of racism, namely, that of making a connection between the lack of a certain category and a physical feature. In this case, it is not one's skin color or the shape of one's nose, but it is nevertheless a physical feature. In this way, the concept of secularism becomes a form of "enlightened" racism. In contrast to older kinds of racism, it is a sort of legitimate racism. And it was people on the political left, or at least who considered themselves as such, who developed this republican, secularist ideology, which has been gradually adopted by the entire political class in France, from the Parti Socialiste to the Front National. Instead of saying that all black people are dirty or that all Arabs are liars and thieves, it sounds "better" to say that certain groups are not secular, that they do not adhere to the universal values of our republic. I believe the development of this secular ideology on the left, which is clearly an ideology of exclusion, is just a vulgar form of racism.

On several occasions you have said that the Parti Socialiste has killed the ideals of the Left in France. Could you explain this? And do you still believe in the role of political parties or parliamentary democracy to change society for the better?

Here I am referring again to the specific French context, though this is part of a more general context. The Parti Socialiste came into power in France in 1980 on the basis of a campaign that adopted the Marxist language of promising a truly revolutionary transformation of society. It wanted to recuperate the legacy of the workers' movement, the socialist movement, and revolutionary movements, as well as the energy of the years from 1968 to 1970. Of course, very rapidly the Parti Socialiste abandoned every aspect of its program. As a matter of fact, it is striking that the French Parti Socialiste has been a party of permanent betrayal. Every time it promises something, one can expect that it will do the opposite.

Obviously, this politics of betrayal had far-reaching consequences. First of all, there is a kind of Left that wants to get power in Parliament and that conducts its governmental practices in the same manner as the Right. Besides this, there was the installation of a hegemony of the intellectual Right. Simultaneous with the socialist government being in power, we saw the development of an ideology that liquidated the entire revolutionary and socialist tradition. This was an operation, as the historian François Furet remarked, that aimed to get rid of the revolution, of communism, and of every other progressive tradition by claiming that all these movements were nothing but totalitarian ideologies. Because this intellectual counterrevolution was really established under a socialist government that constantly betrayed its own ideals, this resulted in a form of discouragement. People who believed in socialist values could either pretend to believe the government was socialist or simply feel discouraged. In the end, this entire dynamic led to a form of demoralization. After all, when a government doesn't hold to its promises, this normally incites some kind of revolt. In the case of France, such a revolt didn't take place. On the contrary, the Parti Socialiste's permanent betrayal engendered a form of consent or resignation. Some people declared that this was just the way capitalism worked and that nothing could be done about this.

Moreover, one should not forget that this dynamic is reinforced by the presidential regime: practically the only "political" question in France—"political" in quotation marks—is the election of the president of the republic. In other words, everything is reduced to the question of who will be elected or who will be a candidate. The enormous power of the president has pushed the representational system to its limits. And a phenomenon like the Front National is, of course, indicative of this problematic situation. That is to say, the monopolization of power by a very small political class explains not only the discouragement on the left, but also the success of a party that presents itself as one that functions outside the system. In fact, the Front National has taken up the outsider position that used to be occupied in France by the Communist Party (Parti communiste français).

As I said, I believe that we are at the point where this type of representational system, and specifically its focus on the president, has reached its limits. By the way, this also goes for the United States. In the United States, the point has been reached where there is nothing democratic about the representational system anymore. However, I do not think all of this will provoke a serious crisis, because, despite everything, there is a certain national consensus that people can live very well for a long time in a rotten system.

If the representational system is rotten, what do you think about popular resistance movements such as the antiglobalization movement or the Occupy movement? Do you believe that such movements can reinstall a political dynamic that has been lost?

Well, I think the problem with the antiglobalization movement is that currently there are no national movements that are strong enough for it to function. What we have, instead, are little groups of, as it were, "specialized" agitators of antiglobalization. This is very different from the traditional workers' movement, which was, of course, taken over by the Communist Party and by the Soviet Union at a certain stage. This movement's role was to connect the different workers' movements so that each had their own autonomous strength. Because there is no such thing today, and because the antiglobalization movement mainly consisted of "specialists of antiglobalization" who did their interventions at every G7 or G8 meeting, the antiglobalization movement has been eliminated.

Concerning the Occupy movement, in my view this has been the only relatively important movement of the past few years because it reminded us of the fact that politics always has to do with the creation of a specific people (*un people*), with its own spatiality and temporality. Essentially, it reminded us of the necessity for every democratic movement to be autonomous, in other words, independent of the logics of the representational system. This is something very important. The Occupy movement has shown that something else is required for politics to exist. Of course, it is a fact that none of these movements has truly succeeded in transforming things while retaining their autonomy. We can think here of the Arab revolutions, which were incapable of forming their own political organization, so that, in the end, the Islamist groups were the only ones organized enough to replace the old dictators. We can also think of Greece and Spain, where a choice had to be made between maintaining the autonomy of the movement and transforming the movement into a radical leftist party. By going down the latter path, the ones in charge hoped to capitalize on the movement by creating an alternative in Parliament. For my part, I believe this is a strategy that will go nowhere. For example, the way Podemos was born out of movements such as the 15-M movement on the Puerta del Sol to eventually become a party negotiating the number of ministers it wants is telling. This is clearly a dead end.

I am not saying that one should remain completely outside of the parliamentary system. After all, this system is there and one should certainly address it. But I believe that the cases of SYRIZA and Podemos have shown that these new parties follow the same parliamentary logic as other leftist parties, namely, a logic that tries to occupy a position of power at the heart of the parliamentary system. I believe this strategy has reached its limits. All in all, while the Occupy movements have indicated other possibilities, they have also left these possibilities open and indeterminate. As a consequence, they were not able to have any substantial impact. Despite the fact that some of them became powerful, there is nevertheless a feeling of impotence and discouragement with respect to the strategy they deploy.

Maybe this can be connected to your ideas about emancipation? You argue that for a true emancipation the idea of the equality of all has to be the starting point. Contrary to this, many social and political movements have regarded equality as a goal to be attained. Could you say a bit more about this? Why do these two positions exclude each other?

Indeed, I have always been of the opinion that the truly democratic or emancipatory idea is that equality is a starting point and not the result of a process. For a political movement this means that one has to assume that equality exists while also finding ways to allow this equality to develop. In other words, one has to develop an autonomy based on the idea of the equal capacities of every person. Hence, the basic issue is that we are confronted with two opposite rationales. On the one hand, there is the logic of emancipation, which is a logic of autonomous development. Its idea is to expand the domain of autonomy to engage the capacities of every individual. On the other hand, there is the logic of taking power, which is obviously a logic where one sets goals, formulates priorities, and selects specific means in order to obtain the designated objectives. In such a context of power, there will be people who claim to know exactly what the necessary means are and how to implement them. Because it is normal for people to ask of a political movement what it wants to achieve, how it will do that, and who it wants to form alliances with, the logic of power is, of course, hard to resist. One can hardly imagine a response like the following: "No, this is not what we are going to do. What we want is to develop autonomous spheres on different levels, collective forms of discussion and organization, as well as forms of knowledge, forms of information, and autonomous forms of manifestation that have been developed out of our movement itself."

All in all, understanding the contrast between these two rationales is very important if we are talking about emancipation. For example, when we think about what happened with the different occupying movements, we can discern a recurring problem, namely, which form of organization suits the principle of equality? As a matter of fact, the organizational form by means of which one usually attempts to realize the principle of equality is that of the assembly in which everybody can take part, in which everybody can speak. Of course, this is all well and good, but I want to point out that equality has to be realized in actions and initiatives. It is not simply realized because of the fact that everybody is gathered in an assembly or by saying that there is no leader and that everybody can speak freely.

I think the issue here is that of imagination, namely, of developing a form of imagination that suits the idea of equality. I think that a truly autonomous and a truly egalitarian political movement today should be a movement that creates initiatives, provocations, and situations. Of course, the word "situation" is associated with the Situationists, who in the end did not do all that much with it. I think that a new and committed movement, if it does not want to disappear or be taken over entirely by a logic of power, should constantly invent situations in the form of redescriptions of the world we live in.

I think there is a double necessity. First, one should develop an internal democracy that puts to work the equality of everybody. Second, one should develop a presence in the public space in the form of initiatives, provocations, and situations. An egalitarian politics should indeed be reinvented. Even though I don't know exactly what such a politics should look like, I do think that its development is extremely important in our current context of politics organized by oligarchies that have a monopoly on the description of the world and on the different possible narratives about the world and its future. So one has to create and constantly reinvent different ways of describing and narrating the world.

Of course, this also relates to the question of diffusion. Here too we encounter a sort of oligarchic monopoly on what is considered an event worth noting. Indeed, we have to turn to alternative channels to high-light certain events that went by unnoticed and to spread alternative narratives. However, today this is easier to do than before because, thanks to the Internet and social media, one can now disseminate other forms of narratives, other images, and other ways of narrating and con-structing the world.

You speak about narratives and images, but do you think that certain political forms or certain forms of organization could better guarantee the principle of equality of all?

I think this is a very difficult issue. Everybody says that we need a kind of organization. Fine, but there are organizations everywhere. Our world has no lack of organizations and not even of revolutionary organi-zations. There will always be a certain amount of people who will continue to protest. The real question is what one understands by organization. What I am trying to say is that in the first place an organization is not a collective interiority that tries to maintain itself, but something that produces real effects. After all, a subject is an operator of narration, of descriptions, of events, of real change in the visibility of our common world. So, of course, one can always have organizations with secretaries and committees. That is easy to do. But, fundamentally, one has to keep in mind that such organizations, not all but most of them, are created for a very specific reason, namely, to take power, either in the parliamen-tary way or in the form of a revolutionary avant-garde or sometimes in the form of a mixture between these two strategies. By the way, this mingling of strategies is exactly what the extreme-left parties of today do when they hold up the flag of the global revolution but, at the same time, try to have one or two representatives in regional councils here and there through the formation of alliances with the dominant left-wing parties. In sum, this is the question of organizations. The aim is not how to install an organizational bureaucracy, but how to invent goals: To what avail does an organization exist? I believe this is the real challenge.

It is for this reason that I try to point out that we have to think about organizations along these two lines. On the one hand, safeguarding one's autonomy from the normal forms of organization that follow the logic of power. On the other hand, thinking about organizations in terms of an internal development of the principle of equality, which implies the production of events that are instances of equality. After all, the main concern in politics should be not just to denounce inequality, but also to create instances of equality.

What could the role of the public intellectual be in the process you describe?

I always have a strong reluctance to speak about the role of the intellectual because speaking about the role of the intellectual means speaking about a social category and about the way one sees and idealizes oneself by presuming one possesses universal capacities, either of knowing the science of society or of being the conscience of those without conscience, and so on. So I would not describe my own work as corresponding to the role of the intellectual. What I have tried to do is to rethink grand narratives a little, such as those about the connection between order and disorder or between history and revolutionary rupture.

As you may know, I have intervened in a conjuncture where one had the old Marxist discourse about science, the avant-gardes' discourse of the revolution, and also a discourse about the end of history. Now, the role I attempted to take up consisted in a reversal of the discourse about the end of history by indicating that that for which one declares the end has never existed in that form. It is clear that emancipation has never been the emancipation of the workers. There has never been a working class that became conscious of itself thanks to the avant-garde that had "enlightened" it. Emancipation is something that has occurred as an operation at the heart of the working class in which people who were workers, in the sense that they occupied a certain place in a system, tried to invent another place in the world for themselves, as well as other ways of living and thinking. In other words, what I have attempted to say is that there has never been a grand revolutionary narrative with a grand working-class subject walking out of the factory. On the contrary, what we had was a multitude of forms of subjectivation that in a way constituted a common signifier, a common subject, but that always remained fragile and at risk. Hence, what I have tried to say is that there has never been a grand narrative, but only little narratives of which the grand narrative has always consisted. This means that we are not at the end of a historical period, although one could indeed argue that we are at the end of a faith in history.

However, the faith in emancipation is not connected with a faith in the kind of historical process that will bring about revolution, socialism, or universal happiness. In sum, I have attempted to redescribe what could have been the history of the workers' emancipation, the history of ideas of emancipation. I have tried to say that we are not in a Marxist logic, which, like the neoliberal logic that has replaced it, is a logic of necessity, according to which there is only one way in which the world can function. In this sense, the role that I give to myself, of course without consciously trying to play a role in the history of the world, is to reinsert again and again an element of indeterminacy and freedom in a history that otherwise would be described as completely determined.

You have spoken about fictions, about representations. What do you think about the use of the term "crisis"? To what does it refer and what is its function when politicians or economists use it today?

Well, I think the notion of crisis is in itself paradoxical. In the nineteenth century, as an economic term, it had the precise meaning of a moment of rupture in an economic cycle. At the same time, it is, of course, a concept that originated in a medical context. In this respect, what I always try to recall is that "crisis" does not mean disease. In ancient medicine, a crisis designated the decisive stage when a disease would reach the moment when there is nothing else one can do, and the patient will either die or recover. What is significant is the way in which this medical notion has been superimposed upon an economic one while at the same time its meaning has completely changed. Today, crisis is the equivalent of disease in the sense that everywhere where there is a problem, there is a crisis. We hear about a climate crisis, a crisis of refugees, etc. But not only is it so that every problem becomes a crisis, but it is also the case that every crisis makes an appeal to a medical treatment, that is to say, to medics who are specialists in dealing with these types of crises.

What is essential here is what this notion of crisis refers to, from an economic point of view. In my opinion, it simply signifies the new form of capitalism. As long as there has been globalization, there have been crises. But globalization is simply the reorganization of capitalism. Now, this globally organized capitalism has caused delocalization and the closing of factories. Moreover, we are faced with a speculative system and all its risks. In short, what one calls "crisis" is simply the normal state of capitalism today. It is described as a pathology against which the individual is deemed to be powerless. Only the medical experts are able to do something and coincidentally those are the same medics who organize the system. In the end, one gets a circular argument in which the term "crisis" is used to say that one should obey those who govern.

You have mentioned the refugees. We see that the political and media discourse surrounding today's refugee "crisis" presumes a division between "us" and "them." Which flaws in our political system are currently being revealed by the presence of refugees, for example, in Calais?

It is really difficult to control that situation. One could say that, on the one hand, there is an economic organization of the world that creates regions where there is no work and other regions where one can legitimately hope to get a job and live one's life. Hence, there has been a concentration of wealth in certain regions so that entire populations living in deprived economic conditions are incited to immigrate to these centers of wealth. This is clear. What is, on the other hand, also clear is that this situation is the effect of a disorganization of the system. With this I mean that it is the consequence of the fact that there are many dictatorial and corrupt regimes that force people into exile. One could think, for instance, of regimes in former colonial states that have never been properly decolonized. Of course, one should keep in mind that the political regimes in the Middle East first had to endure the effects of the Cold War and then the effects of the military operations of the

United States and the Western powers. What we find as a result is a convergence between, on the one hand, the current economic normality and, on the other hand, a huge disorder following the short- and long-term politics of the world powers. All of this plays a role in migration as we witness it today.

Moreover, we are confronted here with a fundamental paradox of what could be called the liberal world, namely, in theory it is based on the free circulation of goods and people, but, in practice, in order for goods and wealth to circulate freely, it is required that people do not circulate freely. This system is really full of contradictions and people like us cannot do much about it. Maybe the only thing we can do concerns the connection of these forms of global migration to their codification as a threat to our national identity, such as when we talk about Islamism or communitarianism. I am not saying that there are no problems with large-scale migration—of course, there are—but what I mean is that the small political intervention we could do is to try to disconnect the problem of migration from the problem of identity.

In the past you have written about the part of those who have no part in relation to what you have called dissensus. *Where can we see this part today?*

Well, I think this is actually very difficult. The part of those who have no part is not the part of those who are miserable, or the part of those who are excluded, or the revolt of those who are starving. The part of those who have no part refers to the capacity of a part of the population to embody the part of those who do not, or no longer, have a part. As a matter of fact, this used to be the definition of the proletariat, namely, the class comprising those who do not belong to a class. Put differently, the class of those who remain outside of the system. What I am saying is that the part of those who have no part refers to the capacity for a universalization of the position of those who are not recognized as actors in the social and political life.

However, today this kind of subjectivation barely exists. Sure, we had the Arab revolutions, the Occupy movement, and things like that, but fundamentally we are in a situation in which groups of people are not constituted as political subjects. For example, the group of migrants in Calais trying to go to England is not a political subject. And even the many groups who want to defend the rights of these migrants or who are there to help—which is, of course, very good—do not yet constitute a political subject that is created as a form of universalization of all cases of equality. I believe this is something that doesn't really exist today. When I think about ways to develop autonomous political groups further, I see that people without a part are actually everywhere, but that we nevertheless remain in a logic of the defense of this or that identity. What is crucial in this respect is that the category of the universal has been completely confiscated by the republican ideology that created this opposition between universalism and communitarianism, while in fact they are only forms of communitarianism that are being opposed to each other. So I think that today there is no true form of egalitarian subjectivation that traverses all identities.

If one thinks again of France, between the people who protest against the expansion of the airport in Notre Dame des Landes and the groups of youngsters who revolted in the Parisian *banlieues* in 2005, there is no connection. There is just a multiplicity of little movements that focus on the defense of one domain. On no occasion have the youth revolting in the *banlieues* attempted to go beyond the limits of their area. Probably, if they'd tried, they would have been beaten on the head anyway—as happened in the *banlieues*. But on no occasion was there an attempt to produce a force that was more than an alliance between people who are angry in this or that specific *banlieue*, that is to say, to produce a true political subject. I think we still remain within a logic of the local and the particular. One could say, to take up the terminology of Lyotard, that there is a universal wrong (*un tort universel*), but it is always approached in terms of particular wrongs, by particular groups.

Do you see ways in which these different groups could become a more universal and connected political subject after all?

I believe that this is an enormous task. We are, in fact, in a situation that is totally blocked. That is to say, the dominant narrative has become so dominant that to oppose it is a task that I don't know how to undertake. So, I must say that for the moment I don't detect the forces that are going to challenge the status quo. Some would say, a bit dishonestly, that what we need is a new form of communism. But I wouldn't know which force of resistance this new communism would refer to in our world today. In sum, we should be radical in the presentation of our diverging views (*écarts*), but we should be modest when it comes to the designation of the possible subjects of a new politics.

INTERVIEW CONDUCTED AND TRANSLATED BY STIJN DE CAUWER
AND GERT-JAN MEYNTJENS

3

The History of the Notion of Crisis

Interview with Joseph Vogl

Professor Vogl, let us start off by defining the object of our discussion. What kinds of situations are denoted by the concept of "crisis"? What is the history behind this notion? What is the main indication that something has reached a state of crisis?

That is, of course, a major question. One can point to three different roots of the term. First, there are its close ties with the classical juridical process. There, crisis refers to the moment of passing sentence. A second significant use is found in medicine, where crisis refers to the transitional phase in which illness evolves for better or for worse (in other words, death). Third, the concept of crisis also appeared in military contexts to denote the phase in which the war is at the threshold of either victory or defeat.

As such, I believe we have already touched upon some important elements, especially that the concept began to move beyond medical and legal contexts into the field of history. It came to be applied in the evaluation and description of historical processes no later than the eighteenth century.

Let us, perhaps, highlight a number of aspects that were central to this crucial moment. First, that there is such a thing as a transitional phase—and, this is important, a phase with an unclear future—when something *will have been decided*, in the future perfect tense. Second, and I think this is truly essential, a historical consciousness is indeed connected to this modern notion of crisis, meaning that we are here and now deciding on historical processes and procedural modes. A third significant point, one that emerges in the course of the eighteenth century, is that the crisis terminology increasingly appears in relation to different systemic contexts: legal systems, political systems, and above all economic systems, which are a decisive motor for the expansion of the crisis concept. Moreover, since the eighteenth century, crisis has also meant a process with a certain expansive character, departing from concrete phenomena and ready to expand into all spheres of life.

I want to add one final aspect to describe the modern scenario of crisis. Also relevant to the crisis concept—and its background in medicine plays a role here—is the interpretation of signs and diagnosis of symptoms. Since the 1770s, the concept has been associated with the omen of revolutionary movements, the foreshadow of enduring revolution. In the United States of America, for example, Thomas Paine founded a journal or pamphlet carrying the title *The Crisis*. This requires a highly specific reading of signs. Kant spoke, for instance, of the *signum prognostikon*. These are medical inheritances, in that "crisis" coincides with a diagnostic and prognostic activity.

So the notion of crisis was mainly applied in medicine. Was what we call a political or an economic crisis today already familiar in classical, for example, Roman, times?

So, the notion of *krisis* was used, on the one hand, to denote a certain processual procedure—be it judicial, medical, or military. On the other hand, it had an intellectual aspect and was tied to the art of judgment. What did not take place, however, was the transposition of the concept to general political processes we find today. But, even though the notion was not used in the modern sense, there were, of course, already instances where its application was analogous.

Take, for instance, the *Iliad*. While the wrath of Achilles that sets off the first Western epos is not described with the terminology of crisis, it similarly amounts to a collapse of social and political ties. The example of Achilles's wrath demonstrates what classical philologists called the "conflictual universe," the caving in of all possible relations between men, between men and gods, and even within the divine sphere.

A similarly relevant example of the crisis format appears in *Oedipus Rex*. In Sophocles's drama, one can observe human relationships collapse in relation to symptoms of illness, the famous plague in the beginning, and the desperation in the face of what is to come—ultimately the issue of royal power. Without the explicit usage of the terminology, we already have here, so to speak, a phenomenon of a social and political crisis with medical characteristics.

Would you agree with the claim that the notion of crisis is used in an inflationary sense today? Or are we indeed experiencing a rapid succession of critical conditions, and, if so, are these causally connected?

I agree with you entirely that the concept is subject to an inflationary use, but there are various historical and contemporary causes of this. One of them is indeed the nineteenth-century origin of the modern notion of crisis, which is related to the genesis of what one could call "crisis theories," which developed at the heart of the economic domain. One might even make the claim that economic theories are genuine crisis theories. Just think of Malthus's principle of population, which states that societies will optimize themselves even by passing through crises, such as hunger crises. Or Karl Marx's prominent crisis theory where crisis appears at any stage where the tension between the "relations of production" and the "productive forces" has become critical. A second area of interest, which emerged at the latest in the nineteenth century with Jakob Burckhardt, deals with issues regarding the relation between crises and cultural development. That is to say, entire cultures will reform themselves or develop according to moments of crisis—and ultimately, these moments are cyclical. Like, for example, in Oswald Spengler. The dissemination of crisis terminology can be considered against this backdrop and I think that the concept was applied in inflationary ways in different areas no later than World War I.

As far as the present condition is concerned, one could perhaps point out two or three aspects. The wide dissemination of the concept of crisis signals above all that the economization of societies is intertwined with the way these societies are represented. The economic notion of crisis, in other words, has a discursive-expansive potential. Second, the use of the crisis notion, especially nowadays, is linked with the perception of instability.

Additionally, it also seems that the discourse on crisis is strategically employed and instrumentalized.

Certainly. After all, the use of the notion of crisis is not only associated with manifest insecurities—meaning that the present is interpreted as a space where the future is obscured, where it is unclear whether prospects are hopeful or hopeless. It also carries a strategic implication. Critical processes and phenomena as such have a character that seems impersonal or influenced by natural law. In other words, certain mechanisms, procedures, or processes have slipped out of our control and have come to represent events signaling reduced responsibility. Strategic use of the notion of crisis occurs when the capacity for decision and action is replaced by a kind of decision and action dictated by the event itself.

As a side note, this is especially dramatic when people talk about "refugee *crisis*." This is a thoroughly corrupt conceptualization. Because, for the refugees themselves, what they are going through is not a crisis, but a catastrophe. When people speak of a "refugee crisis," this suggests in a way that there is a kind of natural process, a surge, a wave that has suddenly swept over Europe as if by a violent natural force. In doing so, one ignores that migration is an essentially *constructed* phenomenon—not just in every individual instance, but also in general. In this sense, I think that using the term "refugee crisis" always carries a trace of resentment for "those people," those anonymous "others," and triggers a defensive reaction in Europe

You are probably aware of the adage "Never let a serious crisis go to waste." Does a crisis indeed entail the promise of purification, of catharsis? Or is this promise of catharsis only a phenomenon, surviving in literature since antiquity, that may lead to an increased acceptance of the abuse of this idea?

That's right. Crisis is in some way connected to catharsis—meaning the passage through difficult times leading to a turn for the better. This appears whenever one speaks of personal crises, psychological crises, crises of adolescence, etc. Essentially, the modern individual is from the outset a kind of crisis-creature that moves through critical situations and dysfunctional phases, and becomes more or less mature and responsible. I believe we are entirely committed to this form of progression, or this idea of progression. Perhaps one could say two or three things on this topic. First of all, I get the impression that the dispersal of the concept of crisis today testifies to something that one might call a persistent awareness of crisis. That is, a reduced power of control in the face of certain political, economic, and social processes where the turn for the better or worse cannot truly be recognized. These are processes in which the present is marked, in a sense, by the uncertainties of the future. This performance of insecurity [*Verunsicherungsleistung*], as it were, is connected to the modern use of crisis terminology and is probably to some extent reality-based. We are living in times of a heightened sense of uncertainty about the future. There is a second aspect that I referred to earlier, namely, in a sense the notion of crisis disposes of possible courses of action. Talk of crisis simultaneously signifies "I can't do anything about this." Or, put even more dramatically, it is the coercion of a particular—between quotation marks—"action without alternative." The ubiquitous use of the phrase "there is no alternative" during the last economic crisis demonstrated this.

There is still another aspect of crisis that we could discuss here, and this one is intertwined as well with the history of the concept of crisis, namely, the notion of criticism [*Kritik*]. Criticism and crisis are essentially complementary concepts. It simply denotes the other, *active* side of things. If the observation of the so-called crisis does not cause losing the power of action and choice, if it does not leave one at the mercy of "the event," then naturally it must yield a specific form of criticism. In such a case, it would mean that crises always pose intellectual challenges as well. Challenges, if you will, to expand one's capacity for judgment, as we experienced during the last financial crisis, when certain orthodoxies and scientific economic dogmas had to be reconsidered and heterodox questions had to be posed.

We were surprised when an IMF article was published in June 2016, in which, after enduring theoretical insistence to the contrary, the claim was made that austerity perhaps couldn't lead us out of crisis after all.

It was actually even more dramatic than that! The IMF made a 180-degree turn with this paper. It dismissed the various austerity programs that were designed since the 1970s and were later combined in the so-called Washington Consensus. It stated that opening up countries to international financial markets and making countries dependent on these markets can be disastrous—and this relates, of course, particularly to indebted countries, emerging countries, and developing countries. That, too, can be read in this paper. This is indeed a 180-degree turn on the part of the IMF, which, unfortunately, has not yet reached Germany and the German ministry of finance.

What is the origin of this remarkable German resistance to all possible alternatives to austerity politics? At times, the Germans were more neoliberal than the Americans.

There are historical and possibly also ideological reasons for this. The historical reasons are, of course, rooted in a highly specific German experience that goes back to the time of the Weimar Republic, which was marked by a very concrete and dramatic crisis. There was rampant inflation and an economic crisis that led to National Socialism. I believe that during the foundation of the *Bundesrepublik*, one had this crisis scenario in mind and therefore identified certain priorities—particularly with respect to monetary and price stability, and what was called "the social market economy" after the war, against the backdrop of ordoliberalism.

A second, more recent reason is the fact that especially in Germany there is a kind of indolence or a certain insensitivity to how the current economic situations are perceived by other countries in the European periphery, such as Greece, Portugal, and Spain. The general understanding in Germany is that we have ultimately somehow come out of all so-called economic crises undamaged or even improved, optimized, with even greater export opportunities, and so on. In other words,

Germany is a poor vantage point from which to observe the misery crises produce.

The final aspect is of an ideological kind. A broad liberal or liberalist consensus started during the early years of the *Bundesrepublik*. This also concerns those political parties that lean more toward the left end of the political spectrum, such as the Social Democratic Party of Germany, especially with its Godesberg Program. One could say that liberalism in all its possible varieties has become a kind of common basis [*Nullstellung*] of political understanding. It is very difficult to foster opposition to the widespread, universally absorbed liberalism that assumes that the market and the rules of the market will ultimately produce social order.

Who enjoys the prerogative of interpretation in times of crisis? What are the mechanisms by which this can be determined? Who gets to pass the verdict on whether or not there is in fact a crisis? Who plays the role of the doctor, so to speak?

I believe that this is a very interesting discursive strategy. The one who is first to declare a "crisis" very quickly assumes the competence of the therapist, the doctor, the evaluator, and as such, of course, claims a certain discursive or interpretative authority. I think that the appropriation of the observation and diagnosis of crisis is one of the most important strategies for assuming power in contemporary discourses. Here, there are two distinct types or characters. A first type is the one who, in declaring a crisis, desires a prompt process, desires a sacrifice, desires blood, sweat, and tears—think of Churchill, for example. It is the one who calls on the people to pass through a vale of tears, and wants austerity, for example. Thus, a state of emergency is declared that signals to those afflicted that you must make sacrifices. This is the first type.

The other type, I believe, is the so-called critical intellectual—a figure that is slowly going extinct, yet that has been strongly connected with the discourse on crisis. It is the one who speaks for others in certain social contexts and gathers "reserves of solidarity" [*Solidaritätsreserven*] around him in times of crisis. One who claims, "I am able, in this situation, to speak for others."

So, the politician declaring a state of emergency and the critical intellectual were, in a sense, organs of power in contemporary crisis discourses.

The first type is then also somewhat of a priest, a sage. Naturally, the notion of sacrifice recalls early societies where there were figures who spoke with the gods.

One could, of course, think of the old institution of the oracle. The mystery of the crisis at the beginning of Sophocles's *Oedipus Rex* is detected by the seer, the fortuneteller, the interpreter, by the one who had the most intimate relation with the oracle. Insofar as the proclamation of crisis is connected to a diagnostic and prognostic function, there is also an old remnant of wisdom that survives in the almost folkloric declamations of all the economic experts acting as economic *sages* [*Wirtschaftsweisen*]. So, there is a "designated space for wisdom" [*Weisheitsreservat*] for the one who joins a prognostic function together with a crisis.

Think also of the eschatological moments that play a role in crisis discourse. In the Bible, for instance, crisis or *krisis* is tied up with the question of the Last Judgment, the separation of the faithful and the unfaithful. Such eschatological remnants subsist in the concept of crisis. If one wanted to draw conclusions from this, I would advise, first of all, to exercise caution in dealing with the notion of crisis. Not because I believe that the use of the notion could not make sense, but because the crisis discourse demands, above all, a great investment of analytical labor.

There is a question that we wanted to ask a literary scholar in particular and it relates to the dissemination of the feeling of crisis by the media: Is there a language, a poetics, or an aesthetic of crisis? Are there specific patterns or cultural models for the representation of crisis-ridden conditions?

There are. At least from the moment literature is considered to be reflecting historical dynamics. One can find the first literary discourses of crisis approximately around 1620, during the first inflation crises on the eve of the Thirty Years' War. For example, we can observe that the so-called economic crisis of 1763, after the Seven Years' War, spawned a specific kind of literature. These literary documents were the products of general crises, such as the collapse of financial markets or the chain of bankruptcies that moved from Amsterdam, over Hamburg, to Berlin and Leipzig. An example of such a document is Lessing's *Minna von Barnhelm*. These are crisis pieces. Or think of *Faust II*, where, in a very interesting way, the modern character Faust (Faust, quite simply, as *the* modern character) can be linked with the question of crisis and even of sickness. At the beginning of *Faust II*, Faust awakes from a wholesome sleep, only to immediately end up in the next political and economic crisis during which, for example, uncovered paper currency is produced.

At every point in time when literature is regarded as an organ that resonates with its historical conditions, crisis is a substantial source of poetic inspiration. The eve of World War I is another example where the notion of the stationary crisis became a proper model for the novel. So when Robert Musil or Thomas Mann were both writing major novels about their times [*Zeitromane*] at the end of World War I, *The Man Without Qualities* and *The Magic Mountain*, these novels were conceptualized against the backdrop of a stagnant crisis that resulted in the First World War. The array of characters in these novels, the relations between them, and the potential for events that can be found there are drawn into the "passe-partout" of a general crisis.

Do you know of any stylistic or topical attributes of cultural artifacts within modern art, literature, or cinema that make you think: here the crisis is already apparent?

Hard to say. On the one hand—and this very quickly comes to mind—one could refer to the popular disaster culture: disaster films that range from terrorist attacks, to ice ages, hurricanes, deluge, all the way to the bombing of the Capitol. However, I believe these are not interesting crisis phenomena. Rather the opposite. I believe that the majority of the American disaster industry conceives of fictional, imminent, or impending catastrophes—from the natural disaster to the act of terrorism—rather counterfactually. It actually demonstrates the points where these societies consider themselves to be immune. Fictional conjectures of disasters play a role in the awareness of one's immunity. Otherwise, it wouldn't be so interesting and exciting. The disaster, so to speak, enjoys the status of being most unlikely, and has become a subject of the culture industry precisely for that reason.

There is a second, more interesting element that leads from the artistic, to the discursive, to the concretely political debate. This is the question—the big question, I think—that permeates all possible debates today, namely, the question of the governmentality of contemporary societies, and ultimately the related question of political sovereignty. I have the impression that most instances where the diagnosis of crisis is made and the bulk of instances of crisis discourse are inspired by the disappearance of *the* sovereign, *the* locus of power, and, with that, the act of governing as such. This leads to all kinds of partially burlesque manifestations, all the way up to figures like Donald Trump. He adopts sovereign features in the most idiosyncratic ways—similar to *Ubu Roi* from Alfred Jarry's play—and demonstrates these when he tells blatant lies or propagates torture, and when he turns the killing and excluding of demographic groups into part of his program, he is able to demonstrate the "pretensions of sovereignty" one is capable of. Such figures are always the profiteers of crisis.

In your last book, you also talked about informal crises that later gain sovereignty in the world of finance. It is also striking that Donald Trump always says: "People call me." The truth doesn't reveal itself on the political forum; it is in the private phone call with Donald Trump that the problem is revealed.

Yes, there's a requirement that could be called the requirement of a direct phone line to "salvation," or something like that. In this sense, it could be said from the perspective of the observer that similar figures are pieced together from the scraps of crisis discourses. In Herman Melville, this was the figure of the *confidence man*, of which Donald Trump is an illustration.

Many of the explanatory models and narratives of contemporary crises seem to represent the problematic situation as a kind of Promethean history of Western hubris: Western capitalism attacked the environment,

which now struggles with extreme weather conditions; Western colonial-
ism reshaped the political geography for its own sake and, today, the
resulting ethnic and religious conflicts in their turn are affecting the West;
racism has intensified and the failure of the West to fully accept immi-
grants from other cultures has led to terrorism against the host societies.
Without wanting to add to (justifiable) talk of Western "self-hatred,"
aren't these different instances of the Promethean myth? Europe as the
sorcerer's apprentice who lost control of his own manipulations? What
does this reveal about the Western self-image? Is it, as Slavoj Žižek claims,
a new form of arrogance to consider oneself the sole originator of these
problematic situations?

I would probably not agree with this diagnosis at all, because I would say that, at least in hegemonic politics, there is the dominance of some-thing that one could call a structural irresponsibility. That is to say, on the one hand, there is a claim of a great potential for political action ranging from the economy right up to military action. On the other hand, one notices highly, highly idiosyncratic responses whenever there are attempts to retranslate this potential for action into an awareness of the implications and the consequences of one's actions. In this respect, I believe that there is a great need in politics to brush off respon-sibility when in doubt—often, in fact, while stressing the unforeseeable nature of the causal processes. This to the extent that Western politics does not find itself in a state of indebtedness and responsibility, but rather exercises its capacity for certain forms of provisional irresponsibility.

One also often hears this argument in left-wing politics: the West is to
blame for these problems, so it shouldn't complain now that it suddenly
experiences them.

Certain aspects of that have some truth to them, of course. All those people who warned against interference in Iraq or Afghanistan had sce-narios of this nature in mind. A form of terrorism was cultivated in Iraq that simply had not been there before. And I believe that this, again, is related to a politics of a reduced accountability marked by an essential principle of action, namely, the so-called *target of opportunity*. So this means that global-political conditions are observed that offer the opportunity to gain access, to advance, to strike, to bomb, but the consequences of these actions and the implications of those consequences were never addressed. There is an excess of a political potential for action and a deficit of political analysis. In the last decades, this constellation has produced the majority of the current disasters, and there are people responsible for this, who should be named, such as George W. Bush.

What are, in your opinion, some of the features required for proposed solutions to gain popular approval? Are there, in this respect, certain rhetorical or aesthetic qualities of a diagnosis that repeatedly emerge and very quickly gain persuasive power?

The first question is obvious and it is a central question for political *publicity*. It is the question of how a general unease is translated into forms of definable resentment. A very significant aspect is the retranslation of a so-called crisis awareness into resentful movements. This is a phenomenon that can be observed in all Western countries, and with great universality at that. A second and relevant important point has indeed to do with the question of the ability and possibility for action and operation, and this is truly decisive for the electorate. Namely, the attempts to minimize the potential for action of those affected within a population, to delegate this potential, and, if you will, to relocate it to an exemplary model.

This means resentment functions best of all when I am not responsible for the consequences of this resentment, when I don't have to drive the asylum seekers out of Germany or I propagate aggressive acts, but nobody really knows how to implement these things politically or strategically.

I believe that both of these things are crucial for the political ability to act within the framework of crises and within the framework of the popularity contest. First of all, the translation into resentment, and second, the transfer or the delegation of courses of action.

In situations of crisis, there is also always the question of populism. How can politics be closer to the people, without at least suggesting solutions for the crisis, and without becoming demagogic? For what reason did populism become such a tainted notion? And for what reason is there often a monopoly on rights?

First, I believe that more or less democratic systems cannot avoid the possibility of demagogy. One can even say that a particular risk of authoritarian structures is fundamentally intertwined with the democratic process. They are, so to speak, an immanent possibility of democratic systems per se. Second, I would say that populism is a thoroughly insufficient concept to describe political processes. I would like to bring to mind that the notion of populism first came about with grass-roots movements in the United States, the so-called *popular* or *people's* movement, a movement of American farmers reacting against the financial aristocracy at the end of the nineteenth century. These were movements that took a stance against extremely harsh economic conditions in order to gain economic rights. In this sense, the notion started out not as a disqualifying term, but as a notion of a certain political movement and struggle.

What I believe to be problematic with the concept of populism and where I approach this concept extremely critically has to do with the fact that it is used to claim a political-ideological normalization [*Normalstellung*] where something like a "representative center politics" is being pitched against a populist politics at the margins. As such, the notion of populism tends to equate political movements that organize themselves in the so-called right-wing margin and the so-called left-wing margin, without taking into consideration the specific subjects of the respective political movements. In this sense, the notion of populism is an eminently *ideological* one.

*What do you think of the many horizontal-democratic [*basisde-mokratisch*]¹ initiatives of today, such as the Pirate Party with its liquid democracy, Nuit Debout, or citizen's parliaments, especially in southern Europe, for instance, in Spain. Is this an opportunity to challenge the conventional political models of consensus and coordination? Could it produce something like a digital social contract? Can social media be instrumental to democracy?*

Of course, these things can only be judged and evaluated from case to case. First of all, the digital contract is one that is problematic to the highest degree, because—and by now this is identifiable in a large number of contexts—it led to what sociology is already calling *echo groups*. These are groups in which the feedback of those with the same opinions is enhanced, and where the platform of digital communication actually minimizes pluralism.

The second aspect concerns the movements that you mentioned. These, of course, are not comparable in every aspect, but one can at least recognize a common tendency in their dependence on the last financial and economic crisis. This tendency exists in the fact that they are out to *repoliticize* certain questions, in particular within Europe, that were purely technocratic questions from a European perspective—for example, monetary policies, austerity policies, budgetary policies, and debt relief. This was the case in the good days of SYRIZA, and it's also the case today with Podemos. To identify social and political conflicts, to name and highlight them, where hitherto a technocratic body of rules had dominated.

This too is a resort to sovereignty: to free the mechanisms of decision from the bureaucratic sphere.

Yes, or perhaps put somewhat more philosophically, the attempt to convert politically rule-guided activities to what Jean-François Lyotard called the "differend": forms of debate where conflicting and irreconcilable interests collide. I believe that this is the accomplishment of these groups.

INTERVIEW CONDUCTED AND TRANSLATED BY SVEN FABRÉ
AND ARNE VANRAES

Note

1. The German adjective *basisdemokratisch* indicates the attempts to make one's form of organization as horizontal and egalitarian as possible. It means aspiring to be democratic at the level of the "basis" instead of having a hierarchic structure or working by means of political representatives.

4

Neoliberalism Against the Promise of Modernity

Interview with Wendy Brown

To start, I would like to address the notion of "demos" or people.¹ Perhaps the central paradox of today's politics, at least in the West, is that the word "people" can be heard everywhere. It seems central to the idiom of contemporary politics, from left to right: from Occupy and Bernie Sanders to right-wing populists such as Trump, Marine Le Pen, or Geert Wilders. Yet, as you claim,² "the people" today have the greatest difficulty in organizing and seizing themselves politically, in exercising their (hypothetical) power. Perhaps you could expand on what seems to be a blatant but structuring paradox of politics today?

Yes, I agree and I think this paradox is a historically specific one. It is not the case that there hasn't been antidemocratic populism or authoritarian populism before—we know there has—but today we have populisms on *both* the left and the right and those don't exactly comprise democracy, either representative democracy or more radical forms of democracy. So let's break up that question a little bit. I do think it is really important to distinguish populism from democracy, and I don't just mean analytically. I mean sociologically and historically. "Populism" is, of course, usually roughly defined as a revolt or rebellion of the people against an elite or perceived elite. There is left-wing populism that does that and there is right-wing populism that does that. On the one hand, there are more emancipatory aims: the kind we see in the

Indignados or Occupy. There is even the populism at the root of SYRIZA. On the other hand, there is right-wing populism: the model of "we the people" chasing out the Muslim immigrants in Germany is probably the most prevalent in many of our minds.

"Democracy," just so we clarify some terms here, means something really different. It doesn't just mean "the people against an elite." It means "self-rule" in its most basic definition. Populism does not always *want* the people to rule. It often seeks fascism or nationalism, or rule by experts, or rule by tradition. It is often a rebellion against the perceived breakdown of norms and the legal instantiation of that breakdown, especially sexual norms or gender norms. On the other side, not all varieties of democracy are necessarily interested in empowering people or in being inclusionist. Ancient Greek democracy, as we know, comprised 10 percent of the population, and there could have been a populist revolt against elitist Greek democracy! Liberal representative or market democracy is not interested at all in empowering people and, from its foundations, tends to be very concerned with how to attenuate the people's power.

Here's what I would say in response to your question about the contemporary predicament of populism in relationship to democracy: it seems to me that one of the things that the combination of neoliberalism and globalization—two different things—has done is to produce both left- and right-wing responses to a sense of *an increasingly disempowered people.* Not just the people who are deracinated or decimated economically—falling middle class, destroyed unions, working class, etc.—but also a people who feel less and less that so-called democracies represent them, their interests, or their protection. Here, I think, is the historically specific predicament of populist movements that arise in response to breakdowns of social contracts, whether social-democratic contracts or contracts just for protection. So we see a populist move against that, and then the question is whether it can also take shape as a set of *democratic* claims or visions. The reason why I think this is so important—and here is my argument with many contemporary anarchists—is that, unless we are able to formulate for the twenty-first century ways for the people to govern themselves, what we will be left with is populist rebellions . . . that burn themselves out. Populist rebellions that either bring into power authoritarian or right-wing governments—Trump, Le Pen, Berlusconi, etc.—or we'll have populist rebellions that are left-wing rebellions that, to put it very bluntly, don't have a plan. What I think is really important at this particular conjuncture for our left-wing populism is to also be thinking about the *dedemocratization* that is so widespread in the West today and the delegitimacy, the delegitimation of democratic forms, as neoliberalism has just gutted the value, the terms, and the practices of even the most modest forms of democracy. This is, to be clear because I am always misunderstood here, not a call for a resurrection of liberal representative democracy, but a call for us on the left to be able to think, in the context of populist rebellion, about new democratic forms.

You also suggest[3] that there is an "antiuniversalism at the heart of democracy": democracy has always needed a (phantasmagorical) "outside" to define itself. This is particularly clear in the anti-immigrant rhetoric of populist demagogues and their promise to protect "our" democracy—and its claims to equality—against the "barbaric other." Can we say we are witnessing a remarkable recuperation of "progressive" themes here: democracy, equality, gay rights, women's rights, etc. are now championed by the Right, even the Far Right?

Here you've introduced another matter into our conversation and one that is really important, which is the shift from thinking about what's happening to democracy and citizenship in liberal democracies *in their own terms*, to thinking about what global movements of people and especially Arab and Muslim immigration have incited *in the West* in relation to those terms. I completely agree with you: it was already clear and obvious in the United States when we had the striking phenomenon of George W. Bush's wife arguing that the wars in the Middle East were important because they would liberate women. The conservative party in the United States has never been much concerned with this issue! All of a sudden, we saw folks that were saying: "We're fighting the Taliban, we're fighting Muslims in the name of Western values," which turn out to be not just "tolerance of," but really *rooted* in the principle of gender equality, sexual equality, the embrace of sexual diversity, and so forth. That is a reminder of the slipperiness of tolerance discourse, but it is also something to be read very carefully, that is, the extent to which both democracy and tolerance—and they're not the same at all—end up being mobilized as signifiers without much specification. They end up being mobilized as signifiers or icons of the West regardless of the extent to which they are actually practiced in the West. I would put it even more strongly: they end up operating to purify the West of any implication in the intolerant or the antidemocratic practices that are being projected unto a fantasized other. Just as a theoretical note: this is why we need not just Foucault here to think about the way that discourses operate, but also Derrida! Because here we are reminded about the fact that one of the ways that conservatives, and even in some cases neofascists, mobilize languages of tolerance and democracy today is by allowing those languages to project onto others the very practices that those same groups might be engaged in on a daily basis. Antidemocratic practices, intolerant practices, homophobic practices, gender-inegalitarian practices. But they all end up being purified from the dominant term, as Derrida would say, and being displaced onto the other. That is a really important thing for us to keep our eye on and to keep us thinking about why we should not jettison terms like "power" and "democracy."

I think the important thing to underscore is that something like "democracy" and something like "tolerance" are not terms that have fixed meanings. They can't have fixed meanings, as they are always about a struggle for what they *should* mean or what they *could* do. The fact that the Right has captured them or the fact that neoliberalism has captured democracy doesn't mean that the Left gives up on them. It means that we try to recapture them!

"Tolerance" is now a much-used rhetorical weapon against the other. As you suggest in your work, what is happening here is the culturalization of political conflict: tolerance and democracy are presented as a cultural marker.[4] Has tolerance, as civilizational discourse, moved from the liberal Left to the nationalist Right? I am even wondering whether neoliberalism, with its emphasis on the democratizing effects of global free markets, contributes to such a culturalization of democracy—in the sense that neoliberal discourse can also be read as a civilizational discourse? The two, nationalism and neoliberalism, seem to go almost too well together . . .

Let's be careful here. While I think there are some intersections, I also think there are some disparities or a lack of convergence in these two discourses. Here's what I mean: the dream of the neoliberals, especially those who had any interest in democracy, such as the Chicago School neoliberals, was the compatibility or in fact the full realization of democracy through neoliberalism. The Ordo-School neoliberalism, on the other hand, was not committed to democracy. It was really committed to technocracy, and saw democracy as quite problematic, as inherently interventionist and clumsy, and actually also inherently cooptable. So we have some differences there. The fantasy that the neoliberalization of the globe will produce democracy everywhere is the extension of that older fantasy that global capitalism would produce a kind of universal culture. The anticipation is that China's open door to markets eventually brings China into modestly democratic waters or brings rights and free elections and so forth. In fact, I believe China is revealing the tremendous compatibility of neoliberalization with authoritarian practices. Yet the fantasy remains that democracy goes with neoliberalism and the more places it spreads, the more it can take hold.

We have that, on the one hand, and, on the other hand, we have what you just identified, which is a *civilizational discourse* organizing the Euro-Atlantic world, in which "democracy" is understood as always already the preserve of the West. Something you try to export to other parts of the world, but it never really works . . . It is always interfered with by religion and tradition, violence and culture, and all the things that democracy imagines itself cleansed of . . . Once again, it's not, but it *imagines* itself cleansed of those things. I think those two discourses are both circulating, but I don't think they're perfectly convergent.

For you the "wall"—but by extension perhaps "the border," which is now a key metaphor in European right-wing discourse—becomes a site for investing (very real) anxieties and "psychic-political desires."[5] The Western subject is made more and more precarious under the pressures of neoliberal policies and economic globalization, and consequently it demands "psychic reassurances or palliatives," you argue. Could we relate this, again, to the question of the demos: those who claim "we are the people" are driven by or fuel this anxiety and the resulting desire for walls?

In the European context, of course, there is an oscillation between the question of the border as a national one versus a European one. Again, between the hardcore nationalist and the hardcore Europeanists, there can be an oscillation that they're not willing to completely avow, sometimes referring to Europe, sometimes referring to Hungary, or Germany, or the United Kingdom, or Greece, or somewhere else. There is no question that one of the things that neoliberalization in the context of globalization has done is to produce a set of concerns related to the capacity of the state to protect its borders or not. More generally, it incited a concern with horizons. What I mean is, at an existential level, it is very difficult, if not impossible, for human beings to live in and conduct their relations in a "horizonless" universe. That is truly what we're looking at with globalization. There are many possible responses to the expanding horizons over the course of the last five hundred years, from communities to nation-state levels, from regional levels to global levels. There are many different levels of responses, but one of them is certainly an intensified nationalism and again a postulation of a purity of the "we" who are *inside* a nation against the contaminating elements who are *outside* and threatening to get in. Of course, that same move includes a disavowal of the colonialism and the imperialism that have produced the world, not to mention the neoliberalism that has set people on the move. But that's a given. We know that frame. I think that one of the things that is crucial to the anxiety about borders is that there is simultaneously an economic and political dimension to it *and* a very deep *psychic* and I am suggesting even *anthropological* dimension to it. I think it doesn't make sense to say that all anxiety about bordering is simply xenophobic. There is no question that there is a mobilized xenophobia in the idea of "fortress Europe" and in the response to the current refugee crisis, but that is to look at the immediate moment and it brings up the question of how communities can be refounded in a globalized world—how they can be democratized.

So there are these two questions: how do we deal with a globalized world in a way that allows us to have some possibility of a democratic organization that can be on a global level, *and* how do we deal with a globalized world in a way that allows having local forms of a "we" that don't turn into violent and aggressive responses to those outside? That is a huge question and one the Left doesn't like to deal with! The reason

I offer it to you in the context of this interview is that I think it's one of the things that the Left needs to put on its agenda.

There is, in fact, a host of contemporary political thinkers, such as Alain Badiou, Chantal Mouffe, or Slavoj Žižek, who, albeit coming from different traditions and perspectives, all attempt to (re)affirm "the primacy of the political" against the rule of the market. You seem to be hesitant toward such fetishizing of "the political," toward the idea, for example, that the primacy of the political can be restored under the aegis of democracy. Perhaps having "the political" or democracy pulling the strings again is not enough to address issues such as globalization or climate change?

Let me just take a piece of what you just said. A host of theorists and leftist thinkers became interested in the "political" in the 1980s and 1990s and early twenty-first century. It was really a post-Marxist phenomenon, reckoning with the fact that part of the reason for the tremendous failure of Marxist experiments in the twentieth century had to do with the failure to come to terms with the power of the political. This resurgence of the sovereignty of the political or the predominance of the political over economics, over economic relations, occurred at the very moment that neoliberalism was insisting on the rightness of the opposite. The neoliberal dream is that markets shall rule. They will be propped up by states—states will be part of their constitution and provide political support—but markets shall rule. The Left inverts that and tries both to think about the problem of the political in ways Marx did not *and* to think about whether it is possible to reassert the sovereignty of the political. Here, I think political theory has to be really alert to the powers of what I will still call "capitalism" to set the terms on which political decisions are made. The fantasy that we can simply get hold of those powers, the idea that you could have political control of economic powers when they are organized by capitalism, just seems wrong. Of course there are redistributions that can be made, of course there are rights that can be redistributed, of course there are policies that can be undertaken, but the idea that you can radically reorganize capitalism in the way neoliberal reason did, the idea that you can actually produce a just order by getting political control of capitalist markets, seems sheer fantasy to me.

That is one-half of an answer to your question, but the other half concerns the fact that our challenge to the values and distributions of neoliberalism, and to the organization of the world by neoliberalism, has to happen in a *political vein*, by asserting an alternative set of political values. Democracy itself is a political project, it's not simply an economic one, as some leftists seem to think that democracy simply means fair distribution. It means much more than that. It means people setting the terms of existence, the values by which we live.

The last thing I want to say here is that what really makes this project complex is financialization, not just neoliberalism. Because today it is not just that the drive for profit rules the world—the financial markets rule the world! I think that democracy and political control of economic life are fundamentally incompatible with financialization. Having said that, what do we do? How do you put this thing back in the bottle? It is literally like trying to put the splitting of the atom, and the nuclear weaponry that emerged from it, back into the bottle. In fact those really are the two giant threats today to the continued existence of the earth. Nuclear weaponry because it can blow us up in a flash, and financialization because it's so fundamentally incompatible with sustainability and with democracy.

In Undoing the Demos *you describe how neoliberalism, over the past three or four decades, has gradually infiltrated and ultimately replaced the democratic imaginary that has been fundamental to our understanding of modern politics. Could we see neoliberalism as a fundamental break with political modernity, if we understand "political modernity" as the politics of emancipation and at least the horizon of popular sovereignty? I was also struck by the fact that you seem to suggest that neoliberalism is an antihumanism, in the sense that it sees human beings not as sovereign but as fungible. Could we say that neoliberalism marks a profound crisis of the humanist idiom that underpins political modernity and perhaps even heralds the end of it?*

It is really hard to tell! Here it would be important to avoid progressive or Whiggish trajectories in history, where trajectories can't be interrupted. But leaving that to one side, let me just start with the antihumanism in neoliberalism. The heart of it is not so much that human beings are fungible. I think that workers have felt fungible for a long time in capitalism! They certainly have been. However, the conceptualization of human beings that neoliberal reason promulgates is that human beings become *human capital* not just for states and not just for employers, but *for themselves*. The reason for that is neoliberalism's fundamental move to economize every field. Once you economize every field, once every field is understood in purely economic terms, every element of our existence and our very being is to be construed in economic terms. In this case, in the case of contemporary neoliberalism, it means as a bit of human capital. That is why you get an economist like Gary Becker very happily talking about thinking of every aspect of our lives, from child-raising to love or family-making, from retirement to work, as simply investments in human capital. Now, what does that mean? It means we are no longer thinking of ourselves, or no longer expected to think of ourselves as creatures who are trying to figure out how to live, how to govern ourselves, and how to govern with others—the promise of modernity.

That is one aspect of the antihumanism. The other aspect of the antihumanism entails that in neoliberalism, and then even more so in financialization, humans are no longer understood as the best governors of themselves. The classic formulation you get from John Stuart Mill that each human being should be choosing the life that they think is best, that they're best suited to, or that they wish for, or the Kantian encomium for moral autonomy, all that's out the door. What the neoliberals have given us is a world in which we are understood to be best governed by markets, not by humans, and what the Ordo-liberals have given us is a world in which we are best governed by technocracy and even by algorithms! The assaults on humanism here are really coming through every door, reducing us to human capital, where increasing human capital value in the present and the future is the fundamental mandate. We are then led to understand ourselves as best ruled by markets, and today by financial markers and the technocracies that go with them, rather than by ourselves.

There we are! Your question at the end of this, I think, is, what is the implication? Does it mean that it is just too late to try to reimagine human beings taking responsibility for themselves, their individual lives, and their collective lives? Or is it the case that this suggests we need other kinds of notions? A lot of the posthumanists go in that other direction: "Forget it! That whole humanist thing, the democracy thing, that was all saturated anyway with brutality toward the human other, whether it was the dark other, animals, or the planet, etc.!" But I think something different here. I think this is a crucial juncture. If human beings at this very moment give up on the idea of taking responsibility for the world that we have made such a disaster of, almost to the point of finishing it off—the irony of it! The irony of being humanist and making this mess and then posthumanists then saying: "Oh well, we're just another bunch of cells like everything else on the earth." The ironies are abundant! But so also is the darkness that falls . . .

To conclude, I would like to ask a question concerning the institutional context in which you write and think, in particular the issue of debt, which you address extensively in Undoing the Demos. *How does a context of financial crisis and the ubiquity of debt affect the ways in which you—or we, as left-wing scholars—practice and, crucially, teach critical thinking?*

Great question. My answer runs in two different directions. The implications of financialization for universities are huge. Apart from the pure economics of it, it has also meant that universities themselves are increasingly governed by ranking and ratings just as everything else is in a financialized world, and that preoccupation with ranking and rating governs the way that universities eliminate programs or preserve programs, admit students or bar students. It affects all of the university concerns with priorities that are so misbegotten in relationship to education and research: what universities put their money in, where they withdraw their money from. There is all of that. But it also has tremendous implications for the kinds of values organizing much of the research in universities, which has more and more to do with a set of rankings and ratings that judge its impact factor not in the world but in research niches that are often irrelevant to the world. The irony is that, even as the cloistered nature of universities has been broken down, they're more and more the heart of financialized economies. At the same time, that saturation has not made universities necessarily more relevant to the problems of this world, and we seek an education that could address it. It has turned us into human capital factories. Understandably, students more and more demand that university research and university education build their human capital, as opposed to their wonder and curiosity and so forth. But the real pressures are not just coming from the students—they are really coming from the ratings and rankings world that governs everything in and about universities.

And yet, it has never been more important for faculty to contemplate what they think students need to learn, and what kind of thinkers they need to be, and what kind of research we need to be doing. I would say that regardless of how our infrastructure has been destroyed, or our research funds have been cut, or various other features of faculty existence have suffered attrition, those of us fortunate to be in this work still have tremendous freedom to teach what we think we should teach, to think what we should think, and to do our research and connect with worlds outside the university that we think we can make a contribution to. Whether that is concern with climate change, or democracy, or political economy, or social relations, or racism on the rise, or whatever else. At the moment I would say that, on the one hand, the pressures in and on universities to simply become appendages to capital are very great. That's a trajectory that one can see: producing little bits of human capital for employment and increasingly looking to the world of corporate sponsorship for research. But on the other hand, it is still quite possible to do otherwise! We actually have a great deal of space and movement for thought and for teaching. I find students enormously open to it, despite the fact that they may arrive at the university with debt and with anxiety, and with concern to be marketable and employable bits of capital when they leave! I still find that the vast majority of them are incredibly available to reading and thinking in ways that open them to this world and that generate their own critical thinking about it. So that, I think, is the dual condition we're in today. It is almost, and I really want to say this, an *ethical* responsibility for scholars and academics to take up!

INTERVIEW CONDUCTED AND TRANSCRIBED BY JOOST DE BLOOIS

Notes

1. Wendy Brown, *Undoing the Demos: Neoliberalism's Stealth Revolution* (New York: Zone, 2015).
2. Wendy Brown, "We're All Democrats Now," in *Democracy in What State?*, by Giorgio Agamben et al. (New York: Columbia University Press, 2011).
3. Brown.
4. Wendy Brown, *Regulating Aversion: Tolerance in the Age of Empire* (Princeton: Princeton University Press, 2008); Wendy Brown and Rainer Forst, *The Power of Tolerance* (New York: Columbia University Press, 2014).
5. Wendy Brown, *Walled States, Waning Sovereignty* (New York: Zone, 2014).

5

The European Union Is a Cage

Interview with Antonio Negri

In recent interviews, you have said that the Left of today should be European. You have stated this in the context of the rising popularity of SYRIZA in Greece. However, today the SYRIZA government in Greece is implementing the austerity measures imposed on Greece by the European Union. How do you see this European Left and do you think this is still possible after what happened in Greece?

It is clear that what happened in Greece was a painful experience, but I am still convinced that there was no alternative. Today, the situation being as it is, there is no possibility for a state to break with the European Union.[1] How could SYRIZA have left the European Union? By forming an alliance with Russia? This is something very unrealistic and, in any case, not a better solution than staying in the European Union. The European Union is a cage. We have to keep it in mind that it is exactly that: a cage. Any attempt to return to the past is a mistake. All this does not mean that the European Union is not an almost-minimal realization of what we hoped it could have been. The European Union is a cage and often it is simply a mess. The European Union—an embryonic but real space—is the place of the realization of and experimentation with neoliberal politics. It is a place where the generalized class struggle against a common enemy, European capital, has become impossible. These are the huge problems that the formation of a European Left has to face. The problem is that there is no way out. There is no plan B. Such a plan B, returning to the nation-state and to a national currency, is unthinkable in the current globalized world. We can see that the Left's anti-European forces—such as in East Europe or in Germany, for example, the group around Oskar Lafontaine—are having difficulties. All this does not mean that there is a politics of the European Left or, even less, that there is a European politics of the Left.

You say there is no alternative . . .

There are no alternatives to remaining in the European Union. There can be internal alternatives, but they are far from being realized.

. . . but you also say that the European Union is a neoliberal construction and that there is no place for the Left in that construction. Do we have to change the European structures or is this a utopia? How could we transform the European Union in a more democratic direction or is this impossible?

I am completely convinced that the European structures have to be changed, and, even more, that the very notion of democracy has to be rethought. The current European structures are the result of fifty years of European history after two world wars. There was the period of war and turbulence between 1914 and 1945, including the Versailles Treaty of 1919. Today we still have wars that are the consequence of the dissolution of the European colonial empires. Present-day Europe is the result of all this history. It is a unity that is born out of the hope to leave all that history behind. The hope to end all wars between European nation-states and the hope to leave the colonial period behind. The European project is completely connected to the problem of decolonization. And the process of globalization has accentuated this problem even more. But what used to be a hopeful project has turned into the decline of the European project. This is the tragic situation Europe is in. Is there the possibility to move out of this situation at the moment when the situation is at its worst? A Hölderlinian question, if you wish. I don't know the answer. I believe that there are still movements possible to invent a new radical form of democracy at a European level. It is clear that the European institutions have to be conquered and reversed, but only a constituent process can touch the European institutions. This is the only thing that the movements can do that take part in European elections, namely, form a constituent group, waiting for the right occasion, an event that would allow for a change of the institutions. The other way is the construction of countermovements on a European level. An example of this is the alliance between the so-called rebel cities, such as Barcelona, and maybe in the future Naples as well. Here we can see the two levels at work: a form of constituent power together with pressure toward the "top." There is the need to change the democratic system itself and the implementation of these new experiments in the form of concrete countermovements, such as the alliance between the rebel cities.

I would like to turn from Europe to South America now. You have always been very optimistic about the leftist movements and governments in South America, but this period seems to be reaching its end. How do you see these changes, especially in Brazil?

The situation in South America today is quite tragic, no? The cycle of very important struggles, of new organizations that have brought us rich experiences and much valuable reflection, is over. In the wake of the global economic crisis—an element I find fundamental—we have seen the failure of these projects, especially in Brazil, as well as the alliance between the BRICS countries. But this is only the surface. Behind all this is the fact that this revolution in South America was a first step in a situation that remains very difficult and dramatic. We always have to keep in mind well that the law in South America is a law based on slavery. The relationship between the classes in South America has never left racial politics. So the question how to get out of this situation is extremely difficult. This is, for example, apparent in the Bolivian fight over the common, such as the struggle over water. Or the *bolsa familia* social program in Brazil. Even in Venezuela—which was, after all, the most problematic of these experiences for several reasons—the development of popular countermovements has produced rich and valuable experiences. The experience of the first government of Kirchner in Argentina was special as well, because there the struggle against the global monetary powers was quite successful. So there was a series of really important experiences and these formed, according to me, forms of constituent power. Like all forms of constituent power, they aim to operate not only at the level of the government but also at the level of society itself. So the experience in South America of the past thirty years was something extraordinary, but in the very difficult context of the economic crisis and the fact that the right-wing parties are more connected internationally. The economic crisis erupted midway through this period, at a moment of a difficult transition.

To this we should add a series of problems that pose enormous difficulties in southern countries and those are the problems with communication. They have to cope with extremely different and highly fractured cultures of knowledge. The monopoly on communication by the big global networks is something tragic and very serious. This problem is also connected with the new function that religion and religious extremism play in this situation. It is also connected with the corruption of the constitutional systems. In Brazil, for example, corruption is basically unavoidable. There are purely proportional representational systems where the worst corrupt forces, especially religious ones, can simply take part in parliamentary politics. In Brazil, the PT² never had a majority. To survive there as a president, one is obliged to circulate money among those who are only out to gain more money. This is a constitutional form of corruption. Constitutional in two senses of that term: because it makes up the constitution of the country and because it is what drives certain representatives—their deepest desire, their craving, their libido—namely, money.

You have witnessed the birth of many resistance movements in your life: operaismo *(workerism), the antiglobalization movement, the Occupy movement, the Arab Spring, different movements in South America, the Zapatista movement. . . . I would like to discuss some of these movements a little bit to know which lessons we can derive from them for present-day political strategies. For example, you seem optimistic, but also with critical reservations, about movements such as Podemos or Occupy. Could you clarify your views on this? What were the possibilities and the limitations of movements such as Occupy or Podemos?*

With the Occupy movement, I never had any big problems. Michael Hardt and I discussed our views on the Occupy movement in a little book we wrote together.[3] According to us, the Occupy movement has correctly pointed out the problem: the degradation of democracy by the contemporary financial system and the impossibility of repeating in one way or another the mechanisms of democracy in its traditional form or of having confidence in the current political structures. Their protests have opened up the capacity to develop new places—places in two senses: places in the sense of an actual space and places in the sense of points of gathering or debate. This was a completely horizontal form of protest that has developed out of the experiences of the antiglobalization movement, such as the protests in Genoa. For me, maybe this is because I am Italian, but I think this is also the case for Alexis Tsipras or Pablo Iglesias; the protests in Genoa were the moment a new form of politics was born. There the problem of horizontality was brought forth. The problems related to horizontality are very old problems. These problems were confronted in a new way when there were a movement and a capacity for mobilization that were connected with new social layers, such as that of cognitive labor, intellectual work, and other forms of labor. Occupy was very important because of this, and not just because many people were involved in it. What happened in New York was different from what happened in Spain or in the Arab countries. In New York they were in the center of domination. There they confronted the real problems in a clear way. They were not confronting a corrupt and declining ruling class in a transition that was never fully realized, such as in Spain. They were also not facing neocolonial powers such as in the Arab countries. The experience of Occupy was more theoretical than political, if you wish. But theoretical with the possibility of putting pressure on the governance of the people, at certain levels.

The problem—and I had continuous discussions about this with the people from Podemos from May 15 onward—is that only seeking solutions by means of centralization or representation, in the traditional sense of a transfer of power, is no longer possible in the present situation. That is why certain positions, such as in the theories of Ernesto Laclau, are very dangerous. We had the experience in South America, especially in Argentina, where we were able to see that such solutions don't work. It couldn't work because as soon as the more vertical axis—even if it stays loyal to the horizontal axis—gains a relative independence, forms of corruption and all the negative aspects of power come into play. It is almost inevitable that this vertical axis becomes autonomous and then all hell breaks loose. This is the absolute evil, if you wish. *[laughs]* So the big problem is that of how to develop a vertical axis, because we definitely need it, but this should always go together with countermovements. These countermovements are the impulse for not one, but multiple vertical axes. This is really fundamental. I had many discussions about this with Pablo Iglesias, and especially with Iñigo Errejón, and other people of Podemos.[4] Their strategy is quite paradoxical. On the one hand, they affirm the party model, but, on the other hand, it is very difficult to align this party with a movement that is so big. If one wants to gain political mandates, such as the mayor of a city, one is obliged to make alliances. But I am not a federalist convinced that this is the right approach. The task today is to develop forms of power without sovereignty. The functioning of sovereignty is horrible not just because it is undemocratic, but also because it is corrupting. The task is not to be against verticalization—verticalization is necessary—but to develop a vertical axis without sovereignty.

You have written that for the multitude the big city is the equivalent of what the factory was for the working class. The big city is the location of struggle par excellence for realizing a politics based on the multitude and the common. You also want to connect political movements more to the outskirts (banlieues) of big cities. Can you explain this a bit? How could this be realized? I have read that you wanted to let your seminar rotate in different spots in the Parisian banlieues.

For example, a movement such as Nuit Debout is very interesting for many reasons, but there are also two problems. One problem is the inability to connect with the struggle of the workers. I know very well how strong the mistrust toward trade unions is. The second problem—and this relates to your question—is the problem of the *banlieues*. I have had discussions about the *banlieues* from when I first came to France. I came to France for the first time in 1983, escaping prosecution in Italy, and at that time there was the first march of the so-called *beurs*: people who are the children of immigrants from Arab countries. This was an incredible experience. Second-generation immigrants organized a march from Marseille to Paris, with the intention to raise awareness in favor of antiracism and democracy, in a time when the spirit of '68 was still more or less alive. After the 1980s and 1990s, I worked a lot in the *banlieues*. I worked there to do research. And there I learned how the *banlieue* functions, because this is something absolutely fundamental. I was working in informal, dispersed networks. And this was a political cooperation around different local struggles, such as the struggle against some far-right mayors, in times when there was still quite a lot of awareness of the *banlieues*. The last big struggle in the *banlieues* was between 2002 and 2005 here in Paris. This was important for me and my wife, who was at that time a teacher in a high school in one of the most "dangerous" *banlieues*. It is not me who calls it the most dangerous, but that is what the state does. There were some really great people involved in the struggle. And the response here in France was absolutely cruel, harsh, and today we can also say stupid, because it paved the way for a certain type of Islamic extremism and for a total absence of a connection between politics and the *banlieues*. The unions are the only ones who sometimes manage to create connections with the *banlieues*, but the mayors, even the mayors of the *banlieues*, are completely disconnected from the people, not to mention the entire system. This is a very fundamental issue. I cannot do much more than point this out. One cannot look at the problem of the city without taking the *banlieues* into consideration.

But we can also see phenomena like those happening in Italy at the moment. The funniest thing, or the most dramatic thing, if you wish, that happened in Italy after the last elections is that the party of the left, the PD,[5] gained a majority in the centers of cities and lost in the suburbs. So even the Blairite social democrats that the communists in Italy have become noticed that something was not right. But this is not only an Italian problem. Here as well [in Montparnasse, ed.], we are in an area full of left-wing intellectuals. The big problem is the problem of democracy. And this is connected with another difficult problem, namely, immigration. Contrary to what should be the economic rationale of acceptance and hence integration of the populations in the *banlieues* and the people migrating to France, one adopts a strongly identitarian, anti-European rhetoric. Concerning the *banlieues*, one adopts a politics that is no longer biopolitical, letting live in order to dominate, but letting die. Here, to dominate is to let die. It's a tragic kind of politics. This counts for the people in the *banlieues* and for immigrants. This is utterly useless and stupid, and even contrary to the logics of capitalism. The logic of capitalism is to have a few years of repression and after that one allows people to immigrate, because this is a workforce they desperately need. In Switzerland, we have seen referenda to make the laws on immigration stricter, and later there was another referendum inviting more people into the country because they needed them. Large-scale automatization with robots has caused an enormous industrial transformation. Every time they show a car factory on television, one does not see people anymore. But it is clear that in different sectors they need people to work to provide for the wealth of others. Today exploitation is no longer exploitation in the factory, but a generalized exploitation of spaces, as David Harvey describes. It is an extraction of surplus-value. This is not the abstraction of all the small-scale use-values produced by people in factories. No, this is extraction of things that are already socialized. And this is why the *banlieues* are so important, because they even exploit those who are excluded. They say I am optimistic when I say that all this cannot last like this. But I continue to be optimistic—if it can be called optimism, because "optimism" in this context sounds not very appropriate, no?

In the time of the operaismo *movement in the 1970s, the strategy of the refusal of work was adopted, precisely to resist the extraction and the exploitation of the general social lives of the people. Is this still a valuable strategy today? Or should it be modified according to the present situation? How can we resist this general extraction?*

The refusal of work was theorized by the theorists of *l'operaismo* as a practice, but the workers themselves were no *operaists*. *[laughs]* Sabotage and the refusal of work were a strategy induced by the Fordist labor model and mode of organization. This strategy was completely connected with a specific situation. The refusal of work, what would this mean today? The refusal of work today would be a form of resistance against the system of financial extraction of social surplus-value, along with the capacity—but in a completely open theoretical domain—to develop a new mode of production. The refusal to work is a demand for liberation and thus a demand for a new mode of production. The refusal of work was never against production. The people working in factories were no ecologists. Often on the contrary, they accepted things such as professional maladies. They knew they were going to die because of their work, but they received a salary for this. So the refusal of work was never a refusal of productivity. It was always a demand for a completely different manner of producing. Ever since, we have seen the end of the prominence of salaried labor in factories. This has been relocated to countries such as India or China. But more and more, this is also transforming in India and China. There, as well, that kind of labor is transforming toward cognitive labor. So, what does the refusal of work mean in this context? It is the capacity to invent a new form of production, where capitalism today already exploits the common. Is the common a form of production? Can we talk about the common as a mode of production? Can we still talk about Fordist, industrial modes of production? I believe that production today arises from the organization of labor. It is a productive form of organization that brings together knowledge and cooperation. Knowledge and cooperation are accumulated by capital. Capitalists provided the knowledge about the machines and organized labor by means of the simplification of the different operations. But people organize themselves by means of communication and by sharing knowledge. All this is recuperated from capital. Today, this problem is still completely open.

You have spoken about the exploitation of the common by capital. In what way do you still see a struggle, a form of resistance, based on the common?

I see several struggles about the common. For example, hackers reappropriating certain forms of knowledge in informatics. The development of open-source software is a form of reorganization of the common. Many of the experiences in South America were a struggle about the common. But there have been important experiences in Europe as well. For example, I am thinking of the struggle about water in Italy: 87 percent of the people demanded the communalization of water in a referendum. They made it impossible for private companies to use water as a means for speculation. The common is not a kind of property. It is neither private nor public property. It is a rendering available by the multitude. These are the ways in which the common can be developed. There are people who try to develop an alternative kind of currency. I believe this can never really work because any currency will always require a form of force to impose itself more generally, but, still, these are important experiments. And there are all the initiatives around immigrants. This is something extraordinary today. But these kinds of experiences are the ways to develop a new form of common. And, understand well, these are the same experiences that allow us to develop a political force that could function as an alternative for the European Union. It is not just the conversion of a social democracy already in crisis, and maybe even finished, that interests us. What interests us is the effective construction of something new that has the same intensity as the movements in Spain had. That's why the May 15 movement in Spain and all the events of 2011 were so important. Even though they were in a sense a continuation of the experiences of the antiglobalization movement at the turn of the century, this was the first time that the problem of how to construct a new form of politics was taken up. And this new form of politics was a politics of the common. This is what was at stake and what recurs in the discussions about it. What, exactly, are we looking for? It is not enough to say we simply want a new kind of politics. And after that, what happens? What do we want and with which means? Certainly, the refusal of work is a means, but the refusal of work is the construction of another kind of order. And what is this other kind of order? Or maybe we shouldn't call it an "order" because that is a dubious term. A new structure, a new commune, a new form of being together. That is the common.

To conclude, a question about the current state of the university system. You speak about the common, but at the same time, we see the expansion of mechanisms of control, of regularization, and the privatization of the common. A notable example of this is the university. Do you believe it is possible to stop the process of universities being more and more organized according to the model of private companies?

This is one of the most evident places where the common has become the fundamental issue. It is indeed the case that the appropriation and privatization of the common have become a central element in politics. The appropriation not just of the public, but also of the common, and we can see this in the domain of knowledge. This industrialization, the entrepreneurial transformation, of the university is a very striking phenomenon. Can we resist this? Well, this is difficult because of the extent to which university employees, especially the professors, are absorbed in this mechanism. I am lucky to have been retired for some time now, so I can watch this a bit from a distance. This mechanism of self-alienation and self-exploitation today is incredible. I can see all these young professors working in front of their computers from the morning to the evening or midnight. All kinds of tasks are transferred to the professors together with the rise in procedures of control that have become crazy. And these mechanisms, in a way, are detrimental to knowledge, because the general quality level of teaching has declined. Precisely because of this entrepreneurial transformation of universities, the quality of education has declined. I am not saying it is at zero level, but very low nevertheless. Can we still transform the university for the better? I believe this is possible. But we will have to make new universities in which the students are protagonists. Public institutions, if they still exist, could provide the money to allow people to develop their knowledge and make their knowledge available to society.

This relates to an important issue of today, namely, that of the guaranteed basic income. It is clear that capital is noticing a problem as well. In the first book of *Capital*, Marx describes the conditions in England during the beginning of the development of capitalism. Physical labor had become so exploitative, with poverty and destruction as its consequences, that the workers became physically worn and alienated. Because of this, capital was forced to introduce a workweek with fewer work hours, and around this struggle the worker's movement was developed. But, on the other hand, why did capital grant the workers this? Because they knew that the struggle around wages and work hours was potentially dangerous for them and even revolutionary. Today, it is the same issue with the guaranteed basic income. There is all this knowledge, but what does one do at universities? Knowledge is being destroyed.

Productive forces are being destroyed. Because it has become so exploitative, they are obliged to consider the guaranteed basic income. Capital is granting this because otherwise the situation would become intolerable and potentially a struggle could arise out of this situation. From this point of view, the problem of universities today is still totally open. The guaranteed basic income would be not a victory of the working classes, but mainly a necessity for the patrons.

INTERVIEW CONDUCTED AND TRANSLATED BY STIJN DE CAUWER
AND GERT-JAN MEYNTJENS

Notes

1. This interview took place before the Brexit referendum, but the aftermath of that referendum proves Negri's point that it is far from straightforward for an EU member state to leave the European Union.
2. The Partido dos Trabalhadores, or the Workers' Party. This is the party of the former presidents Luiz Inácio Lula da Silva and Dilma Rousseff.
3. Antonio Negri and Michael Hardt, *Declaration*, self-published electronic pamphlet, distributed by Argo Navis Author Services, 2012.
4. Pablo Iglesias is the secretary-general of Podemos. Iñigo Errejon is the secretary for policy and strategy and campaigning of Podemos.
5. The Partito Democratico. This party was formed as a coalition between different parties, such as Democratici di Sinistra, the heirs of the Italian communist party, and Democrazia è Libertà—La Margherita.

6

We Need to Have a Clear Alternative

Interview with Tariq Ali

We are in Brussels now. In recent interviews you seemed to have given up completely on the European Union. We have seen how the European Union has dealt with Greece and how it is trying to deal with the refugee crisis. Should we simply give up all hope in the European Union as a political construction and basically reject it, or do you think it is still possible to reform it? Is this a worthwhile struggle?

I have always been an internationalist and very much in favor of an organization on a European level, but I think that if one is hardheaded and realistic, it's obvious the organization we've got is little more than a machine for financialized capitalism. That is its aim. That is what it concentrates on and that is why it punishes governments who step out of line. It's not simply Greece. It was the effective appointment by the European Union of technicians and technocrats to run the government in other parts of Europe as well—Italy, for one—and it is now, after the elections in June 2016, working actively behind the scenes to create a center government in Spain that it can sustain. There will be massive pressure on PSOE to either join a coalition with the victorious PP[1] or pledge to keep it in power for a full term.

So basically, the European Union as constituted at present has become a hangman's rope. It has taken sovereignty away from small countries and it has treated Portugal and Ireland extremely badly, imposing draconian restrictions on spending, etc. There has been a large exodus of young people from both countries. So, what is the good of this European Union, if that's what it does to its own member states? Equality on any level is totally absent from the equation. A few days after the British referendum in June 2016, the German chancellor, Angela Merkel, declared: "We will make sure that negotiations will not be carried out as a cherry-picking exercise. There must be and there will be a palpable difference between those countries who want to be members of the European family and those who don't." We could add, a dysfunctional European family in which the dominant German Mutti and her weak French consort, helped by a butler from Luxembourg[2] and staff from other countries, abuse the children regularly: Greece, Portugal, Ireland (where the European Union's Irish nannies take a special delight in whipping their people and force them to pay for the water necessary to clean the wounds from previous beatings). The children are governed by fear and made offers they cannot refuse.

On the external level, it is completely under the control of the United States. It sees itself as a junior partner of the United States. It works with the United States via NATO, which is the military arm of the Empire, and loyalty to which is a de facto perquisite to becoming an EU member. Increasingly, on every level, it is quite reactionary and we have to say it. I don't agree with this idea that somehow the European Union today is a gold standard or something similar that has to be worshiped. Yannis Varoufakis and others have started to talk seriously about reforming the European Union. How do you do it? You cannot do it just by saying you will reform it. What are the social forces that are going to reform this European Union? And I have suggested that at the very least, even to make propaganda, you need an alternative constitution for this body that can be discussed and debated and published in all the languages, so you have at least some concrete basis for moving forward. At the moment there is nothing. So it is not enough to say: "Yes, we are very critical of the European Union but we will reform it." How are you going to reform it? That is the big question. And after the British referendum, it's becoming crucial, with Denmark, the Netherlands, and perhaps France demanding their own referendums.

As for interstate relations, the European Union is now increasingly dominated by the largest economy in Europe, which is Germany. It's just a fact that they are the largest economy in Europe and as such they are the most important country in Europe. Hence, they dominate the European Union. Britain is half in, half out, in any case, and I think the British elite will try very hard to circumvent the results of the referendum with EU help. Democracy has never been a priority for the elite. Who knows, but the British "No" might force them to rethink and restructure the Union. They won't do it in a way I would like, but at least something would shift and change—though I'm not optimistic. Democracy is not something that the European Union treasures or likes. You remember the referendums in Holland, France, and Ireland. They just ignored them. And those were constitutional referendums. Most politicians of the European Union, if not all of them, had not read the constitution. So, what has democracy got to do with it? It is effectively an institution that has been created to work closely with bankers in order to keep control of the European economies—that's all.

You were particularly disappointed with the choice of the SYRIZA government to implement the austerity measures imposed by the European Union. What do you think is the significance of everything that happened in Greece from the oxi *in the referendum to the current SYRIZA government?*

Let's be blunt: SYRIZA's capitulation in Greece was a huge disaster. For the Left, but more important than the Left, it has been a huge disaster for the people of Greece, who elected SYRIZA. They have betrayed the hopes of their own people. And I can't see them last for very long. The party is in a state of disintegration. Its membership is reduced largely to careerists. People are leaving every day. The party is a shell, like PASOK.[3] Some are not joining anything. Some are joining Popular Unity.[4] But it's a very bad situation. There is economic misery and despair reigns supreme. Overall, the economic situation is a disaster. I have been arguing for a referendum in Greece on these questions for a very long time and I have been arguing with the SYRIZA people that they should pose two questions. One is, should we accept the deal offered by the EU? And the second question should be, if we reject the deal, are you in favor of a withdrawal from the Eurozone? That would have been a good test and I don't know what the result would have been. But they didn't. They got a referendum that was quite decisive, asking to reject the deal being offered by the European Union. Twenty-four hours after that referendum, Tsipras, who we know thought the referendum was going to go the other way, told the European Union: "Yes, I will accept your deal." So, he went directly against what the people had voted for in the referendum. The demoralization this caused! I was in Greece at the time. People were shell-shocked. It was a huge capitulation, of the sort you don't often see in such a dramatic and stark way. Of course it strengthened the feelings of the people who think: "All these politicians are a load of shit. They do nothing for us and look at that." So, I think Greece has been a disaster.

And I think what happens in Spain now will be watched closely. Pablo Iglesias refused to criticize the decision of the Greek government and that was a big political mistake because it is obvious what happened, and of course Iglesias and Podemos share some of the weaknesses of SYRIZA. They are not prepared to make any real critique of the European Union and its institutions. They just think: "We are a large economy, they can't treat us the way they treated Greece." They can if they wish to. They probably won't, but they could if they wanted to. In any case fear is a very strong emotion and reduces people to remaining with the status quo. That is what explains the setback suffered by Podemos in the elections in June 2016.

Do you think this happens automatically when movements that start out more local and horizontal become political parties that want to be part of the government?

Well, SYRIZA didn't develop like that. SYRIZA was a united front formed from different organizations: ex-Maoists, ex-Trotskyists, ex-Eurocommunists, with the Eurocommunists being the largest fraction. And if you look at the record of the Italian and French Eurocommunist parties, what happened to them? You can say that this is the line the majority of the SYRIZA leadership followed. They had a clear opportunist streak in them.

About Podemos, you are right. It grew up as a horizontal movement. And now they've created an organization that in my opinion is top-heavy, though the people in it are excellent people. The circles are not functioning. So you have an ironic situation that the social-democrat leaders are saying that before they do anything they will consult the party. Whatever decision they make, they will consult the party.

The situation in Spain as we speak is a mess. The European Union is trying hard to persuade Rajoy[5] to go quietly so that Ciudadanos[6] can join a coalition with the PP and PSOE can pledge to let the "new" government serve its time. Last time Rajoy refused to go. Will a new investigation commence? Last time the police raided various places to see whether they could find evidence of corruption, which he was engaged in—the whole of Spain knows that. I think they want to drive him out and then set up what I call an extreme-center government. That would leave Iglesias and Podemos as the main opposition in the country, so we will see whether Sanchez[7] will be removed, whether Rajoy will be removed, and whether they can find a compromise candidate. I don't think Podemos can join the government, because a lot of their strength comes from the votes that they got in Catalonia and that were left-wing votes.

You mentioned this idea of the extreme center. Could you maybe explain this a bit more? Given this, what can we still expect from parliamentary politics? People on the left often attach a lot of hope to political figures such as Bernie Sanders or Jeremy Corbyn, but what can we still expect from parliamentary politics?

I think what Corbyn is fighting for—and him I know very well—is not something that is hugely radical but a little bit of social democracy and that is not permitted by the system. That is why I argued that the political institutions created by the neoliberal world make politics redundant because they like the government to be governed essentially by one party with two heads—a left-center head and a right-center head. The differences between these are very narrow. This exists in many different European countries. It doesn't matter much who comes in. The only difference this makes is which companies they favor and who they want to make rich, before enriching themselves. The corruption on a political level is very high. The challenge to this extreme center has come from the far right and groups on the left because a whole vacuum has been created with the expulsion of social democracy, of social-democratic ideas, from mainstream discourse. Corbyn and Sanders are asking: "All we want is a little social democracy. Please, for the sake of our people, let us do it." And the authorities are saying no.

The difference between Corbyn and Sanders is that Corbyn is a radical on foreign policy. He wants to get rid of Britain's nuclear missiles. He is opposed to wars. He wants to spend more on welfare, etc. That is a huge difference. In the British political system we have never had a leader saying that. But by and large, simply relying on a vote in Parliament is not going to work. One has to build movements, and I think Corbyn knows that. That's how he himself got elected. I mean, it was a political insurgency. A social movement with one aim: making Corbyn leader of the Labour party, which has created a crisis for the British rulers. They were not prepared for it. Nobody thought he would win. You had the staff of the British army on television saying that there will be great unrest in the army if Corbyn becomes prime minister and that the army might mutiny. And this is just accepted. So it shows in a strange way that "calm and peaceful England," cut off from the continent and not part of its turbulent history, is actually deep down a reactionary oligarchic state. After the referendum in which Corbyn was for Remain but refused to participate in a joint campaign with the Conservatives, his parliamentary colleagues voted no confidence in him, hoping he would quit. But he has not resigned and will fight for the leadership again.[8] If he does and wins, we have two Labour Parties. A Corbyn rump in Parliament (40 MPs) but with a majority inside the Labour Party and a Blairite New Labour with a majority in Parliament (170 MPs) but having lost control of the party's apparatuses outside.

I see all that is going on as the beginning of something else. People are getting angry. The electorate is volatile. They want something else but are not quite sure what it is they want. And this is what they are getting. But who knows what will happen in twenty years' time? The generation produced by all this might demand something else.

Politically, the "hot topic" in Europe these days is the refugee crisis, which has stirred up a lot of nationalist and xenophobic reactions. Do you think this could lead to a new wave of right-wing politics in Europe? And what do you think about the attitude of most European countries who want to bomb the Islamic State but also openly support regimes such as Saudi Arabia?

This particular refugee crisis, with images of hundreds of thousands of people moving from one country to another, is something that has happened for the first time since the end of the Second World War. That gives you an idea of the scale of the crisis. Second, these refugees are a direct result of war and conflict. This is, as Obama himself has admitted, the result of the American war and occupation of Iraq, which destabilized that whole zone. So at the very least, the countries that made war or supported the war have a moral duty to take the refugees that are the result of their actions. Now these are not economic migrants coming because the economic situation is very bad or because there are no jobs. These are people whose homes have been bombed, who have no hospitals to go to, whose children are dying—direct results of war. I think that the West, which has directly or indirectly taken part in these wars, has to take them in, but they refuse to do so. I have argued—half jokingly, but not totally—that the next time they wage a war, these countries should factor in that they will have to take up a certain number of refugees. It's their responsibility.

Now, of course, it is creating a huge reaction. On the one hand, there is the reaction of the far-right parties for whom this is a gift from heaven. On the other hand, one cannot ignore what happens when countries where there is already unemployment see large amounts of people coming in. Just look at what happened in South Africa when a large number of Zimbabwean economic migrants went to work there, better educated because they had a better education system, getting better jobs. The reaction was violent. Their homes were burned. So this is something that cannot simply be dismissed as racism and xenophobia. It is that in Europe mainly, and the response in South Africa was also partly xenophobic, but the reasons are the same. The people think: "We can't do anything and these people come and do it." This is why this debate launched by the Far Right in Britain on the European Union is an awful debate, because it centers on EU migrants, not on the existing migrants. It targets Poles, Romanians, Eastern Europeans, who come in and who, basically, have made certain forms of labor much cheaper. Everybody knows this. If you want a good plumber, get a Pole. If you want good building workers, get Kosovars or Romanians. This is the market everyone wanted.

But a huge thing is the million refugees German took. I think it is astonishing that the response in Germany is not more brutal. It has been in parts. So, one can't ignore that side of it just by dealing with this thing on a moral level. There are concrete results that we cannot ignore. Of course, the right-wing parties are going to benefit from this. The leader of Alternative für Deutschland said: "Don't let them cross. The German army should be put on the border. If they try and come, we will shoot." This is appalling language. So this is going to happen because the rulers have no way of dealing with this problem. There is all sorts of crazy talk: "Find uninhabited places, etc." But what are uninhabited places: Tiny islands near the Arctic? This is crazy.

There are two more things I want to say on this. One is that, even though the governments are not taking in refugees, the more serious representatives of the European bourgeoisie want refugees, because they are fearful that, with the population in Europe slowing down, in twenty-five years' time they might have a crisis in terms of production. So if you look at the *Economist* and the *Financial Times*—two key publications of the European bourgeoisie—they are very strongly in favor of immigration, for that economic reason. And the Left is in a dilemma. Obviously we support the refugees. We want to give them places. And when it comes to the question of "how many?" we abdicate from the debate. So the Left, which is normally for regulating everything, is for unregulated population, and the Right, which is for deregulating everything, is for regulating migration. This is the contradiction that we face. *[laughs]* I have been asked this many times. When we regulate capitalism and have a planned economy, we will have to regulate migration as well, but till then it's a free market, capital flows in and out, so why shouldn't labor? I make that argument, but I'm not quite happy about it myself. You see? The most recent development is selling the refugees to the Erdoğan regime in Turkey. Paying him a few billion Euros to take them. He jokes about it in public. In bazaari mode he asks audiences: "Do you think we're getting enough money from the European Union? Should I raise the price?"

Many European countries still fully support countries such as Saudi Arabia. Countries such as Egypt, Libya, and Syria are in a dire state. The Arab Spring seems to be dead and buried. You have called the Arab Spring an unfinished project. Do you think it could be revived again in the near future?

Not in the near future, no. I think the defeats have been huge. I think especially the imposition of the military dictatorship in Egypt and the emergence of el-Sisi, who is much more vicious than Mubarak, are a huge defeat. There is no argument here. But for the West it doesn't pose a problem at all. Egyptian people are being killed. Prisoners are being tortured. All that is happening and they shut their eyes to it. It's the way the West works. They do not really believe in any norms at all. For the United States, what is good for their interests is good for the world, and if you don't like it, go take a jump. So, when it suits them, they talk about human rights, but they don't really care about them. It is just used as another stick to beat your enemy. They back el-Sisi and, of course, without American support Saudi Arabia would not be what it is today. The monarchy would have been removed a long time ago, in the 1960s and 1970s, by uprisings. The Americans basically held that country together. And it is no big secret that the Saudis are one of the main forces behind ISIS, Al-Qaeda, and other jihadi groups. They fund them. They arm them, for various reasons.

I have never known the Arab world to be in such a bad state, in my lifetime. Full stop. I mean there are small groups of people who are engaged in radical politics, but the defeats imposed on them and the vacuum created by the defeat of Arab nationalism by the Israelis were not filled in, and then this was filled by different Islamist groups, either extreme jihadi groups or the Muslim brotherhood. Because of this, the Left is totally marginalized. These young left-wing liberals in Tahrir Square couldn't understand this: that once the Muslim brotherhood had started to mobilize, the movement took on a different character. It really became a movement throughout Egypt and a huge movement. It was not a big surprise that Morsi won the Egyptian elections, and the fact that he is a total idiot without any understanding about how to run a country, or run anything, played into the hands of the military, who got rid of him. That is the overall problem in the Arab world. And it's been created—largely, though not exclusively, by the United States and its friend the European Union. Just going and changing regimes, not caring what happens: they did it in Iraq, they did it in Libya, they wanted to do it in Syria, they are doing it in Yemen . . . It's crazy.

We had the financial crisis, we had the situation in Greece, we had the refugee crisis, we had all these wars. It is often said that the Left broadly speaking has never been able to form a strong counternarrative to the dominant neoliberal or right-wing narrative. Do you think this is the case? Why is this the case?

This is indeed the case. In the sense that even the most radical attack on neoliberalism, which came from South America, from Chavez, from Morales, from Correa, did not break from capitalism. So you had a very special kind of progressive social-democratic reforms backed by mass movements but within the framework of capitalism. And it was difficult for them. They had seen the experiences of Eastern Europe and Russia. They said: "We can't be cut off from the world market. Especially in this day and age, we would be screwed." That whole experiment is now coming to an end. As we see in Venezuela: the reduction of oil prices—because the Saudis are producing more and more oil—has wrecked Venezuela. And it had nothing to fall back on. The Left failed to produce, globally and in specific countries, an alternative set of proposals that doesn't immediately get rid of capitalism—because that is difficult—but that presents a transition via a set of structural reforms that make it difficult for capitalism to reestablish itself. In fact, that is what neoliberalism has done—privatize, privatize, privatize—so it's very difficult to turn things back.

You need mass movements. So the Left, of which I am a part, is really living through a transition period. We have to work harder. It's foolish just to talk about reforming the European Union unless you have an alternative constitution, which you can present to ordinary people as well as intellectuals, saying that this is what is possible within the European Union. But we have been very weak at it. There was a plan B in Greece by Lapavitsas and others, but they didn't publish it, because they were caught in the SYRIZA trap, saying: "We are in government, you know." All this I understand. But we really have to find a way now of coming up with a set of ideas that can inspire and build mass movements—a whole set of ideas about how to move beyond this and I don't think it can be done in one country alone. I remember that I once said at a conference in Croatia that it cannot be done in one country—the *kleine Staat* that Germans talk about is not a good policy—nor can it be done in a European Union dominated by German capital. Probably better, though it sounds utopian now, would be the creation of regional entities, of small countries and possibly some big ones, working together within regional frameworks to rebuild their strength and to reestablish their sovereignty. In the case of the Balkans, it's obvious: Greece, Bulgaria, and the former Yugoslav states have a very clear basis to work together. United. One has to think like that.

And one also has to think about how to really democratize countries. We have seen a situation where democracy was hollowed out. The German sociologist Wolfgang Streeck has written about this very well in his work. We say it. We notice it. But we do not have the means to challenge it. Because we have not come up, so far, with a set of alternative proposals. And sometimes people say to me: but these proposals arise out of movements. That is not the case necessarily. The proposals of classical social democracy predated the creation of mass parties. And on the right too: the neoliberal ideas were being discussed in the 1940s by Hayek and such people, who did not even believe themselves that they were going to win, but their time came in the 1980s and 1990s. So it is something we have to do now. There are the campaigns to repudiate the debts of certain countries. All that was very positive, but this was only focused on one issue. We need an alternative plan. Both for Europe and for its regions.

Does such a plan have to be thought out well in advance? Or were you hoping that certain countries such as Greece or countries such as Venezuela or Brazil were actually daring to go further and really break away from capitalism?

Yes, but I think this could only be done by a group of countries. And I think the failure of the Brazilians to understand this was one of the problems. If you remember, during the early years of Bolivarianism, of

Chavismo, the Venezuelans put a lot of pressure on the Brazilians to do as they do. Brazil is the largest country of the continent. Lula wouldn't allow these countries to be attacked by the Americans. He told the Americans: "No, we are not going to do that." On the other hand, he didn't do what he could have done, which is to build a huge fund to transform health education for the poor. At least, the Venezuelans have done that. That has provided the material base. They would have done better in this last election if they didn't have a stupid electoral system, which they copied from Britain and the United States, and which is undemocratic. Under a proportional system, the opposition in Venezuela would not have had the majority it does now. So they made mistakes there.

But coming back to Brazil, the Brazilians turned their back on all of this and went for the neoliberal model, with everything that happened—huge amounts of money disappearing, corruption on a big level for which they are suffering, and then these big prestige projects that cost millions. I mean, to have huge street demonstrations by students against the World Cup in their country! Football! People have to be very angry to do that. And it is not sufficient to say that the Right maneuvered and manipulated—why wouldn't they, they exist in that country. But the protests initially were very genuine. So Lula's decision not to go that way was a problem; it could have made a big difference. If you remember, if you look back at the economists from that period, they would say that there are two ways in South America: the Chavez way or the Lula way and the Lula way is better. All over, this was the line of the European economists. What Lula does is acceptable, what the Venezuelans are doing is not acceptable. Now they are both gone or going.

We have seen many protest movements come and go. There were the different Occupy movements and before them the antiglobalization movement. Every time, there is a lot of enthusiasm and there is a reflection on how that movement can become more lasting and more sustainable, such as, for example, by creating the local and global social forums, but after a few years all these movements fade out. Do you think there is a way to create a more solid and lasting left-wing countermovement?

I think one feature of all these movements is that by their very nature they cannot go on for long. The Occupy movement very definitively rejected politics, very openly: we do not want a political program. I pleaded with them in two or three talks I did at the Occupy events. One was, I believe, in the Bay Area and the other at Harvard or Princeton— I cannot remember. And I said: "You have to have a minimum program, OK. Just six things you want, which is obvious in the United States." The reason is that when this movement stops you leave behind a legacy of demands showing that this is what they wanted. The anarchists didn't want that. Nor did the liberals, and the Left is weak. So that's what happened there.

The most interesting case of a movement transforming itself is Podemos. And here the jury is still out, as we say. And we will see what will happen. My fear is that some of their leaders think that by clever maneuvering and manipulation one can create a shortcut. I don't think it works like that. This is like defending NATO by saying that we want to be in NATO because NATO will democratize the Spanish army. I mean, this is a joke. When has NATO democratized itself or anything? *[laughs]* That's crazy. So I am nervous. But otherwise, I think that the model of Podemos is not such a bad one as it developed. Circles all around the country. Huge debates in these circles. That is the way forward. People are involved by presenting a global alternative, but they stopped doing that. But when I spoke to Iglesias, he denied that the circles had stopped and he said that they would come again, but they haven't come again. And because they did so well in recent elections, his leadership position has been strengthened. But these are temporary things. They don't last forever, and the same counts for movements.

The movements in South America were successful because they produced political attachments or parties that came to power, and they actually did some good things—they didn't do everything, they couldn't—but they did some good things in these countries. And that, I think, remains the model. You need to have a mass movement and a political party, or whatever you want to call it, that challenges the other parties and their ideology on every level. There is no other way. We haven't found any other way yet, and I myself cannot think of another way. Politics cannot be excluded. The Occupy movement and others like it were searching (at least subconsciously) for politics and parties. What we see, to a certain extent, in the campaigns of Sanders and Corbyn is the return of the political, and that political is social democracy or

Keynesianism. It is coming back now. People are discussing it and the interesting thing about the States is that Clinton had thought that, being a woman, she could do with women what Obama did with the black population, but that is not working. In fact, it has backfired in a huge way, with a large majority of young women working and voting for Sanders. So it is a strange mix. Identity politics, as you know, is not the solution. Identity is one part of a human being. Everyone has multiple identities. So for the people who decided to go that route and that way, it hasn't exactly worked out. We need a very clear alternative that can be understood by everyone. Tell people: "This is what we are going to do and this is what it will take." This is absolutely necessary. Fashionable antipolitical discourses on the left, usually in times of defeat, always reach a dead end.

INTERVIEW CONDUCTED BY STIJN DE CAUWER

Notes

1. The PSOE (Partido Socialista Obrero Español) is the Spanish social-democratic party and the PP (Partido Popular) is the conservative party.
2. The French president at the time was François Hollande. Jean-Claude Juncker, the president of the European Commission, is from Luxembourg.
3. PASOK is the Greek social-democratic party.
4. After the SYRIZA leadership chose to accept the proposed deal from the European Union, a group of SYRIZA members of Parliament separated to form the party Popular Unity.
5. Mariano Rajoy, of Partido Popular, is the current prime minister of Spain.
6. Ciudadanos is a Spanish liberal party.
7. Pedro Sanchez was the secretary general of the PSOE at the time. He resigned in October 2016.
8. In September 2016, Corbyn was reelected as the leader of the Labour party.

Finance Is an Extractive Sector

Interview with Saskia Sassen

In your recent book Expulsions *you analyze phenomena as diverse as the mortgage debt crisis, environmental devastation, and land grabs. You describe them as new forms of exclusion called "expulsions." What do you mean by that term? What holds all these phenomena together?*

Let me start with the second part—what all these examples have in common. My basic argument is that in the 1980s we entered an epoch where the organizing logic of capitalism fundamentally changed. Even if it is not fully present in countries with a mixed economy like China, I am still talking about most of the world economy. The new logic that marks this epoch is a logic of extraction, like mining. In a mining operation, you go to a place, you extract resources, and, when you have finished extracting, you are done with it and leave. I argue that finance has become extractive and has moved to the center of capitalism. This constitutes a major shift from traditional banking. The latter thrived on selling money and on the gradual improvement of purchasing power as the population became richer, generation after generation. The logic of mass consumption that dominated the post–World War II era was a very different kind of capitalism from the one that took off in the 1980s and 1990s and that we are experiencing today. A logic of mass consumption meant that the more money the households of a country had, the better for the whole economy and specifically the large corporations that began to dominate mass consumption. There was a push also by corporations to enable households and their children—health care, subsidies of all sorts, student support, etc. Better-off children would become better future consumers. This organization benefited the corporate system, which began to take over what was previously done by small family-owned businesses. So, through the logic of consumerism, capitalism happened to largely coincide with the interests of the population. The same argument also applies to firms. Banks thrived because firms thrived and this created a virtuous cycle between increasing sales and affordable business loans. Traditional banking has a very different logic, with its focus on enabling consumption, compared to today's financial logic. The traditional bank in a town benefited from the sons and daughters of the middle class doing better than their parents so that they would take out bigger loans. Finance does not make its money based on loans.

And today you believe this traditional form of banking has been transformed?

Today we have a shift to another logic, one of extraction. This is the most provocative claim I make when giving this talk in certain settings: finance is an extractive sector. Finance goes somewhere, removes whatever it needs, and then leaves. And to do this it has to invent complex instruments that require great minds—it is mostly algorithmic math, the math of physicists. Once it has extracted what it wants to extract, it does not care anymore. Simplifying a bit, we could say it is the opposite of mass consumption, where corporations push governments to enable consumption by investing in the consumer community: "Give them medical insurance, social security, student support, etc." These public investments allow for and support mass consumption. Finance financializes the wealth produced by others and succeeds in extracting often much more than the original value. It does take some brilliant minds to do this, but . . .

What is the connection between extraction and expulsion?

Expulsion is the consequence of changes in a complex system of flows when capitalism became extractive. These extractive practices produce so-called systemic edges, which are analogous to, but still different from, regular interstate borders. Today everyone is talking about globalization and the abolition or return of borders, but I think the critical development is the multiplication of systemic edges, which are a kind of border *inside* national territories. A systemic edge marks the moment when a familiar condition—independently of the question of whether that condition is simple or complex—becomes so extreme that our existing categories, concepts, and policies cannot get a grip on it. For example, a very long-term unemployed person is after many years no longer counted among the "unemployed" and becomes invisible to the eye of the law. New social divisions and connections appear, but are not included in our categories because these were not designed to capture a condition that exits "normal life." Some crucial realities become conceptually invisible.

That is why I have called one chapter in *Expulsions* "Dead Land, Dead Water" rather than "Climate Change."[1] We kill the environment, and once the land is dead we forget about it, because our focus is on what is working, not what is dead. It is quite interesting how these environments disappear. In Europe you have far less territory and consequently it is better protected, but the United States is my number-one example. I like to ask, a bit as a provocation, how much of the land of the U.S. national sovereign territory is actually being governed, or, more radically, is under government control? We have vast stretches of land that are basically dead due to mining and other environmentally degrading operations. One catastrophic event that happened recently is a mine that had been closed for twenty years and where the degrading metal container eroded. There was a massive spill of a very toxic element into a river that took it all downstream on a very long contaminating trip. The mine had been abandoned, so nobody noticed. That mine's dead land had simply become invisible, as if it did not exist. But the river brought the toxins to human environments. These dead lands start to intrude in our living environments, but scientific categories still fail to make the connections visible.

Behind my argument lies the assumption that we humans are essentially theoretical beings. I mean that in the Aristotelian sense of *theōria*, that is, knowledge as a way of seeing intellectually. If I would walk into a room and see *everything*, I would not be able to see or think it all.

Everything would just come at me all at once. You can explain this with a famous story about the Inuit. According to some, they have numerous words for "snow." Since snow constitutes their everyday environment, they see differences that we do not see, and thus have far more words for snow than we do. So, when I say that we do not see the extreme version of the familiar, I am bringing in a whole set of elements (theoretical, practical, customary) that mediate between the actual condition and how a given actor (a person, measurement system, research method, etc.) sees or does not see that condition. This makes me argue that at least some of our social-science propositions and theories are no longer enough or adequate to identify particular shifts and transformations. Consequently we may fail to see or factor into our research, measurements, or interpretations things that we ought to notice.

Social or conceptual exclusion is not a new phenomenon. Yet you have chosen to coin the new term "expulsion" for your research. Could you state your motivations for this conceptual shift? What is the difference between exclusion and expulsion?

I opt for "expulsion" because social "exclusion" happens *inside* a system and under mostly clearly identifiable circumstances. What happens inside the system is very important: it is a question of "will the system incorporate black people?," "will it give equal rights to women, gays, transgenders?," etc. There is a preestablished system of rules and norms and the question is, who gets access? When I found that there was a multiplication and growth of even more acute conditions (the radical eviction of people, land . . .), I decided that I needed a specific term to capture systemic "expulsions." Social exclusion continues to be very significant, but it happens in plain sight. People recognize what needs to be done, or what it means to have "equal rights" or "equal access." The problem with expulsions is that they are the empirical equivalent of a no-man's zone. Conceptually expulsions are hard to study because our traditional categories fail to address the issues crucial to these cases. So, for instance, in my chapter "Dead Land, Dead Water," I argue that the language of climate change is almost too pretty. It actually sounds quite inviting. *[laughs]* No, let us name it "dead land." I argue that today dead land is invisible, no matter its materiality, because once it is dead it ceases to exist for our economic, political, and social system because it has lost its utility. If a piece of land is dead, it ceases to be part of our lives. In the book I am currently writing on the territorial, part of my research is to map dead land, the *terrae nullius* of our epoch.

Expulsion remains, however, a very ambiguous moment, because those systemic edges are ambiguous. These concepts primarily serve to raise a whole new set of questions. So in *Expulsions* I argue that we need to detheorize much of our understanding of diverse conditions, nail the different concepts and categories to the ground, and then retheorize them, without respecting their prior hierarchy. The moment of detheorization for me is the moment when we actually interrogate currently prevalent categories. We have to allow for the possibility that our specialized research fields might actually make it difficult for us to see that there are conceptual similarities between what are today very disparate knowledge silos that do not "talk" to one another. So, for instance, I raise the question of whether the world's displaced people (due to land grabs, or massive expansion of cities, or floods, etc.), the long-term prisoners in the United States for minor offenses, and the refugees do not all share a core condition—the fact of being expelled? To what extent do we need to retheorize their condition, to get out of the usual conceptual silos, that is, to invent new transversal categories to connect these seemingly unrelated cases?

So, when I talk about detheorizing, it is not just about celebrating empirical data for its own sake. It is an empirical moment to get rid of these existing silences caused by conceptual gaps. In my book I give the examples of Norilsk, a major nickel-producing operation in Northern Russia, and Zortman-Landusky, an American mining conglomerate, and ask: "What matters more today?"[2] That the one has a communist and the other a capitalist history, or that both are spaces of extraordinary environmental destruction? Today, I argue, the defining vector is their capacity to destroy the environment. Destroying the environment would not have been as pertinent fifty years ago, when the communism–capitalism axis dominated the social sciences. But today the communism–capitalism axis is no longer informative in debates concerning environmental devastation. So we should retheorize with new variables and new questions to criticize existing categories. Expulsion is one moment in a messy set of conditions that require us to detheorize and to revisit familiar categories.

The same argument holds, for example, for the disaster of long-term prisoners in the United States. These are mostly just as much cases of the displaced, that is, the expelled from normal life, as are third-generation refugees, people who have lived in refugee camps for three generations. The latter were not meant to be there for so long, but they are not allowed to move or to make their camps into cities, which they are already in many cases, due to UN regulations. When refugees build more permanent structures for housing, they fall outside the jurisdiction and the support systems of the UNHCR.[3] There is a whole movement, people I have worked with, to make some of these refugee camps into real cities. But the United Nations does not allow for these projects, even though some Palestinian youths now say they will build these cities anyway. Long-term prisoners are just as much people not allowed to settle or to build meaningful communities. Should we then not look for meaningful ways to study both phenomena in parallel? I find various types of unsettlement marking contemporary politics: so it is not enough to simply have experts on long-term imprisonment evaluate prisons. We might learn from refugee urbanism. We need transversal categories to make visible how a given extreme condition of expulsion can take multiple forms, and we might learn from this how to devise solutions. More deeply, is there a connection, albeit elusive, an underground conceptualization that puts diverse forms of expulsion on the same transversal vector?

You mention finance as the core problem or source of these expulsions. Have you noticed any changes before and after the financial crisis? A lot of people have pressed for financial reforms to enhance accountability and responsibility. Do you see any of those objectives realized?

It is a bit more intermediated. The issue is the capacity of finance to "financialize"—from student loans and home mortgages to commodities and, above all, debt. Over the last thirty years finance has developed an increasing capacity to extract financial value from a larger and larger range of conditions and operations. As a growing number of experts have come to understand the negative impact, some critical exposés are beginning to come out. Quite frankly, I think finance has not been seriously reformed, even after all the major banks were found to have engaged in fraudulent behavior. One really important point is that crises are constitutive, not disruptive, of finance. *We* might call them crises, but top financiers have known how to turn it around: one mechanism is the "too big to fail banks," which means they can go to their governments and ask for money in the name of avoiding a larger economic crisis for a country. If you look, for instance, at the chart that plots corporate profits and corporate assets over time, you see a few years of crisis and losses and after that returns that are even higher than before the crisis. At the same time, millions lost their jobs, millions lost their small businesses, governments got poorer, and so on.

In short, you see quite different results in charts that describe the economy as a whole compared to finance. I was researching some of the earlier changes in the 1980s, when I was working on *The Global City*.[4] You see the curve changing shape in the 1980s, dramatically moving up vertically. This was the beginning of the new neoliberal era that followed postwar Keynesianism. Afterward comes the crisis of 2007, where you see a sharp fall for the corporates. Very soon, however, the line moves up again and actually gets even higher than before, an almost vertical line of growth. Finance reached over a quadrillion dollars in each of the last few years—the standard measure for finance is the value of outstanding derivatives. It is worth noting that before the 2008 crisis the global value of finance stood at "just" around US$600 trillion.

For some of my other books, especially *Territory, Authority, and Rights*, I have done a lot of research on these financial crises. During the 1990s, when the globalization discourse really took off, over seventy countries implemented the neoliberal program, while at the same time financial crises start surging. We call it "financial crises," but what really happened there was the repositioning of finance, which thrived on policies that opened up and deregulated economies to the benefit of large financial institutions. These crises actually resulted in benefits for the major financial firms and markets because they forced the deregulation and opening up of small, often vulnerable national markets to the major financial firms and markets. Thus, while a crisis produces losses for finance, it often results in power concentration of the large financial

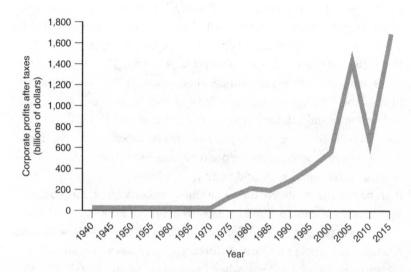

Chart 1 Corporate profits after taxes in the United States, 1940s–2010s (in billions)
Source: FRED Economic Data, St. Louis Federal Reserve Bank. Published in 2012 on
http://research.stlouisfed.org/fred2/graph/?s[1][id]=CP#.

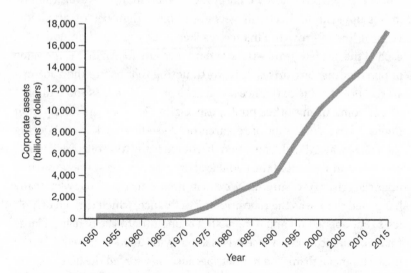

Chart 2 Corporate assets in the United States, 1940s–2010s (in billions)
Source: FRED Economic Data, St. Louis Federal Reserve Bank. Published in 2012 on
http://research.stlouisfed.org/fredgraph.png?g=eco.

markets and most powerful firms. So the language of crisis camouflages some real underlying trends when we are dealing with finance. But that is actually a fairly long history. It is not the first time that economic and everyday discourse obscures what is really happening to finance. So the notion of a "financial crisis" needs to be handled with some critical distance. Otherwise one simply thinks that financial firms were hit because they were too greedy and brought that down on us. This is only one bit of the story. It misses the more systemic developments animating the movements of finance.

When we look at the U.S. government responses to the crisis in 2008, we can distinguish two moments. Right at the beginning of the crisis the financial system had sharp losses and because it is involved in so much of the economy via financialization, the government comes to the rescue. There were two simultaneous interventions—one public and one highly secret. The public one was in the U.S. Congress: it debated an injection of 700 billion dollars into the economy—of which around 324 billion dollars were to go to finance—to help the economy survive the crisis. This was actually a genuinely informative public debate.

At the same time, however, I had my ear close to the ground, so I knew that there were other measures being discussed behind closed doors. But it was very difficult to get the data. So the second, hidden intervention came from the U.S. central bank—the Federal Reserve. Central banks are public institutions and one function is to do research about current economic developments and inform the people of that country. There was quite a bit of speculation about whether the U.S. central bank (the Fed) might be secretly passing on money to the banking system. One move came from Bloomberg News when it filed a freedom of information request with the Federal Reserve regarding what other support it might secretly be passing on to the big banks. The Fed should have promptly responded.[5] It did not. It took two and a half years to comply, which was far too slow. It also meant that by then the lively public debate in the legislature, during which the whole country had been focused on the issue of the government passing on money to the banks, was long over. The Fed's report could have made a real difference in the public's understanding of the relation between "its" bank (the Fed), a recipient of the people's tax payments, and the Fed's transfer of that money to the big private banks. By the time the information was finally sent to Bloomberg News and the media could finally publish it, the public debate had been over for two years and people were no longer paying attention. Bloomberg News published the data and it was a front-page story in the *Financial Times*. And the big banks were getting their billions from the Fed. The data showed that the Federal Reserve transferred not just the publicly announced US$324 billion, but $7.7 trillion to the global banking system. German, French, Swiss, Austrian, and of course American banks profited; even companies like General Electric, which had no business being there, received funds from the government. And another $7 trillion were transferred to the big U.S. banks in the form of quantitative easing—a nice term to describe what is basically printing money to give to the banks. All of this, without any public debate and, further, some of it kept secret even though it is the people's money, so to speak.

When this came out, you would have expected at least some reactions, but it seems that few saw the news or knew how to interpret it. And the financiers were not going to talk about it if no one was asking. From the average U.S. politician we heard nothing. One might still think that the average politician does not do his or her homework anyway, but even the average academic working on finance remained silent. About $80 billion a month are still being transferred to the banking system now.

At the same time, banks regularly broke the law, although the big financial firms primarily solved these legal issues through settlements, avoiding a trial. Consequently they succeeded in securing that there is no legal record. They settle and pay fines, but they avoid a criminal record and their reputations stay "clean." A thirteen-billion-dollar fine for Goldman Sachs, however, for a firm of that size is a joke. It is a fairly low price for the privilege of being able to say to their future investors that, in the history of Goldman Sachs or City Bank, they have never had a criminal indictment. Of course, they did break the law continuously, but settlements keep it all in the family, so to speak.

In finance a crisis is often not an obstacle, but an occasion to reinvent a system and get support. Further, a crisis in poorer countries—notably those seventy-plus mostly Global South countries where the forceful implementation of neoliberalism produced the crisis—weakened both the governments and the banking systems. This enabled the implementation of neoliberalism and the entry of the big global banks into economies that had been fairly closed and national until then. During a crisis it is easier to open up a national, fairly closed system in ways that would not be acceptable in normal conditions. The sad images of financial traders being fired and leaving their offices obscured a far deeper and consequential transformation that strengthened the global banks.

How come those proposed reforms and regulations are so unsuccessful? What hinders the introduction of a more just financial system? Is it due to complexity or is something else going on?

If the financial sector wanted to implement changes, they would have already done that. Elizabeth Warren, a legal scholar specializing in consumer banking and the protection of consumers, has frequently pushed in the direction of reform. She has made very sound proposals, but they are not picked up by the political establishment. Some Members of Congress are not interested in confronting or regulating the financial system. They support it and gain from it—donations during elections, a job or reference after retirement, and so on. Further, most legislators in Congress think that finance is too complex and that we should hence leave it to the experts, that is, the bankers, to come up with governance proposals. The same mechanism is at work, for instance, in the telecommunications industry: when politicians are not too keen to do their homework about the sectors they are meant to regulate, complexity incentivizes politicians to trust the industry itself more than they should.

The Democratic Party is, by the way, not moving in a promising direction in this domain. I am rather skeptical about the current front-runner of the Democratic Party, Hillary Clinton.[6] Her campaign team has cheated during the primary elections. They have kept other reasonable Democratic candidates out of the race. Bernie Sanders is a hero for me, but there were also other good candidates who did not get the chance they deserved—as the commentary in the press has put it, the Democratic Party leadership "anointed" Hilary Clinton. The Democratic Party has also played dirty on occasions. The media was pretty clear that in Iowa the party leadership claimed to have thrown a coin at the end when the results between Clinton and Sanders were too tight. The press had a lot to comment on about this and this is just one of the dubious decisions from the leadership that wound up to the advantage of Clinton. Also the primaries in Massachusetts, where he lost by very few votes, became the focus of complaints, especially when afterward news media caught photos of Bill Clinton walking by people queuing to vote and talking to them. This is actually forbidden and not how a democratic process should be handled.

The Democratic Party leadership has sidetracked a figure like Elizabeth Warren, for instance. Even Obama failed her when he did not appoint her for offices she should have gotten, because some people in the government and the financial sector were terrified to have such a knowledgeable person taking on some key issues—because she would have done something. We could, thus, have been far tougher on finance, but it was a matter of putting the right people in the right place. Obama has intellectual courage and he has definitely achieved some very laudable objectives. He lacks a stronger attachment to the political Left though. He did not know quite enough about economics, which made him oblivious of what he could have done to improve the economic situation.

On the other hand, when we go back to Europe, we have had similar kinds of debates around the issue of austerity measures . . .

I love this language of "austerity"! *[laughs]*

. . . and there has been a leftist response coming especially from SYRIZA in Greece. How would you evaluate their political strategy?

I got quite involved in the Greek story. I went there several times and spoke to all kinds of people. Now I joined Varoufakis's DiEM25 (Democracy in Europe Movement 2025). I think Greece in the end would not have been allowed to implement what SYRIZA wanted to do, no matter who was negotiating. In *Expulsions* I explain how in the Greek situation the discourse of austerity covers up some forms of expulsion.[7] For instance, while the conservative Greek government in office before SYRIZA patted itself on the back for renewed economic growth and employment, the graphs obscured the upsurge in unregistered unemployed people, suicides, and emigration. I think of measures of the economy that exclude most of the negatives as a form of economic *cleansing*, an issue I discuss at length in *Expulsions*.

You mentioned earlier that before the 1980s capitalism thrived thanks to an evenly distributed economic growth. How could this system transform into a discourse about collective asceticism?

Yes, but not "evenly distributed growth." In capitalism there are always inequalities, but the difference of that period was that even as the rich were becoming richer, the modest middle classes and the working classes were also gaining ground, and their sons and daughters were doing better than they themselves. This made the fact of enrichment at the top more acceptable. In *Expulsions* I posit that the shift is from a logic based on mass consumption to a logic based on extraction, which I explained in an earlier answer. I first looked at what happened in the Global South, where debt long ago became a mechanism for extracting resources instead of enabling a country to develop its economy. In the end even the IMF itself had to acknowledge in 2001 that in most of the countries where the IMF and the World Bank instituted their development programs and structural adjustment policies, these projects did not work out. They had to acknowledge that their programs had failed, and that the governments of these countries had accumulated debt levels they would never be able to pay back. Most of these countries were paying more in debt than they were investing in schools, hospitals, etc. What we call "economic restructuring of the Global South" sounds so reasonable. So do terms like "underdeveloped" countries, but these words mask more grim realities.

The same mechanism was applied to the indebted European countries, but what I found so interesting about the European crisis is that in the Global North we call this conundrum "austerity." In other words, the discussion is referred back to morality. Although the fundamental principles are simply a type of neoliberalism not that different from the programs in the Global South, this moralizing was less apparent in the Global South. In my opinion, the whole neoliberal project is essentially extractive. The austerity programs are geared toward extracting resources. The middle classes are getting poorer, also in Europe. The sons and daughters of the middle class are worse off than before. This shows that the logic of mass consumption and somewhat evenly distributed economic growth is no longer working in Europe. It has been replaced by a system that extracts value out of the population, but gives nothing in return. On the contrary, the discourse of austerity demands an increasingly ascetic lifestyle from the modest working and middle classes.

Not only the people, but also our governments are getting poorer. To take an example from a fully functional economy, the debt of the German government was 13 percent in 1980. That was not so long ago, and that was a time when the government was doing a lot more in the fields of building and investments. Now the national debt is over 50 percent. That is still very reasonable for a contemporary government, but it is quite telling, since today's German government cannot maintain or rebuild what it did twenty or thirty years ago. It just does not have the money to finance the same level of public goods. So, to summarize, we have poorer governments and significant sectors of the population impoverished, especially if we look at the data from an intergenerational perspective.

On the other side of the societal spectrum, we see at the same time a sharp increase in private wealth, mostly thanks to finance. Over a quadrillion dollars, as I just said, circulates in the financial sector in the form of outstanding derivatives. Before the crisis it was "just" six hundred trillion. That is almost a doubling over just a few years. We have corporations with more money than they know what to do with and a new, unimaginably rich class; I think it is important to include here not only the top 1 percent but also the top 20 percent (see chart 3)—a new kind of very rich upper middle class. You can barely call them a middle class; they are better described as the new kind of upper professional and managerial class.

So, when you take a step back and look at these numbers, you must say that the language of austerity is just one way of rationalizing that most are getting poorer for some to become incredibly rich. Many small businesses and family enterprises have gone under with this new type of economic logic, while multinational financial firms profit more than ever before. So you have a system that contributes, on the one hand, to

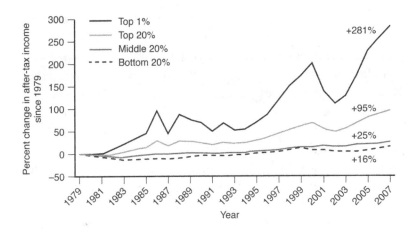

Chart 3 Percent change in after-tax income since 1979

a general impoverishment, even in rich countries, and, on the other hand, to an extraordinary concentration of wealth at the top in a way never seen before.

And then let me just bring in a transversal: Google. This is one of the booming firms of the last decade because it has thrived on the shift toward extraction. Search engines are the ultimate extractive sector, similar to finance even though the methods and tools are very different. Google has made extraordinary profits by basically extracting information from all of us and then selling it back to us and to firms. Using complicated, secret algorithms and all the extracted information, Google is able to predict and shape consumer behavior. This constitutes valuable information Google can then sell to other companies. Google manufactures a few products as a side business, but its core endeavor is not manufacturing but extraction. We do not *think* of finance and Google as extractive, but once we begin to look at them through that lens, we can explain some of the outcomes you see today, like Google's extraordinary wealth even though nobody exactly knows where that is coming from.

I discover these transversal similarities by going into the innards of the system, just like a surgeon checks out his patients' liver, heart, colon, etc. My research focuses on the *innards* of a system rather than the surface descriptions economic sectors provide of themselves.

In what sense does Google differ from other multinational companies?

A car manufacturer, for example, can get heavily criticized in public for every little thing that goes wrong. Each time a firm has to recall thousands of cars, which is costly and a PR nightmare, that firm is under public and media scrutiny. On top of that, these manufacturers have to pay exorbitant fines. I am not saying that they are simply "the good guys," but that they are producers who can be—and frequently are—held accountable. Google, on the other hand, just navigates in between spaces and accumulates vast wealth in the process without being noticed. Let me be clear, I could not live without Google anymore. But we have to acknowledge that its logic is extractive. Just like finance can extract value by financializing and concentrating at the top without any substantial compensation or even recognition of the sources or the consequences of that extraction.

In Expulsions *you have linked austerity not only to moralization, but also to ways in which official government data no longer adequately reflect reality. This generates consistent misinformation. What is the impact of this data on the discourse of austerity?*

"Austerity" is a very peculiar word that we should not accept without some hesitation. Some moralists call the current government policies austerity, but a more adequate description would be extraction of value from certain actors for the profit of others. We call that "austerity," because it gives a legitimating sound to these policies of extraction. Our governments are simply unable to stand back and say: "What the hell happened here over the last thirty years? We are so much poorer while there is so much wealth in the extractive sectors that they do not know what to do with it." These are questions that need to be asked. So in my reading, austerity policies are an instrument for economic cleansing—eliminating from official data a lot of that which has collapsed (bankrupt small firms, impoverished middle classes, hospitals, schools, etc.).

There are hence two separate aspects of the austerity discourse. First, austerity is a series of statements that tries to justify and *moralize* a set of policies, as opposed to the discourse of mere economic restructuring, which is more morally neutral. In the developing countries they could just blame bad management to justify extractive measures, but here in already highly developed Europe we are becoming poor. "Austerity" shifts the focus away from extraction to bad *self*-management. "Austerity" makes it sound as if governments spent too much money in the past and now have to cut their budgets to keep afloat. But in reality a better term would have been "maldistribution of wealth." Wealth has been shifted from governments and middle classes to a small corporate and financial elite (besides old inherited wealth).

The second aspect, intimately connected to austerity, is the way we measure economic growth. The United States is an extreme case in this regard. A long-term unemployed person is no longer counted in the official unemployment statistics after a while. In the United States, for instance, a few months after you get your last subsidy from the government, you simply fall off the charts. In addition, many individuals are not counted in the official statistics because they have held irregular jobs. Another number that gets overlooked is failed small businesses. If you or your business goes bankrupt and you do not declare bankruptcy formally, and commit suicide, which is what happened frequently in Italy and Greece, you are simply not counted in the bankruptcy or unemployment statistics. If you submit papers saying you are bankrupt *before* you commit suicide, then it gets included in the data, but if not, it looks as if you have not gone bankrupt at all. These and other practices and rules can make governments' data look more optimistic than the actual reality.

At one point Greece was a telling example of some of this. The statistics provided by the conservative government estimated that Greece had a 2-percent economic growth. But it was a complete fiction! The numbers did not include the suicides, all the people who lost their jobs, all the small businesses that went broke. Middle-class families had to give up their homes and drop their children at churches, because they no longer had the money to feed them. These people were not counted. One can hardly call such statistics reliable. That is what I mean by economic cleansing: you "measure away" the pieces of reality that disagree with the political message you want to get across. These are mostly highly technical issues that have to do with the way GDP per capita is calculated. If growth actually means bigger middle classes, then this standard measure would actually be a good metric, as it was in the post–World War II decades of mass consumption and growing middle classes. But today, when you have growth only at the top and impoverishment at the other end of the spectrum, the middle classes are actually getting poorer and even decimated, as in Greece. In that case GDP per capita is not a good measure. Its positive number is actually shaped by the massive growth at the top of the economic spectrum, but masks the hardships of the majority of people. Nicolas Sarkozy of all people has hosted an effort to generate an alternative set of measures launched by Amartya Sen and Joseph Stiglitz, among others. These alternative measures should give a more reliable picture of the economic situation, which in most countries has moved from a big middle to two extremes— the rich and the poor, thinning out the big middle.

We have a whole bunch of similar statistical measurements that are inadequate today. Given the reality at ground level, that is, the new trends and patterns of the last thirty years, some data suggest that you are counting growing middle classes, but are actually masking growing disparities. Growth used to mean growing middle classes, which made GDP per capita a very helpful tool, but realities have changed now and our conceptual apparatus to study reality should change as well. It will never be a perfect measure, but then again there are no perfect measures for complex, continuously changing systems such as those studied by the social sciences. GDP per capita has turned into a somewhat useless measure. For instance, today we are very proud in the United States of having created seven million new jobs since the crisis in 2008. In itself that is great, but we should also interrogate what we are talking about here. Thus 65 percent of the jobs that were lost during the crisis were middle-class jobs—broadly speaking, not incredibly fancy, but still fairly stable and well paid. But of the new jobs, only 22 percent are middle-class jobs. The others are either at the top or at the bottom of the labor market. This fundamental restructuring is not captured through the simple number of seven million new jobs. Politicians know that, but from their perspective it is much easier to just say they created seven million jobs. Consequently you have angry working- and middle-class people who are thinking: "Sure, they created more jobs, but I am making less money than before." The anger and frustrations this realization triggers work to the advantage of the likes of Donald Trump and his populist rhetoric.

This illustrates what I call "economic cleansing." I consciously suggest the analogy to the horrifying notion of ethnic cleansing, because this confusion of data *is* a horrible story we are not recognizing as such. The modest and hardworking middle classes—whatever their political preferences—who hoped that their children would be better off have been the ones really hit. They are the ones suffering, while their losses are rendered invisible through inadequate conceptual frameworks.

There are, for instance, fourteen million households that lost their homes in the subprime mortgage crisis.[8] And the loss is due to a financial manipulation that had nothing to do with traditional mortgages. For about six years before the crisis, intermediate agents sold these instruments as if they were regular mortgages. Each agent had to secure five hundred contracts a week to make it all work. The instrument has now been declared illegal by the U.S. government, but it is circulating in Europe and beyond. The key element in play was the demand for asset-backed securities by the big investors—who were getting tired of instruments based on long chains of speculative derivatives and no material asset. The subprime mortgage provided a bridge into an asset, the home. These were almost all fairly modest homes, since that was the population in the United States that still did not own a house; there were also second-home mortgages. Because the instrument was actually not about securing housing for people, the sales people rather quickly simplified the process and brought it all down to "All you need to do is sign this contract and you don't have to pay anything for many years."

The instrument was about creating a high-level investment instrument. And one challenge was to hide the modest value of the asset—the little house, or part of it. So it was mixed with very high debt. Naturally such a system breeds multiple abuses. Furthermore the subprime mortgage instrument consisted of sixteen extraordinarily complex steps, making it difficult to decipher by accountants and lawyers representing buyers. These formulae have nothing to do with microeconomics. The larger public has not been educated to handle these complex materials, not by academics at least, since the latter all stick closely to their models. That is why I think that one of the first tasks of researching a subject is to go into the innards of the system, a collective project to investigate how the system exactly works and what realities our current conceptual paradigms are unable to see.

Have you found any solutions in the innards of finance?

Well, I have a few comments, though no solutions. Finance needs to be confronted. We need to recognize that it is not banking in any traditional sense of the term. We need to recognize that it really is all about extraction. Different countries have different instrumentalities, but there are some driving forces that are now happening in most countries in the world that we have to deal with on a collective level.

When we begin to look at all these sectors, we should not accept their old definitions. As social scientists, we have got to take some distance. We think of finance in the terms that it describes itself with. We think of Google just as a digital-information provider and not as the extractive business it really is. I am really astonished that so many academics fail to interrogate what happens in today's economy. Social scientists, very broadly speaking, too easily use the categories of the sector they try to analyze. That is a lost opportunity. We cannot just use the standard descriptions the sector itself uses to explain its own activities to nonexpert outsiders. My project is to also use *social* categories to analyze the digital and the financial. Then you can really discover something not already obvious to insiders.

The prevalent mode in the social sciences, and this is very strong in the Anglo-Saxon tradition of the United States and the United Kingdom, is replication. And replication means that you are basically working inside a given paradigm. You are not working toward fundamental discoveries, but only propose minor additions. I take a different approach, namely, going to the innards. I do not accept how finance describes itself, but I go inside the financial system to unravel dynamics previously unnoticed. That means I am not so much interested in descriptions but in finding what we need to know in order to generate appropriate solutions. Right now we have all kinds of solutions, but they are all framed from outside (for example, policy), rather than from the innards of the system. This needs to change and I am trying to contribute to this project.

INTERVIEW CONDUCTED BY TIM CHRISTIAENS
AND MASSIMILIANO SIMONS

Notes

1. Saskia Sassen, *Expulsions* (Cambridge, MA: Harvard University Press, 2014), 149–210.
2. Sassen, 156–64.
3. The United Nations High Commissioner of Refugees is a UN agency responsible for the protection and support of refugees and displaced persons.
4. Saskia Sassen, *The Global City: New York, London, Tokyo* (Princeton: Princeton University Press, 1991).
5. A freedom of information request is a citizen's request to access information gathered by a U.S. public institution. This right of access is guaranteed by the Freedom of Information Act of 1966.
6. This interview took place when Hillary Clinton was still running for president.
7. Sassen, *Expulsions*, 35–54.
8. For details, see Sassen, 117–48.

How to Think a War Machine?

Interview with Maurizio Lazzarato

You are well known for your theory of debt. What is debt according to you and why do you consider it to be at the heart of contemporary capitalism?

The full argument is to be found in *The Making of the Indebted Man* and *Governing by Debt*,[1] but shortly I can say that debt is a power relation between a creditor and a debtor, but more abstract than the relation between capital and labor. Throughout its history capital has presented itself in different forms, such as commercial capital, industrial capital, and today financial capital. The latter has risen since the end of the nineteenth century, even if it was temporarily withheld by two world wars and the crisis of 1929.

How should we interpret this hegemony of financial capital? It is, first of all, an abstraction in the sense that it moves away from real production and, second, a generalized power relation between creditor and debtor. In nineteenth-century capitalism, debt remained solely a relation between capital and the state, or between the state and its colonies. Nowadays, however, it is everyone's predicament. Consumption and production, the whole life of individuals, are captured in the financial sphere by debt. Take credit cards as an example. Everyone carries one around and each time you buy something with it you actualize the creditor–debtor relation. You enter into a financial affiliation. This displaces the class struggle because it abstracts from clearly defined classes. It is no longer as easy to clearly individuate the prevalent powers, as it used to be in industrial capitalism. It is consequently more difficult to combat capital and to self-organize. Because each debtor is individually targeted, each also assumes the indebted relation to him- or herself alone. I therefore think that the paradigm of debt is an efficacious tool for the study of power relations today. That does not mean that other forms of power disappear, but the dominant relation in production and consumption, from the viewpoint of capitalism, is debt. It is a strategic product.

Furthermore I have discovered a book by two Chinese strategists, Qiao Liang and Wang Xiangsui, that is called *Unrestricted Warfare*, and that attracted a large following in multiple languages.[2] They introduce the theory that war today has moved beyond traditional warfare and has incorporated other domains, such as finance. That is how they interpret what happened in the Asian Financial Crisis of 1997. They argue that war's capacity to destroy used to reside solely in the army, but has now been taken over by finance. So finance is a form of war. This means that it is no longer necessary to use armies in order to make—let's say Greece—the enemy. The Chinese authors distinguish in this regard between bloody and nonbloody wars. They claim that the Chinese Red Army forgot about these nontraditional forms of war. Both the army and finance refer to networks of power relations that permit the destruction of countries like Thailand and Indonesia in 1997 or Greece today.

Last, I have used the paradigm of debt because Nietzsche and Deleuze argued that the relation central to capitalism is that not of exchange, but of debt. They claimed that the encounter of two free and equal individuals agreeing on a contract is a myth. Instead there are only unequal power relations governing the conduct of the weaker. I have applied this thought to the contemporary context.

You are now working on a book about war and capital. What do you think about the connection between the two? What can such a study illuminate about the new wars of the twenty-first century?

I am indeed writing a book on this subject, together with Eric Alliez.[3] The main claim is that war has an ontological function in capitalism. It is not a merely accidental phenomenon. Even in a book like Marx's *Capital*, economic production is intimately linked to war. One cannot separate war from capitalism. Its role is absolutely fundamental to the latter.

On the other hand, war has changed a lot, because capitalism has changed a lot. In the book we talk about this history from the phase of primitive accumulation until today. Explaining this whole history would take too long for an interview, but what I can say is that, linked to the rise of financial capital, a fundamental shift occurred at the end of the nineteenth century. Certainly, with the First and Second World War we have seen a new alliance between capital and the state. The state was so important because it had captured what Deleuze and Guattari called "war machines" in the army. In the end it is capital that appropriates these war machines through the state and subordinates them to its functions. So both war and the state become resources of capital through the process of imperialism. At the end of this process the state becomes the instrument of capital.

If we then want to define contemporary war, we only have to look at what the two generals wrote. Just as in China, there is intense debate in Europe about the nature of war. This started with the defeat of the American army in Iraq and Afghanistan. This army still thought along the lines of the old industrial war model of the two world wars. Their framework was that of an army with the objective of fighting another army. But Iraq and Afghanistan have revealed this system to be ineffective. The United States won the first battle easily, but the enemy did not disappear. On the contrary, it emerged everywhere. When the American troops left, there were still the conflicts to control Al-Qaeda and now ISIS that are difficult to control. So the reflection of these Western generals starts from this failure: How could such a great army with the most advanced technologies fail to win against a band of unarmed men or gangs armed only with Kalashnikovs? This constitutes the main problem.

Their answer is that war is today fought *within* the population. The enemy is not a state, but a population, so one must manage the conduct of the population. Parallel to Foucault's thought of the governmentality of the population, we can describe a governmentality of war. War used to be oriented toward the instauration of a social contract or toward the installation of a constitution. Nowadays this happens with wars within the population. As Carl Schmitt foresaw, we moved from a war between states in the Westphalian tradition to an internationalized civil war. That is what is happening in the Middle East, civil wars between Sunnis and Shias. These wars are not conducted between states, but between tribes. So an army, to intervene within a population, needs another toolset. Social and political techniques are necessary beyond military means. All these techniques have to be deployed simultaneously. If not, then victory is impossible. These wars, however, no longer talk about "victory." The generals talk about "permanent warfare," not in the same sense that Bush did, but to convey the idea that one has to continuously intervene in the population.

This phenomenon is quite interesting because it is also happening in Europe, even if it is in a different form and with different measures. The European debt crisis is also a conflict conducted within the population. This is not some abstract concept, because the idea that the conduct of the Greek population has to be governed continuously in order to suppress enemies and install a social contract is very present today. The debt crisis is one such regulation internal to the population.

What do you think about political parties like SYRIZA and Podemos, who have won in recent elections? Can their proposals combat such a European governmentality of war? Is parliament the right strategy to transform society?

I do not believe parliaments will be very effective. After the First World War a radical shift occurred in the organization of the separation of powers. A lot of power was concentrated in the executive branch to the detriment of the legislative branch. So this is not very new; it has a history spanning a century. Parliament consequently has no other function but to legitimate whatever the executive decides. If one looks at this evolution in the long term, one can see that with neoliberalism parliamentary elections have had no capacity for reform. Certainly parliaments have been set aside in countries such as Greece, Italy, France, or Spain. Podemos's case is quite similar. If they launch a political project beyond the European framework, they will be massacred by the financial markets. It is as simple as that. I am not saying that these initiatives are completely in vain, but it is very difficult to effect any real change. Podemos's situation is comparable in this respect to SYRIZA's, although for the latter the struggle is at an end.

How to think a war machine that can really approach things differently, that is the task facing us today. At the moment I believe Greece's story has ended with an enormous defeat for the Left. In Spain I do not know, but I do not think they will be able to leave the grip of the European neoliberal collective. In such a condition, how to think the continuity of political movements, struggles, and means of expression—that is the issue we are facing right now. We have seen that countries hit by the financial crisis, like Spain, Portugal, and Greece, have had protest movements because they tried to reform salaries, social security, etc., too radically. They need an organizational form not yet discovered, one that fights the state and finds the capacity to put together multiplicities of experience. We have not found that yet. SYRIZA is over and I do not think Podemos will win, even if they have a more articulated plan than SYRIZA. The latter was mostly the old communist guard, the old "commie" ways. Podemos is a different, more contemporary form of articulation.

If we compare what you are saying now with your earlier writings on the antiglobalization movement, such as in Seattle, you seem less hopeful today than ten years ago.[4] What has changed since then? Why can't we find alternatives today?

At the time I thought the antiglobalization movement could open up an important constitutive sequence of political movements and politico-theoretical knowledges, but that was not the result. This cycle of struggles has in fact ended in failure, even if we do not yet know what to make of this past. We have not found adequate organizational forms because at that time we still relied on an antiquated picture of capitalism. We are always running behind capitalism. In my opinion, that is the main problem. At that time we were not yet aware of the centrality of debt, but in reality capitalists had been introducing debt into the system since the 1970s. We always see that afterward, but we are incapable of anticipating these developments. If one would really want to break with capitalism, then one would have to anticipate the movements of capitalism, to be one step ahead, or aside. We had not seen the possibility for defeat there, which would be repeated in Latin America. That was the experience repeated throughout the decade.

We do not have the theoretical or organizational frameworks to think about past failures. Consequently, we repeat old ones. I believe we are even encountering a conceptual crisis in contemporary critical theory. People like Rancière, Badiou, or Negri face grave difficulties. They do not quite get there. They have not, for instance, foreseen the issue of debt. People like Rancière do not even think about it right now. He does not believe the economy to be an important issue. Capitalism, however, functions in a very specific way with the economy, since the latter is the politics of capital. If one does not understand this story very well, one risks talking around what is of real political importance. So to sum up, I believe that the opening created in Seattle came quite swiftly to an end.

What we need is a political form of organization that can not only effectively answer war and finance, but also develop the multiplicity of different political movements. This would require the construction of a war machine that is not yet available to us. One can criticize Lenin, but at least he had the Leninist gesture of thinking a subversive war machine within capitalist military structures. No one can even imagine a repetition of that gesture today. For my part, I think that Lenin for that reason is one of the greatest political thinkers of the twentieth century. He could efficaciously think an anticapitalist form of political organization, even if he used concepts now outdated such as ideology, historicism, progress, class struggle, etc. Those are now finished, but he did make an effective organizational form within capital. No other thinker has done that. If we do not succeed at finding one today, then each attempt is doomed to fail. We kept repeating the Leninist form, even if it was outdated. I do not think Podemos will succeed because there is not a new form of thinking or even the imaginary resources to conjure up a new war machine against capital. And another mode of government, because, as Deleuze and Guattari argued, such a war machine is not solely concerned with waging war. So we do not know how to oppose war or how to develop new forces within capitalist government. This initiative is in the capitalists' hands. Now we can only defend ourselves and follow, but in that way we will always lose.

Recently you have proposed the right to be lazy as a mode of resistance against financial capitalism. You find that, for instance, in the work of Marcel Duchamp. How can we think laziness as the manifestation of contemporary work refusal? How can laziness be an act of resistance?

I have written *Marcel Duchamp ou le refus du travail* because it is an interesting case.[5] But between the micropolitical and the macropolitical there is a gap not so easily bridged. We cannot say that ruptures in literature are immediately political. Those are two different levels. According to Deleuze and Guattari the micropolitical has to enter into the macropolitical and reconfigure it in order for real political change to occur. So Duchamp might be interesting on the literary or artistic level, but not necessarily for politics. Marcel Duchamp was interesting because of his way of life, but he does not provide a project that can be passed on to politics. Even though he is of importance for individual conduct, I believe that for politics we need a war machine. Only a war machine, and not contemporary art, can be effective.

Duchamp never stayed when war came. He always left, so he is obviously not the ideal political model. During the First World War he was in Argentina and during the Second World War he was in the United States. He did not get involved in the resistance, like Samuel Beckett and others. We do not have to make a political hero out of him.

Even if there is no direct translation from art to politics, I have tried to politicize Duchamp's idea of laziness. Work refusal has to be defined differently today and this book serves to provide such a modification. Italian workerism (*operaismo*) had a very specific understanding of work refusal, but should we not rethink this notion today? When people obtain one, two, three, or seven master's degrees, only to be forced afterward to work for next to nothing, is it not crazy that we cannot find any means of resistance? In that case it would have been better if these people had not studied at all. Or take a look at the contemporary Uber-ization of the economy or the zero-hour contracts in the United Kingdom. This is a duty to be available all the time, while only getting paid for the hours one actually works. We are approaching situations of slavery here. One is constantly available without knowing how many hours one will work that week. One hour, two hours, or twenty-four hours straight, that is madness. But it will continue nonetheless, if nothing is done about it. In France the socialists are lowering the standards right now. They are talking about lowering unemployment benefits. If people are able to suffer these losses indefinitely, then we are in serious trouble.

The only escape is to find new forms of work refusal. This would be a work refusal of *that* specific kind of work. Now we are dealing with students who study until they are thirty-five years old, but who cannot pay the university back afterward. They remain in precarious job situations, without pension or health care. They only have debts to reimburse until the end of their lives, like the Americans or the British. One has to refuse these injustices, or they will continue to proliferate. We could even go along this track until we are back in the nineteenth century, with the total dependence of the worker on the entrepreneur. At the university I see numerous hypereducated students with no future for a job or a decent salary. This evolution toward precariousness is everywhere, but it does not constitute a political movement. People do not refuse and accept this dynamic, but I do not see why. So I have written this text on Marcel Duchamp to politicize his notion of refusal. I like Marcel Duchamp because he questions employment and the idea that one has to work in order to live. His notion of laziness gets to the heart of the fact that the workers' movement was also founded on nonmovement. A strike is not only a movement of rupture, but also a nonmovement.

Where are there perspectives to be found to criticize such a system? In France during the 1960s, for instance, the university and the philosophers played a crucial role in the critique of society. Can the university or the academic philosopher still fulfill that role today?

It has become much more complicated, because the university has radically transformed since then. In France there are still some relatively free spaces left, but when the British and American models arrive in the universities of continental Europe, the results will be catastrophic. For instance, there already is this movement toward evaluations in Italy. They want to evaluate everything, each moment, each student, and each professor.

The people from '68 have a problem with that in my opinion. The failure is always the same: they have not found an alternative organizational form. In the history of the revolutionary movement, military strategy has always been critical: Lenin, Mao, Sun Tzu, Clausewitz, etc. The only ones who tried to really think through Clausewitz after 1968 were Gilles Deleuze and Michel Foucault, by reversing Clausewitz's formula. War is not politics through other means, but politics is war through other means. They tried to think war as the foundation of social relations. They posed the question, although they did not work out an answer. So the limits of the thinkers of '68 are of not having thought through the consequences of this idea. Even forty years later the reality of war is still there without a thorough theoretical investigation.

Why haven't we found a form of organization that can stabilize all these political energies? There are numerous movements, organizations for women, precarious workers, civil servants, etc., but sooner or later they all have to find an answer to the question of the war machine. This question has almost been ignored within critical theory. Only Foucault, and to a minor extent Deleuze and Guattari, have explicitly dealt with it. But at that time the political movement of '68 was already in decline. In the 1960s and 1970s the only form of organization available was the Leninist one. They have repeated things wholly inadequate to the specific time frame. So, similarly to the Italian resistance movements, they constructed organizations more or less along Leninist lines; '68 did not produce theoretical or practical knowledge about organizational forms that could oppose capital. Afterward neoliberalism introduced new forms of warfare, as Qiao Liang and Wang Xiangsui argue. It has installed a civil war by other, nonmilitary means. I think this constitutes a defeat for critical theory. At the moment I do not really see how to escape this conundrum.

If there are no effective macropolitical movements against capital, can we then find individual initiatives or forms of life that, similarly to Duchamp, escape capitalism?

Such a strategy is deeply complicated by the rise of the extreme Right in Europe. We do not know how to retire from capitalist civilization. Franco "Bifo" Berardi argues for such an escape along the lines of medieval monasteries, because the monastery was a space outside of feudal power relations.[6] Today, however, capital is everywhere, we cannot escape it. We are moving toward a Europe consumed by war, racism, and closing borders. We can try to change the political system, as in Latin America, but that does not work. The neoliberals returned to power both in Argentina and in Brazil. And Europe is turning more and more toward the extreme Right. The latter is not only embodied by extreme-right political parties. In France the socialists are putting forward rightist legislative proposals, not the Front National. Social Democrats all over Europe are introducing this form of government. In countries like Denmark we are even approaching Nazi practices. They are now forcing refugees and asylum seekers to give up everything they own above ten thousand kroner.

We have to recall that Europe is not only the Europe of peace, but also that of colonization and two world wars. We have to be suspicious of this Europe, because it tends to return sometimes. It might be another type of fascism today, but it is still in some sense a repetition of past wrongs. Each day the signs proliferate. I do not wish to be too alarmist, but this situation is quite regrettable. Even more so after the political defeat of SYRIZA, which incarnated a kind of hope for new possibilities on the European level. The extreme Right might not grow in Greece itself, but it does in the rest of Europe.

How would it be possible in such a situation to conduct some form of escape? I do not think one can take a wait-and-see attitude. If someone had said to wait and see at the time when fascism and Nazism were rising in Europe, he would have been very wrong. We have to be inside the development if we cannot flee. I do not see many alternatives or possibilities on the individual level though. We do whatever we can, and everyone has to live his own life. However, the possibilities are limited. The economy no longer provides the same assurances that it used to thirty years ago. There might be some individual forms of resistance, but I repeat that the main issue is to find a collective form of expression.

The extreme Right is very skilled in exploiting the injustices of debt and the impossibility of instigating economic growth. These problems will, however, continue to trouble us: only weak or no growth at all coupled with increasing debts. At the same time Europe continues to wage wars in the Middle East. European armies keep bombarding villages there and create catastrophes in the process. In a not-so-intelligent way, they have created or sustained Al-Qaeda in the past and ISIS now. The Arab Spring opened spaces that were immediately closed by Europe's contributions. So, in the end, nothing has changed. We cannot escape, even with interesting movements like the Arab Spring. The neoliberal initiative is stronger, although at the same time it is very weak. It cannot determine a new world order or establish a new economic and political stability. That is why wars have taken these new forms.

On the other side of the spectrum there is jihadism as a kind of counterpart to the extreme Right. Is this also a reaction to capitalism and its wars? Is it connected to the extreme Right?

Jihadism is also a form of fascism. Naturally it is linked to the history of European colonialism. One century ago, after the First World War, France and the United Kingdom divided the territory as if it were a cake. Today the French act as if they have forgotten this. There is a total denial. But the French only stopped the colonization because they lost the conflicts in Algeria and Indochina.

Afterward came the phenomenon of internal colonization. The sons and daughters of immigrants coming from the old colonies are treated within the country as if they were colonial subjects. Their resistance consequently takes the form of a Muslim fascism, if you could call it that. So the core of the problem is still capitalism, which organized the colonization and maintains it at home. I do not think that religion is really the issue here. It is more likely a political appropriation of religion, since they use it quite arbitrarily. They do with it whatever they want. They do horrible things with it, but it is nonetheless a political response. There no longer exists a strong movement of hope stemming from Marxism, so they cling onto other sources for inspiration.

There is also another connection to the neoconservative movement, especially in the United States. Bush and his allies have pushed for and defended strong ties to Saudi Arabia and the European countries later followed. One could call that a fascist country as well, even if it would have another meaning than in Europe. So I think there are ultimately political answers to neoliberalism, but at the moment they move to the right.

INTERVIEW CONDUCTED BY TIM CHRISTIAENS AND STIJN DE
CAUWER; TRANSLATED BY TIM CHRISTIAENS

Notes

1. Maurizio Lazzarato, *The Making of the Indebted Man*, trans. Joshua David Jordan (Cambridge, MA: Semiotext[e], 2012); Lazzarato, *Governing by Debt*, trans. Joshua David Jordan (Cambridge, MA: Semiotext[e], 2013).
2. Qiao Liang and Wang Xiangsui, *Unrestricted Warfare: China's Master Plan to Destroy America* (Los Angeles: Pan American, 2002).
3. Éric Alliez and Maurizio Lazzarato, *Guerres et capital* (Paris: Éditions Amsterdam, 2016).
4. Maurizio Lazzarato, *Les révolutions du capitalisme* (Paris: Les Empêcheurs de Penser en Rond, 2004).
5. Maurizio Lazzarato, *Marcel Duchamp et le refus du travail: Suivi de Misère de la sociologie* (Paris: Les Prairies Ordinaires, 2014).
6. Franco "Bifo" Berardi, "Nove Anni dopo Seattle," Centro Studi Sereno Regis, 2008, http://serenoregis.org/2008/07/02/nove-anni-dopo-seattle-franco-bifo -berardi.

9

The Creativity Dispositive: Labor Reform by Stealth

Interview with Angela McRobbie

In Be Creative, *you described the rise of a new economic discourse with a focus on creativity and on creative entrepreneurship.[1] You call this the creativity dispositive and you regard this as a transformation of the labor and welfare system as we know it. Could you explain this a little bit?*

Well, one way of interpreting the rise of the creative economy and its particular address to young people is to see it in terms of a neoliberal effect wherein a younger generation is being prepared for work in which there is no protection. There are a number of elements or dimensions inscribed within this process, one of which is that it is a kind of labor reform by stealth. Governments do not need to confront the trade unions as they would have done in the time of Thatcher and even after Thatcher. In many ways you could see this process of building up the new creative economy not just as a way of bypassing the trade unions and bypassing normal work with normal entitlements; it is also a way of creating a generation who have no experience of protection in work and therefore who have no reason to look at the past in terms of protection and entitlement. So it creates a kind of generational cleavage. Young people might say: "Well, we don't have these protections, why should we even think about them? Our generation has to do it for ourselves." That becomes part of the very powerful forgetting mechanism of neoliberalism, that is to say, a dehistoricization, making a break with the past, just as happened with feminism, so that there is no need anymore.

If I am teaching a group of students, who all want to work in documentary filmmaking, in photography, or in the fashion industry, about what a trade union is, what the struggles were in the 1960s, 1970s, or 1980s, and what kind of protections there were for maternity or for sick pay, the students are likely to say: "Why is this relevant to us?" It doesn't have a natural place, even in the sociology of work. So, I think this is one of the key dimensions. By stealth, it implies a kind of generational break, a forgetting mechanism, a dehistoricization, and a way of creating a new generation in its own bubble who don't need to feel any responsibility for the past generation.

That is one dimension. The other element is that there is the process of middle-classification. It is not a conspiracy thesis ("by stealth, governmentality has done it"). You can pin down the different steps in this process. You can pin it down historically to the early days of the New Labour government. It is very interesting that it is nominally a social-democratic, left-of-center government who really pushed this through. But this middle-classification process is interesting and particularly relevant in the United Kingdom, and it is very much tied into two elements. One is the expansion of higher education. More young people are going into university degree courses, which you've had in the rest of Europe for a long time, but Tony Blair really pushed that through. So many more people, young women particularly, but also lower-middle-class or upper-working-class young people.

The other element is the gravitational pull toward enjoyable jobs, and this was, if you like, the seduction element. They weren't just saying: "We are going to throw you out into unprotected work and sink or swim." Rather, there was a promise made to this generation of having the possibility of fulfilling oneself, which had great appeal. You won't be working nine to five in a local office. You won't be wasting your talents. This was a powerful appeal to young women. The result of this is the huge expansion of certain kinds of media, cultural, or creative courses within particular sectors of higher education. Photography, media arts, creative entrepreneurship, and so on.

That is what I mean by the "creativity dispositive." I also wanted to encompass the power of pedagogy. That is the key instrument. It undergoes all kinds of different changes. It is not pedagogy in the old sense of the university. It is now coaching and mentoring, tool kits and one-on-one: a customized pedagogy. In a classic Foucauldian sense, pedagogy is really the primary instrument of contemporary power. Everything is pedagogic, for example, when you are looking at television programs about how to be a chef or how to set up your own business, the way in which it is done is to follow the example of the "master chef," to emulate the success of Jamie Oliver or Nigella Lawson. That really connects with Foucault's notion of the pastoral. It becomes part of a longer argument about how pedagogy itself undergoes a transformation. This is really the question then about the entrepreneurial university, and about what happens to the teachers themselves, when the teachers are expected to do one-on-one coaching. It is individualized teaching. What are the consequences of that?

You describe the rise of this situation under the New Labour government. Ever since, we have had an economic crisis, we have had austerity policies, we had the rise of tuition fees. . . . How has this entire situation impacted the situation you describe? Has it made it worse?

My book *Be Creative* documents a decade of extremely active governmentality, from 1997 to 2007. So I am not making claims about austerity or about new forms of activism since austerity. However, there are a number of things that one can see. There has been some continuity. There has also been exacerbation. There were shifts since the election of the coalition government and then the conservative government. I would say it is true that at the level of pure governmentality, the creative economy has slipped further down the hierarchy of importance. Where Tony Blair's government was really pushing ahead with culture and creativity and media and art and doing this very much through the Department of Culture, Media, and Sports, the Tory government since then has really not got the same interest in the creative economy. They do not have this focus on the artist, for example. The role of the Department for Culture, Media, and Sports is diminished. Does this mean that creativity no longer carries so many expectations?

On the contrary, it is more about delegation. The creative economy finds itself embedded in education and higher education. So I would say there is more of a quiet atmosphere, but nevertheless a sustained emphasis on this kind of training and education. Not because the current government wants to train so many thousands of documentary filmmakers, but because this kind of training, at a higher-education level, is still relatively cheap to do. What was developed in the early 2000s has this lasting effect. There are also changes, but the changes are very much within the educational apparatus. For example, there is more of a business-school emphasis, with less critical thinking, bolstering the business side of the cultural economy.

In answer to your question, it is certainly true that the prominence of the creative economy has somewhat diminished for sure. You could also say that in many ways there has been a sectoral redifferentiation. Where Tony Blair was generally celebrating the multitasking, portfolio-holding creative entrepreneurs, more recently these sectors have tended to reprofessionalize themselves separately. So the fashion industry is actually doing very well thanks to a much more aggressive business agenda with the British Fashion Counsel, with the Greater London Assembly, with this huge inflow of students from China, and so on. You could say that each of these sectors has developed a more professional lobbying power: broadcasting and television, film, the gaming industry, fashion, and the arts, they all have separated out again, which is quite interesting.

In your book Be Creative, *you argue that new forms of solidarity should be formed from within the creative industries. For this you take inspiration from volunteer and grassroots movements.*

I outline some of my slight disagreements with some theorists who somehow want to immediately connect the critique of the creative economy with the post-Occupy activist movement. I think that there is a tendency there for the activists, coming out of the kind of movement around people like Lazzarato, Negri, and others, to gloss over the profound class differences of themselves as activists and what they see as grass-roots politics. I think there is a tendency to romanticize a connection between, for example, semiunemployed graduates in performing arts and working-class mothers living in housing estates.

It is almost a form of going back to discussions in the 1970s of what activism would be, minus all the complicated questions, for example, around black politics and race politics. When some of the theorists talk about the exodus and working-class struggle, I think: "Hold on a minute, how do you do that? What does it mean to imagine a new kind of housing economy where unemployed people or single moms are sharing a house or a squat with, for example, academic activists?" It leaves out all of the important debates that took place in the 1970s, 1980s, and early 1990s, often led by feminists, around race and class and around community politics, the slow politics of working (for example, with refugees and battered women), and the awareness of the difference between the vocabularies of middle-class activists and the needs of uneducated, unemployed women, and this is why I have recently sometimes disagreed with the assumptions of the "precarity" activists. Entire libraries of books have been written about cultural values and about not imposing your assumptions on poor, disadvantaged people. I actually think that it mirrors, to an extent, contemporary neoliberal thinking, if you look at the neoliberal idea of social enterprise—"Make a difference! Go and work with prisoners!" Actually, there is a whole bibliography of sociology of working with prisoners. It glosses over those debates, particularly around race.

Do you have examples of what kind of activism or solidarity movements, for example, aimed at single mothers, you would like to see happening more? What would they look like?

I would say it is important to talk about history. If younger people have perhaps not been educated in the politics of race, even if they have done some urban activism, if they haven't read Paul Gilroy, if they haven't read the work of critical race theorists from America, if they haven't read Ruth Gilmore or Angela Davis on prisons or Loïc Wacquant, then it is very easy to have this idea of just going into a prison. One way I see this happening is through doing art in housing estates. "We are going to work in a housing estate in Peckham. We are going to do performance art and we have a project." The recent writing of the feminist geographer Heather McLean is very useful here, for the reason that she has actually carried out ethnographic work that looks at the way in which precarity politics can be sucked into ideas about "cleaning up" areas of the city where vulnerable people try hard to earn some kind of living.[2] So again, one needs to have a slower form of reflection when young activists want to work with and alongside "local" people. You don't just go to young black girls in gangs with your camera. I'm a little bit wary of the enthusiasm on the part of artist/activists to "work with the community" but not to engage in a meaningful dialogue with social workers, with trained youth workers, etc. So there is a need to look back at radical social work theory and critical social policy.

In your book Be Creative *and also in other articles, you describe how women are actually in an even more precarious position than men, especially in the portfolio-driven creative industries. How do you think that education, because you mentioned education, and cultural studies in particular can prepare them for such a situation? Can they be prepared? Can anything be done in order to make the students see certain dynamics in order to change the situation?*

I think there is a longer discussion to be had about what we mean by entrepreneurial culture and about people who are really living from project to project, particularly young women. What will that mean in terms of family and lifestyle and security and stability? Some studies done by one of my colleagues, Lisa Adkins, show that when a couple decides to become entrepreneurial, when they say, "OK, let's go and set up an art gallery together, let's do a business together," often forms of gender retraditionalization become embedded. So, when the family works as a unit of self-employment, with freelance work or with a small business model, what does one find? Traditional gender positions can so easily reemerge, for reasons of convenience. By the way, this point is made wonderfully well in the film *Eine Flexible Frau* by the German feminist filmmaker Tatjana Turanskyj. There is almost an inherent social conservatism that kicks in when we are thinking about small business culture, and as Tatjana's film shows this is compounded when there are new pressures on young women to be the perfect mother, that is, the new neoliberal version of "family values." This connects with the desires of recent governments to reduce the cost of welfare, as David Cameron was known to have said: "The family is the best system of welfare there is."

I think that is one aspect to be concerned about: the family business. So the family business is often predicated on gender normativity, but more than that, the family business is also often predicated on a prefeminist financial dependence. For example, if the family income is tied up with staying together and with the mother saying: "OK, I'm working freelance because then I can be with the kids. My income will drop, but I am very happily married." But what if the relationship breaks down? Who is more disadvantaged? The person who is much more disadvantaged, as in prefeminist times, is the woman who gave up the full-time job and who is absolutely much more precarious than the husband.

Do you see the answer to this more at a policy level?

It is very difficult, however, to make again the old feminist argument about non-family-based benefits and tax credit systems when profamily policies are so embedded in contemporary taxation systems and when the family has become this unit for all kinds of privileged systems of taxation. But I think that feminist campaigns around women and pensions, around independent financial provision to women, is really important, but it is also important for women to be more aware that becoming self-employed or becoming freelance has got all kinds of costs. Of course you could also make an argument for better forms of protection for freelance work. I would definitely go along that road. One other way of seeing this, however, is to consider the portfolio jobs and the high level of freelance work as something of a testing ground that over a longer period of time individuals seek to stabilize. The period of entrepreneurship or indeed of intense creative practice can often give way to paid employment. How does this tally with having a pension to retire on perhaps, nowadays, at age seventy? Overall young women have to become more informed about their earning futures, about pensions, and about taking care of their financial independence.

Now, some people in the rest of Europe would say: "Who are you kidding? Those jobs don't exist anymore. The kind of ordinary jobs with protection are also a thing of the past." For example, in Germany, lots of people would say: "Well, I have been going from one project to the next for the last ten years." Or people who are academics who get a five-year job, and then a three-year job, and then a two-year job. There is little debate about the future of work that is really tackling these issues. How do you improve protection for people whose precarious careers are beginning to become the norm? It used to be the case in academia that you would think: "OK, I will have five years of temporary jobs and then I will get a permanent job." But how can you say in somewhere like Germany: "OK, you must get a full-time job if you want to protect your own livelihood in the longer term," when there is an oversupply of people and they are not getting those jobs? Here in the United Kingdom I would say to my students: "You know what, take a job in Aberdeen or go to the north of Scotland, if it's a full-time job." But people often want to stay where their friends and their family are.

And do you also feel that the "club to culture" that you are talking about is more friendly to men than to women—the work/club scene where you go out and you network. It seems to be advantageous to women when they are young, but . . .

The question is, Is it advantageous anyway to women when they are young as well? It just might mean that it is easier to pick up a job in a bar and then to get more opportunities. Sure, but that in itself is also predicated on a certain kind of freedom and on always being available to go out at night and having no obligations. So it cuts out a lot of people who maybe have to care for older relatives or have to be parents themselves. So it is a very narrow sector. You can say here in London: "OK, it seems like there are hundreds of thousands of young women from all over the world able to take a job in Shoreditch House, able to take a job in an art gallery." But actually, they are from a relatively small sector of the privileged middle class where parents think it is a good investment to come to London for two years and see what you can pick up. So it always was quite exclusive.

You have written that you have stopped teaching theories about subcultures for a while.

Forever! *[laughs]* I find that subcultures became seen as very easy translatable into a celebration of consumer culture at the expense of a more critical and historical vocabulary that was embedded in the original work by Stuart Hall and others. And to make a Boltanski and Chiapello point again,[3] it was something that could really so easily be transformed into its commercial opportunities. Something for people working for an advertisement agency. "Oh, I know my subculture theory. I know my Dick Hebdige." Actually the currently voguish fashion label Vetements (housed under the Balenciaga brand) really excels on this front. They have applied just about every conceivable aspect of youth culture theory with unbelievable commercial success. So, in effect, subculture theory became denuded from all critical and historical understanding. More specifically it got translated into what Sarah Thornton called "subcultural capital," reflecting Bourdieu: knowing about underground DJs or about new music genres became something that would get you a job. After a certain amount of time, subcultures became so instantly synonymous with the mainstream and with consumer culture. You might just as well be teaching consumer culture then. Fashion students as well as employees would be told: "Go and look for interesting-looking fourteen year olds in poor parts of London. What are they wearing?" Either you do it wholly in a critical vein or you stop doing it. It became something without any political or theoretical framework.

This subcultural capital is also something that you notice in today's hipster generation. You describe their deeply individualized stance and their lack of social responsibility. Do you think something can be done about this? How could we get them more committed?

What I described in the book was very much a London effect. In comparison to other European cities, particularly Berlin, there was—in this period I was writing about, this neoliberal moment of celebrity culture with people such as Tony Blair and Damien Hirst—an absolute absence or disavowal of any social responsibility in favor of a celebratory effect. It was a completely apolitical decade, from 1997 to 2007. And during that period there was not a vestige of the existence of an antigentrification movement, never mind activism.

This had a long spillover effect: the fact that there was a decade without the politics of the neighborhood, of the black people living around the corner, of poor people living on the street. It's not because post-Occupy there is suddenly a little bit more political awareness that this somehow compensates for this lack. What happened during this decade was really powerful, really deep-rooted, really embedded. It is this that transformed the landscape of London, that made rent in London go sky-high.

And again, I find that my students have an incredible lack of knowledge of past models of more socialized urban living. So I teach a module called "The City and Consumer Culture" with one session on gentrification. And the students had no idea of the landscape of London before its recent transformation, of housing associations, of the fact that young people in the past were involved in the community and not just looking for trendy bars. How they could do a deal with the local authority to take an empty house (short-life squatting) and create connections with the neighborhood. They had no idea of that level of neighborhood community awareness with questions of poverty, of disadvantage, of not being patronizing, etc. For example, they had no awareness of the history of housing associations, whether they were living in Islington or Peckham. It is interesting. There are all these trendy shops on one side of the street and a black no-go area on the other side of the street, and let's take some photographs!

This swooping in of trendy-looking photojournalists is something that so-called locals are beginning to contest. In Berlin especially, people who have lived for decades found themselves being photographed as "local color" by busloads of architecture students from wherever. It even happened to me in the less-hipster area I live in in Berlin, Friedenau, whose only claim to fame is that Marlene Dietrich is buried in the local cemetery. Having a coffee in the café overlooking the beautiful Friedhof, I was joined by a bunch of fashionable-looking twenty-somethings all in skinny jeans, and they actually turned to me and, without saying a word, took a picture and then walked out nodding and semismiling as if I should be grateful. I was totally infuriated by this idiotic behavior. This desperation to find new hip locations with "local people" for Instagram or whatever. Unfortunately I just didn't get the chance to jump up and challenge them.

Do you think something can be done about this apolitical "doing of culture"? For example, is there a role for education?

Yes, but it's a bit of an uphill struggle in terms of education. We all work so hard. That's what we have been doing for how many years. Students would say: "Thank you, Angela, I loved your course and I have become more aware." But they are completely starstruck and then they say: "Oh, I want to go work with Vivienne Westwood." *[laughs]* And I am a wet blanket, you know. It's a slow process, like Stuart Hall would always say.

I think in London the battle has been lost. It is now an impossible place. The only way in which one can think about creative economy in the United Kingdom is to think about regional investment and job creation outside of London, about how you can build stronger local economies in different parts of the United Kingdom. If I worked in cultural policy, that's what I would say, because London is just a place where the wealthy flow through.

Scholars such as yourself often describe a particularly British situation, but at the same time you write about Berlin or Italy. Do you see this as a more general European trend?

What I wanted to do in this book is refer to a more embedded and long-standing tradition of, for example, feminist projects in the neighborhood or in the community or working with girls and the kind of NGO culture that has always existed in the European Union and that has actually employed enormously talented academic think tank people.

But I also want to show how the European Union itself is also, of course, profoundly shaped by the same emerging neoliberal discourse. Actually, I do think that the creative policies formulated in the United Kingdom have influenced thinking across Europe. I can see that in something as narrow as the fashion creative economy. Last week we did a seminar in Berlin and what they wanted me to do was to bring some policy makers, some people who set up incubators in London, and talk to people in Berlin about how it worked. So I do think that this kind of Tony Blair effect has had an enormous influence. I really wanted to show in this chapter about grassroots European projects that they were becoming unviable for various reasons.

There is a new shaming on people who are dependent on welfare that amounts to the undoing of welfarist thinking and a lack of solidarity. People say: "Why should I pay for somebody else? They should find a job."

The family has to step in, or so it seems. But why should they be ashamed of being temporarily unemployed? In different parts of Europe, in Greece or in Spain, where so many people are unemployed, maybe 50 or 60 percent of young people, there cannot be that shame. And that is where activism does come in. It should be antishameful. There should be an antishaming, prowelfare movement.

That is also very much what I argue in the book. If you "middle-classify" people and you also shame welfare or the fact that you might be unemployed for three months, then very few people will actually go to a job center and find out what they are entitled to, even if it is just fifty pounds per week. There needs to be a new form of activism around welfare and the benefits system. Whereas in my generation, this would be a normal thing to do. But now young people would rather just live at home and ask their parents to give them fifty pounds per week. Or they will do interning and basically work for nothing. The family is relied upon. I would say: "That is what I pay my taxes for. Of course, go and get the benefits!" What if I was suddenly sick, what would I do? I would need sickness benefit.

The benefits are also tied to the fact that people do part-time or temporary jobs. What do you do when your temporary job ends?

Exactly! They are both disavowing welfare and pushing people into this kind of project work, making it much more socially unacceptable to be dependent on benefits.

INTERVIEW CONDUCTED BY STIJN DE CAUWER, GERT-JAN
MEYNTJENS, AND HEIDI PEETERS

Notes

1. Angela McRobbie, *Be Creative: Making a Living in the New Culture Industries* (Cambridge: Polity, 2016).

2. Heather McLean, "Cracks in the Creative City: The Contradictions of Community Arts Practice," *International Journal of Urban and Regional Research* 38, no. 6 (2014): 2156–73; McLean, "Hos in the Garden: Staging and Resisting Neoliberal Creativity," *Environment and Planning D: Society and Space* 35, no. 1 (2017): 38–56.

3. Luc Boltanski and Eve Chiapello, *The New Spirit of Capitalism*, trans. Gregory Elliott (London: Verso, 2005).

10

The Idea of Crisis

Interview with Jean-Luc Nancy

Until recently, when we used the word "crisis," we thought of the big oil crisis of 1973. That was a shocking experience. Suddenly our Western self-confidence was shattered. What was perhaps worse: the price of life went up spectacularly. But it still remained a crisis within the world. This crisis was resolved by the Western economy, with the aid of Western economic models, and the world remained the same. Now, it seems as if the world itself is "in crisis," as if the world today is crisis. Does it concern the world as such or only processes within the world? What does it mean when people say: "We're in a crisis"?

This oil crisis was indeed clearly a crisis within a system, but within a system that was already transforming. In fact, I prefer the term "mutation" to "crisis." I think we are living the beginning of a mutation that could be as important as the capitalist mutation or the mutation from Antiquity to a Christian Europe. These processes develop slowly, of course. The passage from Antiquity to Christian Europe, that is, from the fourth until the tenth century, prepared what eventually led to the Renaissance and the birth of capitalism in the thirteenth century. So, a crisis is indeed the announcement of a mutation, but a mutation that was already on its way and that continues for a long time afterward. Before the oil crisis in 1973, there was the famous crisis of 1929, the crash with the Great Depression. This was also a crisis within the system that urged this system to adapt, to rearrange itself. Out of these crises rises the necessity to transform capitalism. With the aid of economists like Keynes, capitalism slowly left its essentially industrial model that still largely hinged on family property. After the Second World War, the West entered an era of monopolistic enterprises.

These enterprises were also multinationals, with all their political impact.

Precisely. This process had its political effects, as we can see by the transformations of nations and their international relations. It is also necessary here to point out what was then the beginning of the end of decolonization. Its real meaning is not the superficial fact of independence but rather the expansion of a worldwide political, economic, and technological network. This alleged independence is an illusionary one. The large part of Africa still finds it impossible to arrive at political autonomy. It can be said to be economically colonized—for example, by China. Dictators succeed in remaining in power. The state of political autonomy in Africa is in some cases almost shameful. Finally, there is this major technological development. A nation's need for energy beyond its own resources is symptomatic of the crisis, due to this development and its effect on, for example, transport. And of course, nuclear energy and the invention of the computer contributed largely to what I called the mutation of capitalism.

In Europe, the oil crisis relates significantly to a political enervation. Recently, Régis Debray wrote an autobiographical little essay, full of anecdotes, called *Madame H.*[1] Madame H., that is, History. Debray describes how he has seen History "taking leave." I agree with him. I grew up in the complacency of technological, political, and moral progressivism. We had great, almost-mythical statesmen like de Gaulle and Pompidou. They represented "high culture," they talked like masters of rhetoric. And suddenly, in 1974, there was Giscard d'Estaing, who dressed like everyone else and played the accordion. This instrument had nothing to do with "great music" or "high culture." He represented "common people." There was this European experience of a change of civilization. All these crises and changes took place within the system, but at the same time they became worldwide. And now we have gone from crises into what I call mutation. It is only during the last, perhaps not more than two, years that the notion of "crisis" entered its very own crisis (*la mise en crise de l'idée de crise*).

Why have we arrived at the crisis of the idea of "crisis"?

Because we always realize that a crisis is a period where something is revealed. Take a medical crisis. During such a crisis, a symptom breaks out and reveals something about you. Crisis means, and has since Hippocrates, a phenomenon that allows you to judge (*krinein*) what disease you suffer from. At the moment when the symptoms break out, we say that the disease manifests itself. The crisis is the moment of revelation that allows us to judge and also to heal.

We all too often tend to see crisis as a condemnation of a situation or a thought. Critical thought or the notion of crisis was introduced by Kant and Marx, not as condemnation but as discernment or judgment. In his *Critique of Pure Reason*, Kant separated what can possibly produce an object of knowledge from what cannot. That is not a rejection of metaphysics; it just rearranges its reach. He poses an analogy, a postulate that allows thought to think something "as if" it were a realm of ends, "as if" it were God, and so on. One could then think them as if they were objects without having to be able to construe them as objects. It was the same with Marx. Marxist critique was a critique of political economy. His analysis of the production process wanted to distinguish what was socially acceptable from what was not. He discerned the illusion that the value of things was their market value, calculated in terms of capitalist profit and not in terms of labor distribution or exchange-value. Marx did not want to destroy the economy; on the contrary, he wanted it to work better. He did not even want to destroy capitalism as such, because of its historical and dialectical function. Capitalism was necessary to generate the revolution. It would lead to a situation where everyone would own the means of production and thereby benefit from production. Here, we run up against a limit in Marx's critique. He thought that capitalism would, of itself, enter a state of crisis that would automatically lead to a revolution, and at the same time he thought that this enormous production machine or technology was in itself good since it is its own history, it is the history of man becoming the history of nature. But since then, since those great ideas, crisis has come down to depreciation, to condemnation. Crisis became an intrinsically bad thing. We say that something is a bad state of affairs, but we have no more means of discernment, of critique. An operation like those that Kant and Marx accomplished seems to have become impossible. If I were to say, "let us pretend there is a realm of ends," people would laugh at me. So, should we not have utopias? Indeed, I think we should not have utopias, because we would not know how to make them work, how they could function. We know that a utopia is an illusion. The demand for a utopia means dissatisfaction with the present state, on the one hand, and, on the other, the expectation of another state that is sadly impossible, since it is defined as "nowhere," as a place we have no access to. Marx saw this very clearly, which was why he replaced utopian socialism with a scientific one.

But even there I believe Marx was, discreetly, even almost secretly, a bit Kantian where he talked about the "total human." He could not say, "Well, this is what the total human is going to be." This was a projection of a state he really did not know how to define himself. In *The German Ideology*, he talked of a society where a human hunts in the morning, goes fishing in the afternoon, rears cattle in the evening, and criticizes after dinner. This is a utopia. Nowadays, we lack projects like this. People often feel uncomfortable in society as it is, but at the same time there is a tendency to believe that this life, shared in communication, is almost played or acted, in a way. These people know they are playing. Most of them would never admit it; they will never declare that they are involved in what seems a play, but usually they think that political action has become futile. When I was young, political action was what one could call "general." We had the class struggle and the labor movement. There was solidarity, an interdependence between the different production sectors. But now, it seems to me that the national framework for this action has disappeared; political action can only take place in specific economic sectors. Railroad companies are a good example here.

You mean that they internationalized or "multinationalized" after having been privatized?

Yes, precisely. The railroad company is a very old national institution and the railroad unions are very powerful. But the current strikes are directed against the national institutions. Ultimately, this has to do with technological development, and I do believe we should insist on the importance of this evolution.

Why is that?

Because this could possibly be Marx's blind spot. Marx saw machines—machines that made things. Machines were production machines. He did not discern the problems these machines pose. In the technological ensemble hides a certain autonomy. Take the example of traffic, of planes and boats and trains. The production of these machines mobilizes a technological complex that generates specific needs, mainly energy, and that also determines global relations. There is the issue of rare minerals in Africa—that, by the way, contributes largely to the distorted sociopolitical situation in some African countries. We need to understand all this through the notion of a technological revolution that replaces nature, even on the level of production and consumption. Information technology produces immaterial goods: communication, knowledge, etc. Of course, there is always hardware—the terms "hardware" and "software" are, by the way, not coincidental. One needs hardware, but real production takes place by means of software. The notion of hardware brought about a new phenomenon, namely, disposability. Now, we are familiar with this phenomenon, we can even think of humans as disposable (*jetable*). Whereas, before, we had production and consumption, we now add disposal to it. This is rather interesting, the history of the word "consumption." A first connotation could be that of absorption. When we eat, we maintain our resources and eject the waste. It is not like when we use a hammer: there is no waste there, only wear. A hammer can serve for several years, can be repaired to serve for several more years. We used this notion as a representation of production—as a tool. No matter how big the machine was, it was still thought of in terms of "tool." A tool is seen as an extension of human activity. This is in my opinion how Marx looked at machines, whereas, nowadays, we would prefer the word "instrument." An instrument has a very particular function, but no real consistent intrinsic value. An instrument like a computer has its value inasmuch as it belongs to a chain of machines.

This chain is to be understood as a chain of production that produces machines that produce machines that produce machines, etc.

Yes, precisely. We have arrived at a stage where machines have only this end: to become the means of production of other machines. We find ourselves today in a state that can be called "final without end," to use Kant's expression. This expression has a "bad meaning," an endless finality, where finality goes on forever. If I would have to find an example of this, it would be the way we think about health. To many of us, health "suffers" from an endless finality. We all have to remain healthy and avoid death. To me, this opens a really absurd perspective, namely, of an ever-increasing population that in a way becomes immortal. This is why it has to stop: the end of death is also the end of all finality—this is the true meaning of Heidegger's *Sein zum Tode*. Death has a final value, because we can say that we live to die. Death really accomplishes something and it is precisely this accomplishment that we seem unable to think today. We have arrived at a state "beyond" crisis. According to me, we have had two major phenomena: the first was paradise, and that has gone; the second was what one might call "total man," the illusion of a humanity that does not die—and that illusion has also gone.

Could you explain about this immortality without end that lies beyond the crisis?

Well, you can easily see that the number of elderly people in Europe is continuously increasing. The lives of all those who reach eighty or one hundred years of age are not always that magnificent. Of course, everyone says how great it is that people can become that old nowadays, but is it? No one can explain exactly why a life of one hundred years should be better than a life of seventy. Everyone tells me: you have lived on for twenty-five years thanks to your heart transplant. Correct, but these twenty-five years mean nothing *to me*. If I would have died at fifty, I would just be dead now. And then they go on: but look at all the things you achieved during those last twenty-five years. Again, that does not mean anything since everyone else could have achieved the same things.

You really think so?

Sure! I am talking about those things one does for the community, what is useful to the whole world. I am convinced that those things will happen anyway. Take Kant. Imagine Kant not having been born in Königsberg in 1724; would nothing that happened between 1750 and 1800 (independence of America, French revolution, steam engines, vaccination, etc.) have taken place? *Would* they have happened, without a corresponding philosophical event? It would, perhaps, have been different; it would not have been Kant. I am sure the critique of the evidence of God's existence would have been formulated anyhow. In Kant's time, God was not dead yet, but already very ill. Kant found himself challenged with a theodicy or the justification of the existence of God, and when you feel you have to justify God, it means He is not doing well on His own. It is impossible to imagine what would have taken place if the phenomenon of the polis would not have happened or, in fact, any other great social, political, or technological phenomenon that belonged to the great empires of the past. All these events would not have taken place without someone like Plato—but not necessarily Plato himself. I am convinced that the philosophical event itself, the arrival of philosophy, would have taken place anyhow. The event that took leave of the myths, the public declaration that myths are only stories, is probably not dependent upon the person of Plato.

Christianity coincided with a great mutation. The question of why Christianity succeeded is a slightly incorrect one. It is not the result of successful marketing, as if Christianity came up with a better product. Christianity arose in the middle of very strong philosophical and religious agitation. The notion that it "won" somehow is erroneous. "But why?" one asks. This is difficult to answer. In the fifteenth century, Christianity became a disease and later on, in the eighteenth century, it was commonly regarded as a superstition. Even today, there are people who think of Christianity as a cancer that poisons Western civilization. But Christianity was already a response to a crisis, namely, the crisis of Antiquity. This mutation of Antiquity, the event of Christianity, was made possible by Judaism. Something was produced, something that could be summarized as a change in the relation with the infinite. They called it "God," but this God was not like all other gods.

You have stressed the fact that every mutation is actually a change in our relation to the unknowable, the infinite, etc. Is the current mutation also of this magnitude?

Yes. Only, the modern change of Christianity has for a long time approached the unknown as a sort of endlessly reducible quantity. This is the age of science, even of scientism. In the end, we will know and solve the secret of the universe. Einstein believed, and lots of people after him, that $E = mc^2$ could well be *the* formula of the universe. Lots of scientists really believe they are digging a tunnel that leads straight toward the secret of the universe. Only the wisest among them dispute this. They understand that this tunnel only recedes ever further toward this unknowable. Science persists in creating ever-new objects, like black holes and bosons and quarks and so on. This entails the fabrication of ever-new and stronger detection instruments and measuring devices. Some scientists imagine this as progress toward the "secret," but in reality, they move away to something, probably to a nothing. Science is still attempting to theorize the Big Bang, already trying to imagine what might have preceded the Big Bang. This approach, this movement, is endless, infinite, indefinite. We finally start to realize that the "beyond" is precisely not beyond. We are capable of conceiving of a universe that is at the same time expanding and yet finite. There is nothing beyond finite. So, science itself is beginning to think otherwise. There is this book by the physicist Aurélien Barrau on truth in science that shows this.[2]

Is this perhaps the sign of a new thought, when science contends things like "Time comes into being some microseconds after the Big Bang"? How can one measure time before there is time? Is this not an absurdity? Moreover, is it not remarkable that such a crisis does not seem to appear in the Arab world? For example, algebra was known for ages without it leading to the elaboration of what we, in the West, call modern science, including this kind of explanation.

Indeed, the West is, in another word, technology. Again, it remains important to stress the importance of technology. Heidegger put it correctly, namely, technology is the last of "Being's fateful sending." Humanity did not end up with technology by coincidence. This does not mean there is a question of necessity here, like some form of providence. I would say, in short, that we live through an anthropological mutation that is not the first one. Humanity as it was at the end of Antiquity is not the same humanity as the current one. The latter is a humanity from which every sacred presence, of god and spirits, has disappeared. Renaissance humanity was also different—not that much attached to locality, to territory like before. Each mutation is largely influenced by displacements and expeditions. The Renaissance was strongly marked by the great explorers like Marco Polo and Columbus.

Some anthropologists have called this mutation "Anthropocene." This is supposed to be the era that is dominated by humans, when the transformations brought about by humans in the world become most significant. The preceding eras (Pleistocene, etc.) were then determined by a natural agent. But I would say that this Anthropocene can also be seen as the anthropological mutation of human domination itself. Modernity is, after all, the era of human domination. Humans consider themselves lord and master of nature. But now, a double movement is spreading. Humanity is beginning to realize that it has submitted itself to its own productions, because it needs energy, because it produces machines that are much more powerful than humans, because of artificial intelligence. By the way, I always suspect there is something slightly wrong with this notion. I cannot see how an intelligence—if we can call it that—produced by another intelligence can be so much more powerful than that intelligence. No artificial, produced intelligence is capable of thinking the infinite. By this I do not mean the endless calculation of a certain number, but to really think the infinite.

At the same time, there is this sudden grasp of the utter relativity of humans in the universe. Their relativity probably has to be understood as that which is "in relation with." Family members are called "relatives"— that is the meaning of the relativity that marks humanity. Humanity is becoming a world family. More than ever we know how to relate to all other points of the world. So, we have to think of ourselves as natural beings and at the same time wonder how we can produce, by means of technology, the human animal that would be . . . what? A new humanity? Take all these new methods of procreation, knowing that we have only crossed the threshold of this. There is artificial insemination, cloning, etc.

We are asking ourselves what is possible, but is this really a question when we keep thinking the possible in the register of the real? The question concerns more what can become, in the sense not of the possible but of the impossible. Imagine when all is gone and there is no human world anymore. Not like in *Mad Max*, with a few humans surviving. No more humans, no more thoughts. Surely one may ask: If nature no longer produces humans, what will happen with nature? Will nature come to an end? The meaning of history, of the world and of humans, would not disappear into a sort of absurdity—it would just "pass out." There would be no more sense, time, world. There would be nothing, no more problems to pose. When there are no more humans to pose problems, there are no more problems.

Then there is no sufficient reason for it to continue. But when Heidegger talks of a new understanding of Being, this is a sort of basic philosophical faith or trust. Heidegger is confident that there will be sense, that we will never be left behind in total absurdity. We cannot predict or extrapolate the new meaning of Being, or where it will come from.

Indeed, but this may also mean the possibility of Being as nothing. There may be something of this in messianism. This also can mean almost nothing. Christ changes from one who comes to restore the Kingdom of God into someone who tells people to expect something else. His disciples want to know when He will come back and He replies that *kairos*, the moment that is also the occasion, is not their concern. Then what does the coming back of the Messiah mean? All the more because to some people it is not at all clear whether He has not already come back. He has arrived a first time. Why? To die. And then there was the Resurrection, but the risen Christ is probably elsewhere. The coming back may well be the Apocalypse. This is interesting because the coming back is at the same time the final end: Judgment Day. This means that all that was is judged. There is nothing else. There is only God . . . a Trinity that loves itself, as Dante puts it. At the end, there is only light. These are the last verses of his *Divine Comedy*:

> But now was turning my desire and will,
> Even as a wheel that equally is moved,
> The Love which moves the sun and the other stars
> Paradise is when desire is transformed into the endless love-of-self.

Dante must have read Augustine, where the latter says that, in the end, there will only be love, a love that needs nothing but itself, not even hope or faith. God, that is, total love.

Yes, but is it really an end? There is something that haunts Christianity from the very beginning. In Augustine, but already in Paul and John, something points at an infinite, at precisely the absence of an accomplishment, of an end, a conclusion. We have landed beyond paradise. This final love is not an accomplishment but an event that endlessly turns back into itself, as a wheel of desire, to stay with Dante. Desire that desires itself. It is not satisfaction but desire. I think we approach the very core of the mutation we are living. We find ourselves beyond accomplishment, beyond satisfaction. Our society suffers from satisfaction, from consumption, and at the same time desperately looks for satisfaction. The other day, a student asked me how it is possible that we all live very happily and at the same time we are all very dissatisfied with the world. We are unhappy. We, philosophers, think and talk about everything but we also realize that we cannot inscribe our personal action into a great project, like the communist or the Christian paradise. There is still so much to understand, to reinterpret, to resignify.

At least we can see how our time is marked by a clear disconnection between the actual possibilities and a future that cannot be deduced from them. It is a future that borders on the notion of a future without future. Something is on its way. Something is coming, perhaps even the end of the world. Here we can see the disconnection from both sides. On the one hand, there is a crisis from the viewpoint of the project, of a goal, of the representation of a future; on the other hand, there is the mutation—the fact of no longer being in the project, of no longer living the representation of a future but rather the opening toward a to-come (*avenir*). This is always the case with the great mutations, like Antiquity and the Renaissance. A mutation suspends time. Christianity suspends time. Time becomes a time wherein one can leave time. The Messiah will come back as a thief in the night. The Renaissance, on the other hand, is when time produces the promise of accomplishment. This promise is a very important notion, Christian as well as Roman and Hebrew. Judaism is the making of a promise; look at Abraham and how Yahweh keeps delivering promises of posterity. The Christian promise is the promise of salvation. This is no longer a matter of generation, of continuation, of transmission, but rather the deliverance of the subject, of the person. Between those two lies the Roman promise: the promise of a civilization, made to itself of itself. Rome has arrived, has given itself its laws, its nation, its republic, etc. Later, Virgil will supply Rome with its own history, wherein it is told how Anchises promises his son Aeneas a great empire. This is, of course, not what really happened, but it explains how Rome feels about itself, as a promise of itself to itself. The historicity of Rome is not the infinity of Abraham. In this Roman spirit, we can discern what prepares the mutation of the end of Antiquity and that is the spirit of enterprise. They set out to dominate the world, as a plan, a project.

What was special about Rome was its notion of law. Law is, in fact, technology that is conscious of itself. It is technology. It is artificial inasmuch as it emancipated from religion. Roman law is no longer divine or natural. Each year, the Pontifex Maximus explains how the law will be interpreted. Law has nothing eternal. Roman religion always refers to laws and rules and those are always in transformation. Roman law is aware of being artificial. And this architecture of law is the very basis of the spirit of enterprise. It was also the basis of citizenship. No matter what nationality you have, if you belong to the Roman Empire, then this will be your law.

There, I see two simultaneous mutations: the opening toward the infinite, toward God, in other words monotheism. At the same time, there is this spirit of enterprise, the spirit of the world. I mean by this that Rome, for the first time, constitutes a world. Before Rome, there were worlds, places where people thought of themselves as the home of humanity, societies that considered themselves to be the true humans in opposition to the others, who were barbarians, "lesser" humans. Rome did not have barbarians, but it would nevertheless be taken over by barbarians, by the Visigoths and the Germans and so on. This is the first mutation. The second one is capitalism and humanism—the infinite becoming precisely the enterprise of the infinite domination of the world. According to me, this infinite has to be read as Hegel's "bad infinite." It is the infinite growth, increase, accumulation of power and knowledge. In this mutation, humanity appears as the subject of this power and knowledge, of technology. And now, this subject returns to a nature he has transformed in such a way that there is hardly any nature left. Nature is completely marked by humanity. Actually, this return is humanity that relates to itself as perplexity. Humanity started interrogating itself before—even Kant asked about what it means to be human. Pascal said that humans infinitely surpass the human. With this quotation, I believe, Pascal actually heralded the modern world—he was more modern than Descartes. And I do not think it is redundant to question humanism, as many think, because humanism is precisely the idea of accomplishment—it is the old mutation. We have to move on. Things are actually changing.

Then perhaps we should render our discourse on crisis more practical? What to do?

Well, in my book *What to Do?*,[3] I suggest that we transform the question itself. Until now, we understood this question in terms of production: What do we have to fabricate: things or laws? Take the problem of the refugees. This concerns the whole world on a geopolitical and techno-economic level. We have the advantage to notice very clearly the value of human rights, to see the institutions that allow people to apply for asylum, etc. This appeals to our responsibility. But at the same time, it poses the practical problem of how to take care of an extra million people. I think Germany is very well organized and has taken some smart measures, but all the same, these measures are determined by the notion of integration into the economy, by the spirit of enterprise. Is there a way to stop this? It is clear to me that we should stop the war and then stop the economic traffic.

But is this not a suppression of the notion, of the phenomenon, of the experience of "crisis"? Crisis announces a world that changes while it seems that governments are taking measures to keep things the way they are. Shouldn't we allow the world to mutate?

Yes, indeed, we see at the same time the rise of right-wing politics, even extremely right-wing politics, and the appearance of something else, namely, the need for Western nations to welcome refugees. This is, I believe, a very poignant discussion. In these countries, natality is historically low and Europe realizes that Germany, Belgium, France, and the Netherlands cannot survive without reinforcements in their labor force. This is the paradox of Europe at the moment. One wants to preserve national identities but the refugee crisis shows that such preservation is impossible if nations enclose themselves. It is no coincidence that populism and right-wing political thought oppose the notion of Europe. But then Europe is in itself a contradiction. It is at the same time an economic space that aims at self-preservation as well as a political space that is imploding, or exploding, or possibly both. The markets are constantly fluctuating, industries are continuously relocated, etc. The multinational character of economies renders them less transparent. The production of cars, of food, of IT is changing fundamentally and radically. Some will hold on to current production models, others will try to develop new ways of production. Crisis means precisely to balance this twofold being.

INTERVIEW CONDUCTED AND TRANSLATED BY
ERIK MEGANCK AND EVELIEN VAN BEECK

Notes

1. Régis Debray, *Madame H.* (Paris: Gallimard, 2015).
2. Aurélien Barrau, *De la vérité dans les sciences* (Paris: Dunod, 2016).
3. Jean-Luc Nancy, *Que faire?* (Paris: Galilée, 2016).

11

Terror and the Rejection of Sense

Interview with Jean-Luc Nancy

Let us talk about terror. With reference to the "Arab spring," I think I can discern three separate effects: emancipation, radicalization, and reinstallation. What do you think about this?

I think it is precisely as you say. There is liberation or emancipation, there is radicalization, and there is a return to old values. All three are interconnected. I will give a striking example. Take Nasser's Egypt. This was a strong and ambitious Egypt. It was perhaps not a real Arab project, but partly a Western one—a socialist model with strong power. There was certainly a socialist idea behind this project. What happened during Nasser was in fact an emancipation, also vis-à-vis Islam. Egypt achieved a truly modern sovereignty, with the nationalization of the Suez Canal and so on. But at the same time, this evolution went against the Western interests—let us not forget the position of Israel in this. This position has something terrible—a word that, by the way, belongs to the same family as terror—because Israel is not just the outcome of a reaction against the extermination of Jewish people by the Nazis but also the effect of a process that produced Zionism as a sort of socialist ideal, a whole new idea. The *kibbutzim* were very popular here in the West when I was young—we even learned Hebrew chants!

At the same time, this socialist Zionism had already passed through the war with the Arabs. The analysis of this is frightfully complex.

I would even say that Zionism became aggressive and violent at the moment when the operation that started out as an occupation of "empty" territory revealed itself as a great disadvantage to the population that lived there legitimately. I suspect that behind this Zionism lurks a Jewish hyperidentification that resulted from anti-Semitism and from the model of the European nation-state. After all, modern anti-Semitism was invented after the national independencies of Italy, Greece, Germany. We have to take this into close consideration, because I see this anti-Semitism as a striking sign of a division of the West against itself. I do not think we have to separate anti-Semitism from something that is very typical of the West. By the way, many people insist on a difference between Christian anti-Judaism and modern anti-Semitism because the latter is founded on race theory, but in fact, anti-Semitism would never have risen if it were not for anti-Judaism that appeared together with Judaism itself.

What is typical of the West is its self-hatred. This self-hatred is clearly connected to the hatred of the Jews through the motif of money. There is this remarkable connection between Plato and the Gospel, as well as the Letters in the New Testament, for example, the letter of James, and this common connection is the contempt for opulence. This is typical of the general spirit of Antiquity and Christianity. The explanation is quite simple: the sacred opulence has gone—the luxury and treasures of the pharaohs, of the great kings of Babylon have gone. Those were the great civilizations where the leaders gathered wealth to finance their armies, but there was no notion of accumulation of capital. Their opulence was not the result of such accumulation. According to Marx, primitive accumulation began when people accumulated capital that they could invest. Sacred accumulation is an end in itself—it is, in the word of Marx, final. The pharaohs may have had enormous treasures, but capitalism, in its rudest form, came with Antiquity. There was money and also equality—the notion of equality is said to have a Judeo-Christian origin, but is also connected with the idea of democracy. This is actually a presupposition of all philosophy, even if Aristotle recognized slavery—though Aristotle somehow made it complicated. He agreed to slavery by birth, but not to slavery by war captivity. Equality has always been a problem in the West. On the one hand, everybody is declared equal—by law or by grace. On the other hand, differences install themselves: power and wealth, etc. These differences are already suspect because of the contempt for opulence, but also because of the fact that the poor are not slaves by nature but free citizens. This is embarrassing to the rich. Even if the rich were not too embarrassed by this poverty, eleventh- and twelfth-century Christianity, with the rise of the mendicant orders, reaffirmed the value of poverty. The poor reproach the rich. But there is also an extraordinary ambivalence that I detect in the Franciscan spirituality. The Franciscan notion of poverty has this one aspect of poverty that opposes opulence and luxury, of accumulation pure and simple; but they also came up with the idea of getting money from the rich to redistribute it among the people. But the people were not just the poor, but also the bourgeoisie, those who did something useful with the money. In a way, Christianity too, for example, Franciscanism, has produced capitalism. It was their idea to subvert this glorious and ceremonial opulence to the benefit of the people. These people will bring about capitalism. This is the period where great merchants will set up great enterprises by investing wisely. They will even form a new sort of nobility that succeeds the older one. But in the nineteenth century, capitalism becomes dirty. Finally, it becomes technology. This is yet another figure of this self-hatred I mentioned. The last figure is technology, I would say. All technical developments are great, magnificent. But at a certain point, technology becomes unbearable.

And then there is another thing: metaphysics, or, with another word, the West. Metaphysics is a permanent process, an evolution, and at the same time a permanent self-criticism. Nominalism criticizes Aristo-Thomism; Cartesianism undoes the whole scholastic and nominalist scene to come up with something completely different; Kantianism eliminates the whole traditionalist metaphysical project; and Nietzsche eliminates the Kantian project. Nietzsche reproaches Kant for being a metaphysician, etc. And then Heidegger deconstructs all ontology, incredible though it may seem. Yet, despite all this self-criticism, the West is the only civilization in the whole world, I contend, that has installed a technological reason that is being recognized by the whole world. You cannot get away from it. To live without electricity would be very difficult today. And this particular feature generates a sort of discontent, a self-hatred even.

And how does all this relate to the phenomenon and the experience of terror?

Terror is a very typically modern phenomenon. I cannot think of anything like it in the times that preceded modernity. Sometimes, terror refers to national terrorism, like the Jacobins during the French Revolution. In each case of terrorism, violence is inflicted by people who do not represent themselves, but a higher ideal. This is important, because it means that terrorism is not a matter of some rogues. Of course, people were terrified by rogues, but nevertheless, rogues were motivated by something different than what motivates terrorists. They would only kill you for the money, not kill you just to kill you. Terror always happens in the name of a higher abstract principle, like the necessity of the Nation or the necessity of the Revolution. Terror is always organized by the nation or directed against the nation. Terror is intimately linked to the nation.

One cannot deny a nation the right to defend itself. France is internally divided about the current state of emergency, with many debates about it. This is understandable, but at the same time, it does not seem appropriate. The nation is, in a way, the great political invention of the modern world. It became sovereign, independent of the Church, in charge of public goods, but also the subject of revolutionary hatred from the very beginning of modernity, of the modern nation. Even before that, the monarchy was already the object of revolutionary destruction. Modernity gave sovereignty to the people but these people never stopped saying that they do not have it, this sovereignty. Therefore, sovereignty was declared bad and the nation had to be suppressed. This is a very different situation from every other society where there always have been people who fight the power in order to take it. But fighting to gain power is not the same as condemning power as such.

Without offering any alternative.

Yes, that is why and how the notion of anarchy entered the West and has never left. In intellectual circles, this notion of anarchy is still very popular. Take the principle of anarchy and broken hegemonies in Reiner Schürmann's interpretation of Heidegger.[1] This notion can help us understand how capitalism has entered a particular phase when the international monopolies were criticized. On the one hand, capitalism glorifies the principle of completely free trade, of total competition, but, on the other hand each competition that takes the form of a quasi-monopoly is declared illegitimate. So, liberalism can only be an internal contradiction. At the other end of the scale, egalitarianism also shows an internal contradiction, because there can never be total equality between those who have the sole technical power, who make the decisions, and the others. There is the matter of expertise, there is the problem of people telling other people what to do. We cannot have an industry that is managed on the principle of absolute and full equality. That would end up in disaster. The expert has also become a figure as necessary as detestable.

This constellation wherein the question of terror finds itself is marked by very archaic connotations, such as human sacrifice. I can refer to the executions that started with the guillotine during the French Revolution. It is a recourse not only to archaic methods, but also to archaic emotions. Terror finds itself before a superior power. Human sacrifice was also terrorized. If we read all those mythical stories, like the Minotaur who wanted his virgins delivered on a regular basis, they are all versions of terror where demonic powers demand these sacrifices. We can claim to be the civilization that has completely left human sacrifice behind. I can see four major episodes in the history of the West distancing itself from human sacrifice. There is the story of Abraham—very clearly about the interdiction of human sacrifice. Then there is also Iphigenia, again an interdiction of sacrifice. Zeus tells Agamemnon to sacrifice his daughter Iphigenia in order to improve the weather conditions to set out to Troy. Despite some versions where Agamemnon kills her himself, there is also the version where Artemis saves Iphigenia. Then Clytemnestra will kill Agamemnon and so on. The killing never ends. In the case of the Greeks, things turn really bad, whereas in the case of the Hebrews, things turn out very well. Then, later, there are Socrates and Jesus Christ. Both cases have to do with a voluntary passing through death. The former figure of sacrifice installs a connection, a relation with the sacred—he appeases the sacred powers. The latter figure of sacrifice perhaps also installs a relation, but from the other side, so to speak. Socrates opens the gates of the world of ideas, Christ opens the gates of heaven. An element that is quite crucial here is the innocence of the victim, of the lamb that has been sacrificed. The access through these gates depends precisely on this innocence, on the spilling of innocent blood, whereas the innocent blood that is spilled by the terrorists does not open anything, does not achieve or serve anything. There is no one outside the terrorists themselves who recognizes the sacrifice. The sacrifice of terror is like a sacrifice that has no social context. If there is no society, how can there be a sacrifice?

Is there a difference between the one who decapitates someone and has this recorded on video and the one who blows himself up, taking the lives of others with him?

Yes, there certainly is a difference. In the case of a suicide, I kill myself and, doing this, I accomplish something good for my family, for my community, and for myself, for I will enter paradise. We can always ask afterward what the amount of fascination, madness, or drugs was that led to this. But then I often think that the Japanese kamikazes during the Second World War were not drugged, but just shared this specific Japanese spirit. The Japanese empire is a very great living substance with an emperor who is treated as a deity at its head. It is this sacred character that Hirohito relinquished after the war. The kamikazes were totally inspired by this system. Now, in the case of these kamikazes or the suicide attacks, you would expect this to happen in a flash, without time to reflect, in one instantaneous and violent moment. The stories that relate the sacrifice of Socrates and Christ take their time. They both take their time to advance toward their death.

Perhaps we should understand terror as divine violence without any god, when there are no more gods. I use the term "divine violence" in the way Benjamin does.[2] Divine violence is, one way or another, present in any religion, I would say. In all religions, gods can become angry and take revenge, possibly because of the infidelity of their faithful. Christianity is supposed to put an end to God's anger. And yet, there is this trace of divine anger in Christianity, certainly in its Augustinian and Protestant versions, where one could interpret the withholding of grace as a form of anger. This is terror, and it refers to a question that I have posed myself and that I find I am unable to solve. Terror manifests a rampage of violence. On the one hand, there is this abstract violence, as Hegel says, when people cut heads like they cut cabbages. This is the abstract character of violence. But this character is inseparable from another character, namely, that of modern technology. The guillotine is a modern invention, to make decapitation quicker and less painful than with an axe.

It is very difficult to fight terrorism because only violent warfare seems to work. One cannot talk things over with terrorists. Terrorists are not there to talk, but to accomplish terror. There are these remarkable stories about Russian anarchists and communists, where a terrorist is appointed to attack but has second thoughts.[3] He is judged, condemned, and executed by his comrades. He had to be killed because he betrayed the revolution. One could say that the whole history of militant revolution is pervaded with this matter of terror as a categorical imperative. I mean, when one engages in terror, one has to accomplish the terrorist act. If one does not, one betrays the higher principle, which is the revolution itself or the government itself—a government that is not about governing but simply about dominating and petrifying by means of terror. This is what Hitler and Stalin did.

But is it at all possible to understand terrorism and its motives from one principle only? The cause of the terrorist, you seem to imply, can only be understood, or, better, can only be affirmed from "within." Alain Badiou has elaborated a strictly Marxist analysis of terror that is all about economic motives. Is there then no trace of a religious or political motive?

Well, even Badiou has left this viewpoint. Since the creation of ISIS, Badiou talks about an insupportable barbarity. Last time I saw Badiou, in January, we talked it over. At the time of the military intervention in Libya, we had a very serious controversy. I had just published an article wherein I defended the intervention.[4] Well, perhaps I was wrong, but nevertheless, this is typical of a totally new vein of political thought. Even Badiou feels that a single-track Marxist explanation is, if not wrong, at least somewhat short in arriving at an adequate insight into the conditions resulting in ISIS. Social explanation is not enough when we are dealing with terrorism. Social explanation can always lead to all kinds of revolt within society against society, but never to the extermination of this society. The question of understanding terror is just as limited for us as the question of understanding the death penalty. There are a lot of arguments in favor of the death penalty. One of the most subtle things Derrida has taught us is that it is very difficult to contest these arguments in favor of the death penalty. According to the model of a sovereign nation as a body politic, where one amputates one member in order to safeguard the integrity and health of the whole body, the death penalty can appear justified by the necessity of sacrificing what is bad in order to restitute integrity and health. Here we see the problem of the legitimacy of a nation that is recognized by all members, also those who are to be executed. Take Norman Mailer's *The Executioner's Song*. This is about a man who is condemned to death in the United States, who acknowledges his guilt and asks to be executed. But his lawyer and family keep postponing the execution with all kinds of procedures. The execution took place, but very late. Mailer interviewed many people from the man's environment to write this book. He was fascinated by the notion of someone demanding his own execution on the ground of his own recognition of guilt—guilt in the face of the nation and society, so, in a way, in the face of the body that he was part of. If we want to understand terrorism in a nonpsychiatric register, we would have to enter into a state of mind where we see the nation as an organic ensemble that contains the terrorist as well as us and where we have hurt that ensemble. This way, we can understand why the terrorist acts. But why should he kill anyone? Perhaps because, in his logic, anyone still belongs to this society. And then suppose the terrorist uses an atomic bomb. He could eradicate France, Germany, Belgium, etc. Everything would go up into the air, but then again, to the terrorist, we are nothing. Perhaps he wants to start all over again elsewhere.

Then that is utopia. I would say they want to destroy a political system that we rely on here, like democracy, for political rather than religious reasons. When someone sacrifices himself, the sacrifice may have, perhaps, religious motives, but the terrorist attack always has a political motive.

Yes, but there we stumble upon a confusion between politics and religion. There is this submission of politics to religion and the other way around. This leads to a very difficult and complicated matter: the question of politics and religion in Islam. Also already in Christianity (between Catholicism and Protestantism) and within Protestantism (between Luther and Calvin) the relation between politics and religion is very complicated. But in the end, we may say, everything evolved in the direction of a mutual independence (that is, of Nation and Church). Well, at least we think we see this mutual autonomy because politics has lost its authority, that is, it has lost some of its sacred character. The modern notion of sovereignty that was developed by Jean Bodin is in itself, of course, completely nonreligious. Nevertheless, it transfers unto the sovereign something of the sacred. When you look at the French monarchy with its divine law and the English monarchy where the king or queen is actually the head of the Church, which is in fact called the Anglican Church, you can see that these are ways of preserving the sacred character of power. At first sight, the famous principle *Cuius regio, eius religio* looks like a pragmatic principle. When the prince adheres to this specific religion, all his people by force of law share this religion. Whereas this indeed resembles a principle of order, it also establishes a relation between the nation and religion, a relation that can never be totally neutral. Anyway, we still have great trouble recognizing power.

In Islam, something particular happened. There was a religious foundation that did not adhere to an already-existing power. There was Muhammad, belonging to his tribe, being chased away to Medina and returning to Mecca, and this has a military as well as a religious aspect. There is a certain dissemination of Islam that does not look like a political conquest, but that, on the other hand, is installed as a political power. Instead of what one usually hears, namely, in Islam politics is submitted to religion, it is rather politics that submits religion to itself. The political order, the domination by a system that is by necessity at least partly military, identifies itself with religion. The Quran itself yields no political prescription whatsoever. One cannot derive politics from the Quran alone. The Quran consists of a list of commandments and rules for being a good Muslim. But these commandments and rules only relate to God. There is no other authority between God and the faithful than God's word. These rules have no other character or finality or motive than to behave in accordance with the rules. There is no message of love, as in Christianity. Of course, Christianity has its own commandments and rules, but these are always under the sign of the law of love. In my interpretation of Islam, there is no law of love. The God of the Muslims does not love people. He takes care of them whenever and as long as they obey the rules. The prophets of Israel are real, not just symbols. They are there to reprimand the king or the city of Jerusalem and therefore install a distance between politics and religion. They persistently remind the body politic of God's discontent with the way things are shaping. They even criticize religion, when they proclaim that God does not want sacrifices and the blood of bulls. He wants a pure heart. And this pure heart has nothing to do with the king or even with the Temple. But in Islam, it is different. In my view, Islam has succeeded in installing an immobile society. At the bottom of this immobility is the absence of a separation between politics and religion.

Do you mean to imply that this separation is a condition for mobility in the sense of the process of ethical universalization or economic globalization? And that therefore the absence of such separation forms, in a way, a threat to Western ethical and economic values?

Yes, you can see that if you look at a social form that is typical of the modern West: the middle class, the inheritance of what during the French Revolution became known as "le tiers état." This system is starting to crack, in Europe as well as in America, precisely because the middle class is frightened by the terrorist attacks. They affect the economic potential and the middle classes are dissolving. But once one leaves the middle class, one ends up either among the superrich or among the superpoor. These superpoor always find themselves in particular territories. In Africa, India, certain parts of China, and around Russia, you will meet forms of life that cannot be universalized. We seem prepared to appreciate the aesthetic value of what is produced in those particular areas, of everything that differs from our technical objects, of what I could call "local folklore." We want technical objects to be functional rather than beautiful. In order to be beautiful, a car, for instance, has to be old and a teapot has to be Chinese.

But this question about the universal keeps coming back. A lot of philosophers, but also anthropologists, are working on this matter. At the same time, we find ourselves in a multiverse, a pluriverse. Perhaps even from the point of view of physics, the notion of a universe is hardly a tenable representation anymore. Here, we approach a very profound and decisive aspect of the mutation. It is really a mutation of the universe itself. Our representation of the universe, our relation to the world, no longer has the sense of a great cosmic unity. What we are living in can no longer be called cosmos in the sense of a well-organized whole. That still does not mean that we have to call it chaos. Nevertheless, we find ourselves in between. Even our unique position of thinking beings is problematic. Are there other thinking beings? I am sure there are not, because we have produced this multiplicity of thoughts ourselves. I can imagine another population, but not one with which we cannot communicate. Nevertheless, we would share the same symbolic order. Even if they spoke another language, they would still speak a language. I can see a truth of universality there, namely, it is impossible to have several universalities that are incapable of communicating among themselves. But then this would presuppose a sort of superuniversality. I do not see how we can leave the universal behind. Suppose we are visited one day by little green creatures from outer space, like in *Close Encounters of the Third Kind*, and then whatever goes on still takes place within a certain communicability. Heidegger understood the world in terms of *Bedeutsamkeit* or sense. To meet beings with whom you cannot share *Bedeutsamkeit*...

... is precisely terror! This attempt to disorganize, to dissolve this Bedeutsamkeit? *All these analyses that focus on the religious or economic or moral aspects, they all ignore or neglect this basic attempt to undermine Western democracy and to disrupt its self-understanding?*

Yes, yes. But there, it becomes a matter of revising *Bedeutsamkeit*. It could well be that terrorism is directed against *Bedeutsamkeit*. There is this experience of having lost all meaning.

Is there not also the religious or philosophical experience of a meaning that lies below any political signification? Or does even politeness have a political meaning—an ensemble of formalities that make a society function. When we do not answer a greeting, that is also violent.

But I want to come back to the question of violence. With terror, a very particular dimension of violence has appeared, relating to the enormous violence that also came from terror. I am speaking of extermination and concentration camps, of genocides. We are in a state of perpetual war with all the features of guerilla warfare. This is also a new phenomenon that could be something like what Carl Schmitt called the war of partisans, which means that it is not a war between nations. Why do we find ourselves in a state of violence that we understand to be new in the history of humanity? This novelty came about slowly. At the beginning of the nineteenth century, war was fought between armies. By the end of that century, war had become slaughter, which is why the Red Cross was founded. This foundation was a reaction from civil society, against the excesses of warfare. A modern form of violence exists, as Freud said in his *Civilization and Its Discontents*, even before the Second World War broke out. He foresaw that humanity would become capable of destroying itself. And, he said, there is no principle as strong as such violence except Christian charity.

But since this does not exist, at least according to Freud and others, there is no remedy against terror?

What does it mean that modern violence can only be opposed by an impossibility? And what is more, an impossibility that is understood in the register of affectivity, even of the highest affectivity: the sublime, the absolute, love . . . In fact, we do not really know what that is. Freud also says that against violence, there is only the opposite of violence. And what is that? Love. Or is love just another form of violence, perhaps Benjamin's divine violence? Perhaps love is the violence that demands *Bedeutsamkeit*, as the possibility to signify. This possibility always has to be conquered. Every child has to enter language. This comes first, before the issue of speaking well. Language cannot mean the appeal to another by crying. When a baby is hungry or sleepy or in pain . . . it cries.

And a cry signifies anything!

Indeed, language demands that the cry be suppressed: "Stop crying!" This opens the whole process of what Freud calls repression, the repression of the drives—in short, the process of civilization. Freud describes this in a very repressive representation, with disavowal, negation, etc., which is in itself already a violent model. But this civilizing violence is still a form of violence that humanity inflicts upon itself.

Is this then what René Girard claims, that a derivative form of violence is necessary to curb a more original violence that is invisible as such to science, but that takes the form of a religious-cultural motif that pervades and dominates all human culture?

Yes, and this original violence has to do with murder, with the suppression of the existence of the other. And this is at the same time the suppression of the possibility of signification. It is also as Levinas says: the minimal relation with the other is either kill or talk. To talk is to renounce murder, even if I tell you that I will kill you. But this is what terrorists do: they tell us that they will kill us and enjoy our fright. This is why we consider today's violence to be outrageous, in the sense that we do not know what to put up against it, how to oppose it. We need to understand this violence as Girard taught us, as an absolutely original violence, that is, the violence of exclusion, also the exclusion of sense. So, this violence is another violence than the one that urges us to speak. The violence of exclusion contradicts the violence of communication. The Christian commandment to love one another could perhaps be reduced to the commandment to talk. This has nothing to do with positive affectivity: we are not expected to hug the other, only to talk to the other.

This resembles what Gianni Vattimo preaches. If someone wants to kill me, he says, I will talk to him. I will not use violence, because that does not comply with weak thought. I will talk to him until the moment where he no longer wants to kill me.

Does he indeed? In any case, current terrorist violence is that strong because we ended up in a situation where we cannot talk anymore. Communication broke down; there is a crack in *Bedeutsamkeit* in either the sense of a universal communication or that of a communication about something that could be universal even across its particularities. Talking implies taking account of the differences in language. But even that does not impede conversation. Suppose I am in China and am lost. I want to ask for directions, but the one I am addressing does not understand me. Then he can always direct me toward someone who can understand me or a service where I can be helped. Differences in language are not obstacles to *Bedeutsamkeit*—one can always make gestures, mime, laugh, shout, etc.

It is not that we have acquired more means of violence. This is what is often said, that we have so many terrible weapons. I think that we have invested in the possibilities of destruction because signification started to fail us and we entered something like what might be the self-destruction of humanity.

So, terror can be understood as the risk of the world? Terror would then be not only the dissolution of communication but also the rejection of sense.

Yes, rejection is correct. There is not so much a loss of sense, as many people contend, but rather a refusal of sense. But refused by what? Must we say that technology refuses sense? Perhaps this is *the* crucial question. Technology pursues its own ends, and every end becomes a means to a new end and it all ends up nowhere. It makes no sense. Perhaps we have to think that sense is refused. But at the same time, technology seems to offer us the conditions of a new sense. This may be the challenge of the information revolution. This is not what Levinas meant by the alternative between talking and killing. This technology restarts the whole process of communication. It does not just reduce communication to information. The term "information technology" is not really adequate. It is the same with words like "numerical" and "digital." They refer to conditions of production. Of course, computers do work digitally, but what they produce—images, music, texts, etc.—is itself not digital. Here, again, we see this self-hate at play. We have arrived at a severe hollowness and emptiness of sense, and the difficulty is precisely that we cannot make sense ourselves, we cannot ourselves decide to have sense. Sense arrives.

Nevertheless, on a smaller scale, all we can say is that, all in all, the majority of people stay within sense. There are family, friends, colleagues, a neighborhood, work, etc. No one wants this to be suppressed.

One can even have a strong sentiment of solitude, but then again, one can always talk about that. It is as Heidegger said: even solitude is part of *Mitsein*!

INTERVIEW CONDUCTED AND TRANSLATED BY ERIK MEGANCK
AND EVELIEN VAN BEECK

Notes

1. In *Broken Hegemonies*, Reiner Schürmann describes how every great metaphysical system always carries the seeds of its own de(con)struction within itself. Reiner Schürmann, *Broken Hegemonies*, trans. Reginald Lilly (Bloomington: Indiana University Press, 2003).
2. Benjamin distinguished divine violence from mythical violence in "Critique of Violence" from 1921. Walter Benjamin, "Critique of Violence," in *Selected Writings*, vol. 1, *1913–1926*, ed. Marcus Bullock and Michael W. Jennings (Cambridge, MA: Belknap Press of Harvard University Press, 1996), 236–252.
3. Famous examples are Bertolt Brecht's *The Decision* or *The Measures Taken* (*Die Massnahme*) and Albert Camus's *The Just Assassins* (*Les justes*).
4. Jean-Luc Nancy, "What the Arab Peoples Signify to Us," *Critical Legal Thinking*, March 11, 2011, http://criticallegalthinking.com/2011/03/31/what-the-arab-peoples-signify-to-us/. The original French article appeared in *Libération* on March 28, 2011. Alain Badiou wrote a reply on April 4. An English translation of Badiou's letter can be read on the website of Verso: www.versobooks.com/blogs/463-an-open-letter-from-alain-badiou-to-jean-luc-nancy.

12

Community in Crisis

A Letter Exchange Between Zygmunt Bauman and Roberto Esposito

In 2014, Zygmunt Bauman and Roberto Esposito—who have written some of the most original contemporary reflections on the topic of "community"—were invited by the editors of the Polish journal *Znak* to engage in a letter correspondence on this topic. Esposito, with his theories about the relation between community and immunity, and Bauman, with his theories about liquid modernity, have also pointed out the extent to which the communal or the common is increasingly threatened, even more so since the recent economic crisis. The resulting letter correspondence was published in Polish in issue 718 of *Znak*, in March 2015.

NOVEMBER 1, 2014
Naples

Dear Sir,
Responding to the editor's questions and to the invitation for taking up a conversation with you, I take the freedom to address you directly.

I believe not only that the terminologies of philosophy and of psychology are complementary, but also that their critical encounter might intensify the analytical capacities of both. Of such an intensification we have seen significant examples. On the one hand, we need only to think of the Parisian "Collège de Sociologie," the group around Georges Bataille and Roger Caillois at the end of the 1930s; on the other hand there is the work conducted by the Frankfurter Schule, both in Europe and in America, and especially by Adorno, Horkheimer, and Marcuse. In both cases, the terminologies of philosophy and of sociology—and psychoanalysis can be added here—have been articulated with impressive results, when considering not only their potential analogies, but also their respective semantic differences. In the realm of human sciences, the innovative paradigm leaps have started to appear just as their respective terminologies have been put in mutual tension, the one penetrating into the other and, by doing so, exposing their internal contradictions. In this sense one might say that the increase of every form of knowledge always stems from something that puts pressure on its external margins, thereby changing its original identity.

This first observation already takes us to the heart of the topic of "community," as it was addressed, on the one hand, by attentive philosophers in social matters, and, on the other, by an author like you, for whom the label "sociologist" is too reductive, as you are endowed with a strong philosophical sensibility. It is no coincidence that a book like *Modernity and the Holocaust*, from another perspective and with a different methodology, arrives at conclusions that don't differ much from those arrived at by the French and Italian philosophers who worked on the concepts of biopolitics and thanatopolitics. It is remarkable how you also retrace totalitarian crimes to an immunologic practice that leads to excess, to the point of becoming a lethal force. Even if you don't explicitly adopt philosophical categories like those of biopolitics and immunization, for quite some time you have been implicitly relating to them. Starting with the preface of your book *Community: Seeking Safety in an Insecure World*, you grasp the contradiction that pervades both the concept and the practice of "community." As you write on p. ix of the Italian translation of this text: "The community of the communitarian project cannot but exacerbate the condition it had promised to cure. And it will do so while heightening the atomizing pressure, which has been, and will continue to be, the major source of insecurity." In this manner, you perfectly grasp the antinomy of both the immunological and the autoimmunological paradigm, which operates by curing the malady with a fragment of the malady itself, vaccinating the life it intends to cure with a kind of poison. Obviously, in the vocabulary of sociology, such an antinomy appears as the outcome of two oppositional tendencies—toward protection and toward atomization, toward safety and toward exclusion, toward order and toward freedom. Personally, I have tried to advance the same question, in considering such polarities as the outcome of a unique dialectics that connects the concept—and practice—of community with its opposite, that is, immunity.

In the beginning of your text, you consider the meaning and also the emotions brought about by some words, such as, indeed, the word "community." I have also started with an analysis of this term, elaborating on its Latin etymology. *Communitas* and *immunitas* both stem from the term *munus*—which in Latin means "gift," but also "debt" or "duty" in relation to the other. However, while the first term—*communitas*—relates itself to *munus* in an affirmative sense, acknowledging the mutual "law of giving," *immunitas* relates to it in a negative or depriving sense: immune is he who is relieved from the law of *munus* and locks himself in his own identity, differentiating himself from others.

Through this theoretical explanation, the same contradictory polarities that for you appear separate from each other I consider as the front and the rear side of one and the same concept, and also of one and the same reality—the reality indeed of a community that, while autoimmunizing itself when confronted with its original openness, ends up folding back upon itself, thereby risking implosion. This has always been the case: just as the human body could not survive without an immune system that defends it against pathogenic agents, so communities need to defend themselves through their immune systems. For example, as Luhmann claims, justice constitutes the immune system of social organizations. However, when the immune system gains excessive weight, its defensive function lapses into an offensive one, first toward the other and then also toward the self, as is the case in autoimmune diseases. The history of Germany under Hitler has proved to be the most terrifying and extreme example of this tendency, which is typical for the modern condition. This has not happened only in modern times, but it is true that this age has constituted the most fitting background for a series of other factors that have contributed to the development of this antinomy.

There is another striking analogy between our books about community. You claim in *Community: Seeking Safety in an Insecure World* that today we lack community, that we have the need for community without attaining it, which is the contradiction that the title reveals, that is, the incurable contrast between liberty and safety. However, that beautiful title can also be interpreted in philosophical and thus ontological terms: as the constitutive lacking of community, the fact that community is lacking because of its lack of identity or properties. Such a lack derives not from historical contingencies, but from the empty structure of community. Community, as the opposite of self-appropriation, namely, openness to alterity or expropriation, is necessarily lacking, and holds a void of being within itself. Immunization, on the other hand, is the mechanism that tends to fill up that void with new identities, up to the point of canceling it, and turning it into potential violence. For all these reasons, I consider your work fundamental to exploring the dynamics in question.

Kind regards,
Roberto Esposito

NOVEMBER 12, 2014
Leeds

Dear Sir,
The European contribution to modern sociology—in contrast with the American contribution, which is rooted in economics and law—derives from philosophy. I graduated from the Faculty of Philosophy and Sociology at the University of Warsaw. Both disciplines were studied in the same building, which is quite rare, if not simply impossible to encounter overseas. I never asked myself whether the match between sociology and philosophy was made in heaven, or whether it was a morganatic marriage. I would also have difficulties if I wished to establish which aspects of the human world would belong to which spouse. I thought of it as natural (much like the way conjoined twins live together) that both philosophy and sociology would eat at the same table, namely, that of human experience, and that they would operate within the same semantic field thanks to which (according to Hegel) "one captures his own rhythm." And up to this day I haven't changed my mind, even if the administrative division of academia has made incredible progress.

In the work titled *Communitas: The Origin and Destiny of Community*, in writing on *immunizing power*, you have suggested that the individualization to which it leads, deriving from liberation from a "debt" with respect to others, "comes at a very high prize." This is undoubtedly true. But what does this price consist in? According to sociology, and not according to economic theories or banking practice, it consists in the liberation from a debt together with the loss of a credit. Émile Durkheim, the first professor in sociology at the Sorbonne, asked rhetorically, while at the same time proposing an obvious answer for his question, "How could man multiply his own energetic resources, if not by surpassing himself? Would he be capable of surpassing himself with his own strength? The only fire capable to warm his morale is the company of others." And his most talented and important pupil, Marcel Mauss, in developing the master's thinking further, established the obligation to give, to receive, and above all to correspond, as the critical ingredient of the so-called total phenomena, which are the ones that produce not only riches and alliances, but also social solidarity, and which are therefore responsible for the creation and duration of society. Without these, the human way of "being-in-the-world," as Heidegger called it, would be inconceivable. However, both Mauss and Heidegger were preceded by Aristotle (preceded by more than two thousand years), who maintained that only animals or angels would do without the polis. And since man is not an angel, and doesn't want to be an animal...

Being a member of the polis means that one believes one has the right to receive help from compatriots and has the obligation to help them. The law offers a sense of security: I am not alone—if necessary there are people who I can count on. Duty is the price I am willing to pay for safety. The motto of the polis is reciprocity—and reversibility—of right and duty. From the threads of right and duty, the tissue of community is woven. One cannot do without the other: you have them both, or you have none. As it is put in the English aphorism: you can't have your cake and eat it. This obvious truth is hard to digest. The human way of living in the world is torn up on the inside (and not on the outside) by this contradiction that cannot be conquered. Even though the praxis of being human has always attempted to resolve this, it is still trying and probably will continue to try to untangle this Gordian knot.

In my opinion, on the basis of this contradiction one discovers the dialectics of safety and freedom. These are two values that a decent and dignified life cannot do without. The problem lies in the fact that a growing security puts a limit on freedom, while an increase in freedom reduces safety. All important social organizations have tried to find and apply a recipe for the ideal dosage of both ingredients, but in the few cases where it seems that they have succeeded, the success turns out to be only temporary. It is not possible to illustrate the history of safety and freedom with a line of progress. Rather, their history swings between excess and deficiency of one of the two values.

In this matter, *nihil novi*. However, something that constitutes a certain *novum*, without precedent in history and with consequences that are until this day difficult to classify, is the question of who is obliged to search for the equilibrium between safety and freedom (or who, at minimum, is responsible for soothing the unappreciated consequences, when an equilibrium is impossible to attain). This responsibility, which first explicitly or implicitly rested upon the community, is now laid upon the individual. The place of community is now occupied by identity (or, rather, by the process of identification). No longer is community a factor that determines the individual; it is the individual that needs to construct its own (private) "community," referred to as a "network." (However, more precisely it would be a "web.") The role of the spider is appointed to each and every one of us. The faithful service in the name of the community has been replaced with the continuous construction and reconstruction of identity, while the desire to free oneself from the invasive demands of the community is substituted with Sisyphus's efforts to spin one's own network. Both the traditional order and the one that is destined to replace it are contaminated by the same sort of incurable dialectics of safety and freedom—as thesis and antithesis. To date, I don't see their synthesis because I don't believe in substitution by industrial brands, used in our consumption societies to fill the gap that is left by community in the process of self-determination and affirmation.

I have the impression that, in heaven and on earth, signs are building up that the historical pendulum mentioned earlier has swung in the other direction: the kinetic energy that thrusted people toward the pole of freedom has been transformed in an increasing energy of rotational movement directed toward the pole of safety. Community, come back, because everything that was wrong has already been forgotten, but are you also forgiven for that which continues to be remembered?

I leave you with this question and send you my best regards,

Zygmunt Bauman

NOVEMBER 24, 2014

Naples

Dear Friend,

If I may call you so, in what you say about the relationship between sociology and philosophy I sense something that I share with you, something, moreover, that is part of my education. This connection, today suspended or threatened by an educational organization of American origin, is at the heart of European civilization. Unfortunately, at present this awareness is lost and European sociology imitates American social science.

Concerning *Communitas*, I agree with you on the fact that immunization, today ever extending to the point of creating a sort of autoimmune disease, exchanges the liberation from a debt for a loss of credit (or maybe rather for a loss of "gift," as it was defined by Mauss). At present, as a true form of "economical theology"—to use the words used by Benjamin in his text from 1921 "Capitalism and Religion"—the intention to liberate ourselves from the obligation of the *munus* has led us to a situation in which we are all just debtors. Considering what we call with a contradictory term "sovereign debts"—these are the public debts of states that have lost their sovereignty in favor of anonymous powers in the financial world—every European citizen is born charged with a debt of approximately fifty thousand euros even before entering the world. As it is our wish to free ourselves from the "common debt"—and thus, in the end, from community itself—we have become slaves of public and private debt, like those who in ancient Rome gave their own bodies into the possession of their creditors, in exchange for a debt that they could not pay off. Besides, the immigrants that succeed in reaching the coasts of Europe alive spend their lives paying for the debt that was agreed on with the criminals who transported them there. In the same way, it takes years for American graduates to pay back to the State the money that it lent them to pay for their university fees.

Once the communitarian dimension is annihilated or reduced to a minimum, thereby favoring mass individualism, which ends in depriving the same individuals of their singular uniqueness, it becomes clear that freedom and safety place themselves at the opposite poles of a line that continuously threatens to snap. To some extent, it has been like this for a long time. Michel Foucault explains this very well in his lectures on *The Birth of Biopolitics*, when he observes that, in neoliberalism, freedom generates itself while canceling itself out—this means that it is created in one place while it is suspended in another. This is a topic that you have addressed with great efficiency in most of your written work. Even while containing very diverse elements, modernity is analyzable through these contradictory dialectics.

But things have changed and deteriorated for about fifteen years—more precisely starting with the attack on the Twin Towers in 2001. It is paradoxical that the fall of the Berlin Wall, which is rightfully celebrated in the whole world, has generated so many walls. In this way, globalization has been the cause for so many identitarian withdrawals. This is what I mean when I speak of the dialectics between community and immunity: paradoxically it is the extreme interconnection, typical in our times, of man, ideas, and technologies, which generates fear and enclosure within one's own boundaries.

Something of that sort can be said also when concerning the network or, as you term it, the "web." To some extent, it has created a network of relations never before experienced in any preceding society. Never before has man communicated with others so much as today. Every day, we are immersed in thousands of messages that we cannot even answer anymore. Nonetheless, before today we have never felt such loneliness and emptiness. This is the case because these communications, which we can no longer live without, have little to do with a community project—in whichever sense one wishes to conceive of this notion. Not only because the contacts that are determined are virtual and unreal—they don't involve people's bodies—but because the excess of communication beyond a certain limit is equivalent to silence and generates entropy. The idea that everyone in their own home can create their own community through the Internet, shut off from real contact with others, is quite risky. Today, libraries and bookshops, as well as post offices, banks, travel agencies, and all the public offices, tend to empty out because of the loss of jobs. Everything that in these institutions occurred in direct interaction between people can now be done through the network. I don't underestimate the saving of time, of effort, and of work implicit in these changes, but I don't turn my eyes away from the risks of the progressive loss of social bonds that they bring about. The decline in participation in the voting process across all of Europe is another symptom of this model, in which the sense of acting as a group is lost.

Of course, there are phenomena that go against this trend—the great manifestations on squares that were held in northern Africa and also in some European and American cities besieged by the economic crisis. However, the outcome of these movements is not yet clear. We are in a historical period that is marked by growing contradictions, of which the one between freedom and safety might be the most evident. It also seems to me that today the pendulum oscillates in the direction of safety. It is obvious that a social organism (like a human organism) without an immune system cannot survive the conflicts that threaten it from the outside and from the inside. However, there is a threshold that should not be crossed. Otherwise immunization ends by turning against the body that it protects, thereby making it implode. How do these anticommunal phenomena affect that which you have masterfully called "liquid society"? And what is the prognosis for the future society that derives from your diagnosis?
With best wishes,
R. E.

DECEMBER 8, 2014
Leeds

Dear Sir,
I totally agree with your diagnosis on the social costs of the phenomenon appropriately called "immunization." However, I want to concentrate on just one of the lines of thought you have pointed out.

What does it mean, immunization? Liberation or expulsion? Authorization or exile from legally regulated territory? A breaking of chains or a loss of certainty? An act of self-determination or an act of rendering oneself incapable? I think it is both. The official, politically correct term is "deregulation." From the viewpoint of countless human actors, deregulation is a form of slavery hidden behind the mask of emancipation. Its form, its intensity, and its effects are not the same for all social categories.

Its worst and most morally revolting damage to human society is probably the marginalization of more and more people, which is a phenomenon that will increase. Marginalization means deprivation of legal tutelage (as Carl Schmitt said, who identified the sovereignty of the sovereign with the power of exclusion from legal norms). Today Giorgio Agamben observes the same *homini sacri*—people excluded from both human and divine laws, the people whom one can kill without punishment and who are exempt from religious rites. It is a threat that now weighs on the whole of society. The exception is constituted by a small fraction of people who are protected by immunization, while the gloomy consequences threaten all the others: the middle class is forced to face precarity (a life without certainties, under the weight of continuous instability, fearing social degradation), while the ones who cannot afford to resurge after having been hit no longer make up part of the civil body (their voices are not heard, one should not take them into consideration). For that small fraction of privileged people, society, with its codes of behavior and its task of solidarity, is pure torture, and immunization becomes the way to obtain independence from moral norms and remorse (if these have survived the perishing of community). For all the others, a society that resists the negative consequences of immunization appears—at least in dreams—as a lifeboat for the drowning, who can count only on their own weak muscles . . .

Pope Francis has criticized this attitude and reminded us of its negative consequences in his first apostolic exhortation, after having been elected. He restores the moral dimension of our surrender to the malicious market, which has escaped from social control, blinded by the desire for profit and thus blind to human misery: "When the inner life is locked up in its own interests, there is no more room for others and the poor cannot enter anymore, one can no longer hear the voice of God, one can no longer relish the sweet joy of His love, and the heart no longer pounds from enthusiasm for doing good."

As the direct consequence of this situation, we see "the world of empty apartments and homeless people" poignantly described by Joseph Stiglitz, and food being wasted next to starving children and elderly people, or as pope Francis has observed: "Just as the commandment 'Thou shalt not kill' sets a clear limit in order to safeguard the value of human life, today we also have to say 'thou shalt not' to an economy of exclusion and inequality." This economy kills. It should not be possible that an elderly man, forced to live on the street, freezing to death, doesn't make it into the news, while the devaluation of the stock market by two points does. This is exclusion. We can no longer tolerate the fact that food is thrown away, when there are people who starve. This is inequality. Today, everything enters the game of competition and the law of the strongest, in which the powerful eat the weak. As a consequence of this situation, great masses of people see themselves excluded and marginalized: without work, without perspective, with no way out. Human beings are considered to be a commodity that can be used and thrown away afterward. We have initiated the culture of "discard," which is even encouraged. We are no longer simply dealing with the phenomenon of exploitation and of oppression; we are dealing with something new: with exclusion. Society is struck in its very core, since one doesn't have to be at the bottom, in the margins, or without power to be on the outside of society. The excluded ones are not "exploited" but garbage, "leftovers."

The pope's diagnosis corresponds with the data that I have assembled in the book *Does the Richness of the Few Benefit Us All?* These data show the increase of inequality and of social exclusion. The first example that comes to mind: if in 1974 the salary of a company manager was 35 times higher than a laborer's wages, and in 1980 this comparison resulted in the ratio 135:1, in 2000 it increased to 531:1. The frequently used justification, repeated by those who enrich themselves beyond measure and by political leaders according to which "a rising wave takes all the boats up" (that is, growth improves the situation of all citizens), does not withstand criticism. Since the beginning of the recent financial crisis, 93 percent of the growth of the American GDP was absorbed by 1 percent of the richest, while almost the entire middle class has undergone a downturn of living standards and the poor working class has been affected by great economic problems, not to mention the misfits, the lower class of excluded people, the ones who depend on social services and on charity. According to Michael Burawoy, the dominant trend in developed countries is the "ex-commodification" of the excluded. Once they are exploited, they are denied decent employment, or rather they are denied the "modern privilege" to be exploited. Immunization against margins brings people into difficulty, treated like products in the job market. It means for thousands of rejected human beings an expropriation of the right to work and to income, the right to contribute to social welfare, and of a dignified life, and thus, unfortunately, it constitutes a deprivation of human rights.

To conclude, I believe that the four commandments included in the apostolic exhortation of Pope Francis—"No to an economy of exclusion," "No to forms of governance serving money," "No to the new idolatry of money," "No to inequality that generates violence"—should guide all those who are aware of the fact that "in a world where the market is conceived as the solution to all problems, the ideological challenging of the market's dictatorship is," as Burawoy fittingly maintains, "the crucial condition for any efficient counteraction."

José Saramago has written in his diary: "God is the silence of the universe, and man is a cry that fills the silence with meaning." Pope Francis discovers the meaning of this cry, in turning it into a human vocation: "This implies that we are docile and attentive to listen to the cry of the poor man and to help him. . . . We are called to take care of the most fragile on the Earth. But in the current model of success and privatization, there seems to be no sense in investing so that those who remain behind, the weak or the less talented, could move ahead in life."

The problems of our society arise from the fact that it has stopped to question itself. It paralyses the mind with "naturalization": being "natural" means, in the end, to have no motive or objective—it simply means "being." To describe casually created human products as "natural" helps to nurture feelings of tranquility and satisfaction regarding society, which has dropped the ambition to recognize *comme il faut* and *comme il ne faut pas*, to fight the evil that can be defeated, to mend its own mistakes, and therefore to accept the responsibility for its own choices. This "naturalization" is a result of an insupportable and even toxic mix of satisfaction and cheap hypocrisy.

Like many others, this existential problem lies behind the daily hunt for new impulses, the rushing of life, and the activities of myopic consumers (a probably incurable myopia). Problems that (at their own risk) can be removed from sight, but not from the human condition. They ask for an increasingly accurate attention. As long as we deny the human condition this attention, man's autonomy—that cry which gives sense to the silence of the universe—remains far out of our reach.

My prospects are not optimistic, but this is how I see the situation. Greetings,
Z. B.

DECEMBER 27, 2014
Naples

Dear Mr. Zygmunt,
I am also convinced that the most serious problems we experience are born of the exhaustion of our capacity to ask fundamental questions about the condition of our times. And I am also convinced that the danger of this absence of questions is a new kind of naturalization of history—in the meaning that Adorno gave to this expression: just at the moment when human history seems to have embraced every form of civilization, at this very moment, an archaic mechanism reoccurs, which is a bearer of violence and regression.

The category of immunization is set at this horizon, as is clear from its contrast with the paradigm of community—understood in its original sense of mutual obligation. However, as occurs to many decisive concepts of our intellectual lexicon, it is true that the concept of immunization bears in itself two apparently opposing elements—as you say, liberation and expulsion. Immunization dismisses man from certain tasks—first of all, the honor of sharing a common world—while releasing his energies for other objectives directed toward individual well-being. However, this immunological relief is paid for with the individual's emotional weakening, and also with an overall deficit of communal experience. Hence the other perverse effect of the immunological procedure, to which you also refer—that is, the expulsion of everything that breaks this individual logic, starting with social bonds.

In this sense, one can say that immunization is an apparatus of a theological-political nature (what I have described in detail in my book *Two: The Machine of Political Theology and the Place of Thought*), even if it seems to represent the secular side of our society. The reference to the actions and words of Pope Francis can be incorporated in this context, like the battle that he is fighting inside the Catholic Church. The immunological apparatus excludes in various ways. The most violent kind is the expulsion of the ones that need help and hospitality. But also, in an apparently inclusive manner, placing in ghettos those who are admitted to our territory without assigning them the same rights we have. The general crisis that we live in today is also a consequence of this excluding inclusion. I thank you for this conversation, and I hope that in the future there will be an occasion to elaborate on it. I believe that every time we openly share our thoughts with others, step by step we approach community.

Kind regards,

R. E.

DECEMBER 30, 2014
Leeds

Dear Mr. Roberto,
One could not better express this thought! Truly being in community is revealed by the fact that people talk with one another, sharing impressions and emotions, joys and griefs, hopes and fears . . . They didn't pass one another in silence, avoiding eye contact, which expressly communicates that nobody has the intention to speak. In this inverted order of exclusion and inclusion, mutual communication is no longer a given, it is more like a task: it doesn't arise out of itself, as in community, when it was natural; it is a task that has to be taken up intentionally. Normally it is an event with a clear goal: it happens not "because" but "in order to."

For this reason, your hypothesis that the attempt to resume dialogue in this torn-up community could help it to recover is by no means unfounded. And it is certain that the effort of reviving the virtues of communal coexistence cannot do without dialogue. And this dialogue should be the first thing to do in the process of reconciliation. A better start would be hard to find, because, as in the communal way of being-in-the-world (and in contrast with the market's competition or with the competition for social privileges), the real dialogue does not consist in distinguishing between winners and losers, between excluded ones and included ones, but in the mutual exchange of thoughts and experiences that can enrich all spirits and dignify all actions.

I thank you and send you the kindest regards,

Z. B.

TRANSLATED BY JOLIEN PAELEMAN

Contributors

TARIQ ALI is a British-Pakistani writer, journalist, and activist. He is part of the editorial board of *New Left Review*. Already in the 1960s, he was a famous antiwar activist, inspiring John Lennon to write "Power to the People" and the Rolling Stones to write "Street Fighting Man." He writes contributions to, among others, the *Guardian* and *London Review of Books*. His books include *Clash of Fundamentalisms: Crusades, Jihads and Modernity* (2002), *The Obama Syndrome: Surrender at Home, War Abroad* (2010), *Street-Fighting Years: An Autobiography of the Sixties* (2005), and *The Extreme Centre: A Warning* (2015).

ZYGMUNT BAUMAN was a Polish sociologist and philosopher. He was professor of sociology at the University of Leeds. He wrote on diverse topics such as modernity, the Holocaust, and community. Of his vast number of books, some of the best-known are *Modernity and the Holocaust* (1991), *Globalization: The Human Consequences* (Columbia, 1998), *Liquid Modernity* (2000), *The Individualized Society* (2000), *Liquid Times: Living in an Age of Uncertainty* (2007), and *Strangers at Our Door* (2016). He passed away in January 2017.

ROSI BRAIDOTTI is distinguished university professor and founding director of the Centre for the Humanities at Utrecht University. Her latest books are *The Posthuman* (2013), *Nomadic Subjects* (Columbia, 2011), *Nomadic Theory: The Portable Rosi Braidotti* (Columbia, 2011), and *Conflicting Humanities* (with Paul Gilroy, 2016). She has honorary degrees from Helsinki (2007) and Linkoping (2013); she is a fellow of the Australian Academy of the Humanities (FAHA, 2009) and a member of the Academia Europaea (MAE, 2014).

WENDY BROWN is Class of 1936 First Chair at the University of California, Berkeley, where she teaches political theory. Prior to coming to Berkeley in 1999, she taught at the University of California, Santa Cruz, and at Williams College. Wendy Brown has held a number of distinguished visiting fellowships and lectureships. Most recently, she has been a member of the Birkbeck Critical Theory Summer School faculty (2012), a senior invited fellow of the Center for Humanities at Cornell University (2013), and a visiting professor at Columbia University (2014). Her recent books include *Undoing the Demos: Neoliberalism's Stealth Revolution* (2015), *Walled States, Waning Sovereignty* (2014), and *Regulating Aversion: Tolerance in the Age of Identity and Empire* (2008).

TIM CHRISTIAENS is a PhD student and teaching assistant at the Institute of Philosophy of the KU Leuven, Belgium. More specifically, he works in the Research Institute for Political Philosophy Leuven (RIPPLE). His research mainly concerns contemporary Italian political philosophy (Agamben, Lazzarato, Negri, etc.) and their historical influences, and his PhD project focuses on Agamben's theory of subjectivation and capitalism. His most recent publications deal with Lazzarato's critique of financial markets (2016) and Agamben's interpretation of Aristotle's Book Thèta (2015). Tim also teaches tutorials in ethics, philosophy of science, and philosophy of mind.

JOOST DE BLOOIS is assistant professor in the Department of Literary and Cultural Analysis at the University of Amsterdam and researcher at the Amsterdam School for Cultural Analysis. He has published extensively on the nexus between culture and politics. Recent publications include *The Irregularization of Migration in Contemporary Europe: Detention, Deportation, Drowning* (with Yolande Jansen and Robin Celikates, 2014) and "The Death of Vitruvian Man: Anomaly, Anomie, Autonmy," in *The Anomie of the Earth: Philosophy, Politics and Autonomy in Europe and the Americas*, ed. Federico Luisetti et al. (2015). He is currently working on a book-length project on anthropogenesis, precarization, and racialization in the Anthropocene.

STIJN DE CAUWER is a postdoctoral researcher in literary studies and cultural studies at the University of Leuven in Belgium, funded by the Research Foundation Flanders (FWO). He is also a member of the MDRN research group and founder of the interdisciplinary IdeaLab "The Biopolitical Condition." In 2014, he was a visiting scholar at Humboldt University in Berlin. He obtained his PhD at the University of Utrecht in 2012 and published his dissertation as *A Diagnosis of Modern Life: Robert Musil's Der Mann ohne Eigenschaften as a Critical-Utopian Project* (2014). Together with Joost de Bloois and Anneleen Masschelein, he coedited the book *50 Key Terms in Contemporary Cultural Theory* (2017). He is currently coediting a special issue of *Angelaki: Journal of the Theoretical Humanities* about the recent work of Georges Didi-Huberman and he has coedited a special issue of *Configurations* on the topic of "Immunity, Society, and the Arts" (2017) together with

Kim Hendrickx. He has published articles in, among others, *Symposium—a Quarterly Journal in Modern Literatures, Orbis Litterarum, Interiors: Design, Architecture, and Culture*, and *Neophilologus*, and he has taught courses in cultural studies and literary studies.

ROBERTO ESPOSITO is an Italian philosopher at the University of Pisa. Special issues of *Angelaki* and *Diacritics* have been devoted to his work. In his books *Bíos: Biopolitics and Philosophy* (2008), *Immunitas: The Protection and Negation of Life* (2011), and *Communitas: The Origin and Destiny of Community* (2004), he analyzes the complex interaction between community and immunity. Other works include *Third Person: Politics of Life and Philosophy of the Impersonal* (2012), *Terms of the Political: Community, Immunity, Biopolitics* (2012), *Persons and Things: From the Body's Point of View* (2015), *Categories of the Impolitical, Living Thought: The Origins and Actuality of Italian Philosophy* (2012), and *Two: The Machine of Political Theology and the Place of Thought* (2015).

SVEN FABRÉ studied Dutch and German linguistics and literature and economic policy in Leuven, Belgium. He finished his PhD at the University of Leuven in 2016; the title of his dissertation is *Das Credo des Kaufmanns: Über Poetiken kreditökonomischen Wissens in der Prosa von Freytag und Keller*. He is an associated member of the PhD Net "The Knowledge of Literature" at Humboldt University of Berlin, Germany. His research topics include historical poetics, the history of the novel, and economics and literature. He has published articles in *Orbis Litterarum, Victoriographies*, and *Zeitschrift für Deutsche Philologie*.

MAURIZIO LAZZARATO is an Italian philosopher and sociologist based in Paris. He started his philosophical activism within the Italian workerist movement of the 1970s. He is the author of books such as *The Making of the Indebted Man* (2012), *Signs and Machines* (2014), and *Governing by Debt* (2015). His latest book is *Guerres et capital*, written together with Eric Alliez (2016).

ANGELA MCROBBIE is professor of communications at Goldsmiths College, University of London. As a cultural theorist, she is particularly interested in popular culture, feminism, and the modern work economy. She has conducted postgraduate research at the CCCS (Centre for Contemporary Cultural Studies) in Birmingham and taught at Loughborough University before moving to Goldsmiths. She is a member of the editorial boards of several journals, including *Journal of Consumer Culture, Communication Review*, and *Journal of Cultural Economy*. McRobbie's most recently published works are *The Uses of Cultural Studies* (2005), *The Aftermath of Feminism* (2008), and *Be Creative* (2015).

ERIK MEGANCK studied philosophy, theology, and psychology in Leuven, Antwerpen, Gent, and Rome. He wrote a dissertation titled *From Veritas to Caritas: On Nietzsche, Heidegger, Derrida, and Vattimo*. His research and publications deal mostly with contemporary continental thought, the critique of metaphysics, and philosophy of religion. Forthcoming publications are "Re-Telling Faith: A Contemporary Philosophical Redraft of Christianity as Hermeneutics," in *New Blackfriars*; "Ratio Est Fides: Contemporary Philosophy as Virtuous Thought," in *International Journal of Philosophy and Theology*; and "'Spem in Aliud . . .': What (Other) May I Hope For?" in *Ethical Perspectives*. He also coordinates the teaching and research department of the social doctrine of the Church at International Institute Canon Triest.

GERT-JAN MEYNTJENS is a PhD researcher at the research unit for literary and cultural studies of the University of Leuven. Besides teaching in the MA programs of cultural studies and Western literature, he is currently conducting research on the poetics and institutional embeddedness of French creative writing workshops and handbooks. An article based on this research and concerning the author François Bon will be published in *Nottingham French Studies*. Apart from French literature and literary and cultural theory, his other areas of interest are theories of (post-Fordist) work, craftsmanship, and leisure.

JEAN-LUC NANCY was professor of philosophy at the Université de Strasbourg. He has written and contributed to over a hundred books, articles, and interviews. He has written about philosophy, psychoanalysis, art, politics, and religion. He stands in the tradition of Nietzsche, Heidegger, Blanchot, Bataille, and his friend Derrida. Together with his friend and coauthor Philippe Lacoue-Labarthe, he set up the famous colloquium on Derrida "Les Fins de l'Homme" and subsequently the Centre de Recherches Philosophiques sur la Politique, which was closed down four years later. Some of his publications are *Being Singular Plural* (2000); *The Inoperative Community* (1991); *The Sense of the World* (1998); *The Creation of the World or Globalization* (2007); *Corpus* (2008); and the two volumes of *The Deconstruction of Christianity*, *Dis-Enclosure* (2008) and *Adoration* (2012).

ANTONIO NEGRI is an Italian political theorist, philosopher, and activist. After his involvement with the Autonomia Operaio movement and the subsequent trial, he went into exile in France. He is mostly known for the trilogy he wrote together with Michael Hardt: *Empire* (2000), *Multitude: War and Democracy in the Age of Empire* (2004), and *Commonwealth* (2009). Some of his other books are *Time for Revolution* (2003), *Political Descartes: Reason, Ideology, and the Bourgeois Project* (2007), and *The Savage Anomaly: The Power of Spinoza's Metaphysics and Politics* (1991).

HEIDI PEETERS is a postdoctoral researcher in cultural studies and literary theory at the University of Leuven. She completed her PhD on the topic of novelization—the adaptation of a film or television series into a novel or another written format. She has published on novelization, on word and image interactions, Peter Greenaway's *Tulse Luper Suitcases*, the semiotics of music videos, the specificity of the photographic medium, multimodality in adaptation, the audiovisual poetry of Pierre Alferi, documentary cinema, and fan fiction. She has taught courses on film and literature (KU Leuven), semiotics of film and photography (Luca School of Arts, Genk), and theory of visual communication (University of Antwerp). Her current research is embedded within the international Literature and Media Innovation (LMI) research team and deals with the phenomenon of manuals for creative writing and screenwriting.

JACQUES RANCIÈRE is a French philosopher, teaching at the European Graduate School and the University of Paris St-Denis. He is especially influential because of his political theory and theories about aesthetics. Some of his most famous books are *The Ignorant Schoolmaster: Five Lessons in Intellectual Emancipation* (1991), *Disagreement: Politics and Philosophy* (2004), *The Politics of Aesthetics: The Distribution of the Sensible* (2006), *Proletarian Nights: The Workers' Dream in Nineteenth-Century France* (2012), *The Future of the Image* (2009), *Aisthesis: Scenes from the Aesthetic Regime of Art* (2013), and *The Emancipated Spectator* (2009).

SASKIA SASSEN is Robert S. Lynd professor of sociology at Columbia University and centennial visiting professor at the London School of Economics. Her work mainly focuses on issues related to urbanization, globalization, and international migration. She is the author of eight books, including *The Global City: New York, London, Tokyo* (1991) and *Territory, Authority, Rights: From Medieval to Global Assemblages* (2006). In her latest book, *Expulsions: Brutality and Complexity in the Global Economy* (2014), she argues that contemporary globalization is linked with various types of systemic expulsions, exemplified both in environmental issues and in the recent financial crises. She is currently working on a new book, *Ungoverned Territories*.

MASSIMILIANO SIMONS is a PhD student at the Institute of Philosophy of the University of Leuven, Belgium, funded by the Research Foundation—Flanders (FWO). He is associated with the Centre for Metaphysics, Philosophy of Religion, and Philosophy of Culture. His research explores the different conceptions of constructivist claims concerning nature and science, related to the fields of synthetic biology and metagenomics. His most recent publications are "The End and Rebirth of Nature?: From Politics of Nature to Synthetic Biology," *Philosophica* 47 (2016): 109–24, and "Beyond Ideology: Althusser, Foucault, and French Epistemology," *Pulse: A Journal of History, Sociology, and Philosophy of Science* 3 (2015): 62–77.

EVELIEN VAN BEECK has a degree in family sciences and master's degree obtained at the Institute of Philosophy of the University of Leuven. Her research focuses on the reenchantment of the world within the tradition of the critique of metaphysics from Nietzsche to Nancy.

ARNE VANRAES is a doctoral researcher at the University of Leuven, funded by the Research Foundation—Flanders (FWO), mainly active in the fields of cultural studies, literary studies, and dance studies. He has done dramaturgical work in dance and currently teaches theory of contemporary dance at the KU Leuven. His recent publications deal with affect theory and literature and with kinesthetic empathy in Butoh. At present, Arne is collaborating on a book about the literary advice industry and is preparing articles on handbooks for creative writing. The topic of his doctoral thesis is the notebooks (theorized as *nodebooks*) of Roland Barthes, Hélène Cixous, and Bracha Ettinger.

JOSEPH VOGL is a German philosopher, literary theorist, and media theorist. He is professor at Humboldt University in Berlin and visiting professor at Princeton University. His works in English include *The Ascendancy of Finance* (2017), *The Specter of Capital* (Stanford UP, 2014), and *On Tarrying* (2011); his works in German include *Kalkül und Leidenschaft: Poetik des Ökonomischen Menschen* (2008) and *Ort der Gewalt: Kafkas literarische Ethik* (2010).

Index

Ben Ali, Zine El Abidine, xiii
Benjamin, Walter, 178, 184, 187n2, 194
Berlant, Lauren, xxvi
Berlin, xiii, 69, 154–56; Berlin wall,
    5, 17, 195
Berardi, Franco "Bifo," 142
Berlusconi, Silvio, xx, 22, 77
beurs, march of the, 92–93
biopolitics, 24, 36, 37, 189, 195
Black Lives Matter, xii, xxx, 35
Bolivia, xxxi, 89
borders, xii, xvi, 79–80, 106, 115, 143
Bozalek, Vivienne, 28
Braidotti, Rosi, xiv, 1–46
Brazil, xxvii, xxxii, 89–90, 98n2,
    109–10, 143
Brexit, xi, xx, xxi, xxii, 4, 10–11, 16–17,
    23, 30, 98n1, 100–101
BRICS, 11, 89
Brown, Wendy, xxi, 75–86
Bulgaria, 109
Burawoy, Michael, 199
Bush, George W., xx, 72, 77, 137, 144
Butler, Judith, xxi, xxxii, 37–38

Caillois, Roger, 189
Cameron, David, 11, 152
Canada, xiii
capitalism, xv, xvi, xxii, xxiii, xxviii,
    3, 4, 11, 12, 15, 19, 28–30, 45n48, 50,
    57, 70, 79, 81, 83, 94, 95, 97, 99, 106,
    108, 109, 113, 114, 117, 125, 134–36,
    138–40, 142, 144, 159–61, 171,
    174–75, 177, 194; cognitive
    capitalism, 15, 28, 30, 33–35, 42,
    96–97
cartographies, 3, 16, 19, 20, 30,
    31–32, 37
Césaire, Aimé, 8
Chavez, Hugo, 108, 110
Chile, xiii
China, 11, 32, 35, 79, 95, 113, 136, 149,
    160, 182, 186

Chirac, François, xxiii
Chomsky, Noam, 34
Christianity, 165–66, 169–70, 174–75,
    178, 181
Ciudadanos (Spain), 103, 112n6
Clausewitz, Carl von, 142
Clinton, Hillary, xxi, 11, 13, 16, 112,
    123–24, 133n6
Coetzee, John Maxwell, 32
Cold War, 2, 5, 6, 7, 57
colonialism, 1, 5, 6, 8, 16, 17, 22–23, 28,
    31–32, 35, 57, 71, 80, 88, 91, 134, 143,
    144, 160; decolonization, 2, 10, 15,
    28, 30, 31, 57, 88, 160
common(s), xxxi–xxxii, 13, 29–30, 89,
    92, 95–97, 188
communism, 6, 8, 9, 49, 51, 60, 102,
    117, 138, 169, 179; in Italy, 93, 98n5;
    Parti communiste française
    (France), 50
communitarianism, 47, 58, 59, 189, 195
community, xxvi, xxvii, 5, 10, 19, 27,
    35, 36, 114, 150–51, 155, 156, 165,
    178, 188–202
Conservative Party (UK), xxiii, 104, 148
constituent power, xxxvn10, 89–90
Cooper, Melinda, 37
Corbyn, Jeremy, xviii, 103–4, 111,
    112n8. *See also* social democracy
Correa, Rafael, 108
corruption, xxvii, 57, 90, 91–92,
    103, 110
creative industries, 149, 151
creativity dispositive, 146–48
crisis, xi–xii, xiv–xix, xxii–xxiii,
    xxxii, 1–4, 16, 22–24, 50, 56–57,
    61–72, 74, 82, 89, 90, 96, 104, 108,
    125, 139, 159–66, 169, 171–72, 188,
    201; as a cultural notion, xiv, 63;
    financial crisis, xi, xviii, 22, 65, 74,
    84, 108, 113, 118–19, 121–23, 126,
    130–31, 134–35, 138, 148, 188, 196,
    198; as a legal notion, xiv, 61–62; as

a medical notion, xiv, 61–63, 65,
161; as a military notion, xiv,
61–62; oil crisis of 1973, 159–60;
refugee crisis, xi, xvi, xxii, 57–58,
64, 80, 99, 104–6, 108; of sovereign
debt, xi, xxii, 137; as a theological
notion, xiv, 68
critique, xvii–xviii, xix, xxx, 2, 4, 6–7,
8, 16, 20, 21, 29, 30, 31, 33, 35, 40,
65, 102, 141, 149, 161–62, 165
Czech Republic, 10

Darwin, Charles, 7
Davis, Angela, 150
debt, xi, xxii, 13, 15, 22, 66, 71, 74, 84,
85, 109, 113, 118, 125, 126, 131,
134–35, 137, 138–39, 141, 143, 190,
192, 194
Deleuze, Gilles, 3, 4, 6, 14, 15, 17–21,
25–27, 33, 35–38, 41, 135, 136, 139,
140, 142
democracy, xii, xv, xxi–xxii, xxiv, xxv,
6, 7, 9, 11, 14, 22, 27, 28, 35–36,
49–53, 73, 74n1, 75, 76–85, 88–89,
91–93, 96, 101, 109, 110, 111, 174,
180, 183; de-democratization, 77
Democratic Party (U.S.), 123–24
Denmark, 100, 143
Derrida, Jacques, 1, 6, 14, 78, 180
Descartes, René, 171
d'Estaing, Valéry Giscard, 160
de Gaulle, Charles, 160
dialectics, 3, 12, 18, 21, 33, 40, 41, 161,
190, 193, 195
DiEM25, xxv, 34n16, 124
Digital Humanities, 28, 33, 34
dissensus, 58
Divine Comedy (Dante), 169
Duchamp, Marcel, 140–41, 142

echo groups, 74
economic cleansing, 125, 128,
129, 131

Ecuador, xxi
Egypt, xii, xiii, xxx, xxxi, 107, 173
elections, xx, xxiii–xxiv, xxix, 79, 89,
93, 99, 102, 107, 111, 123, 137
el-Sisi, Abdel Fattah, 107
emancipation, 8, 24, 39, 52–53, 55–56,
75, 82, 170, 173, 197
environmental humanities, 34
Erdoğan, Recep Tayyip, 106
Errejon, Iñigo, xxxivn8, 92, 98n4
Essed, Philomena, 16
Esposito, Roberto, 24, 37, 188–202
Executioner's Song, The (Mailer),
180
Europe, xi, xviii, xxi, xxii, 1–2, 4–8,
16, 17, 23–24, 28, 64, 66, 71, 73, 74,
79, 80, 87–89, 94, 95, 99–103,
104–6, 107–9, 110, 115, 124, 126,
129, 131, 136, 137–38, 141, 142–44,
147, 152, 154, 156–57, 159, 160, 164,
172, 174, 182, 189, 191, 194, 196;
Eurocentrism, 7–12; European
Union, xi, xii, xv–xvi, xviii, xxi,
xxii–xxiii, xxv, xxviii, xxix, 7–8,
10–11, 13, 14, 16, 23–24, 32, 34, 36,
43n13, 87–89, 96, 98n1, 99–103,
106, 108–9, 112n2, 156;
Euroskepticism, 10–11, 16
expulsions, 113–18, 124, 125, 128

fascism, 5–8, 12, 17–18, 22, 24–26, 36,
76, 143, 144
family, 83, 114, 122, 126, 151–53, 157,
160, 167–68, 178, 180, 186
Fanon, Frantz, 8
Faust II (Goethe), 69
Federal Reserve, 120–122
feminism, xxx, 2, 8–9, 16, 21, 22, 24,
25, 35, 39, 147; postfeminism, xxx
financialization, 82–84, 121
Finland, 13
First World War, 63, 69, 137,
140, 144

National Socialism, 5, 7, 22, 66, 143, 173

NATO, 100, 111

necropolitics, 8, 38

Negri, Antonio, xxix, xxxvn10, 87–98, 139

neoliberalism, xvii, xviii, xxvii, xxx, 2, 4, 11–13, 29–32, 35, 56, 66, 75–83, 87–88, 103, 108–10, 119, 122, 123, 125, 137, 138, 142–45, 146–47, 150, 151, 154, 156, 195

neomaterialism, 4, 18, 19, 33, 41

Netherlands, the, xiii, 9, 13, 16, 32, 100, 172

New Democracy (Greece), xii

New Keywords Collective, xv–xvi

New Spirit of Capitalism, The (Boltanski and Chiapello), xxix, 154

Nietzsche, Friedrich, 5, 14, 16, 135, 175

nomadism, 3, 19–21, 25, 28, 29, 33, 41–42

Nuit Debout, xxiv, 27, 73, 92

Nussbaum, Martha, 29

Nuttall, Sarah, 28

Obama, Barack, xx, 105, 112, 124

Occupy, xii, xxiv, xxxiii, 27, 32, 39, 50–53, 58, 75, 76, 90–91, 110–11, 149, 155; Blockuppy, xxvii

Oedipus Rex (Sophocles), 63, 68

organization, xiv, xix, xxii, xxiv–xxvii, xxix, xxxiii–xxxiv, 51, 53–55, 57, 74, 80, 82, 89, 94–95, 99, 102, 114, 137–39, 142, 190, 193, 194

Paine, Thomas, 62

Parikka, Jussi, 27

Partido Popular (Spain), 112n1, 112n5

Partij voor de Vrijheid (Netherlands), xxi

Pascal, Blaise, 171

Pasolini, Pier Paolo, 8

Patton, Paul, 37

pedagogy, 31, 148

people, the, xxi–xxii, xxxii, 75–76, 79, 91, 176

Peru, xxxi

Piketty, Thomas, 14

Pirate Party, 73

Plato, 165, 174

police violence, xii, xxx

political, the, xxxivn8, 18, 27, 81, 111,

Podemos (Spain), xii, xxv, xxvii, xxxivn8, 12, 51–52, 74, 90–92, 98n4. *See also* Errejon, Iñigo; Iglesias, Pablo

Poland, 102–3, 111, 137–38, 139

political modernity, 36, 82

Pompidou, Georges, 160

Pope Francis, 197–99, 201

Popular Unity (Greece), 101, 112n4

populism, xxi, 4, 12–14, 16–17, 24–26, 32, 72–73, 75–77, 130, 172

Portugal, 66, 99, 100, 138

posthumanism, 19, 29–42, 84; critical posthumanities, 31–36, 42

posttruth, 14, 26

Povinelli, Elizabeth, 41

power, xiii, xviii, xxi, xxv, xxvii, xxxivn8, xxxvn10, 3, 6, 11, 12, 15, 16, 19–21, 22, 24, 29, 30, 40, 49, 50, 52, 53, 55, 63, 65, 67–68, 70, 72, 75–76, 78, 81, 89–92, 119, 134–35, 137, 143, 148, 171, 175, 176, 177, 181, 192, 194, 197

precarity, 29, 30, 45n48, 79, 141–42, 150–53, 197

prisoners, long-term, 117–18, 150

public intellectuals, xix, 11, 55

racism, xxi, xxx, 8–10, 15, 16, 22–24, 39, 40, 48–49, 71, 85, 93, 105, 143

Rajoy Brey, Mariano, 103, 112n5

Rancière, Jacques, xv, xvi, xviii, xxv, 47–60, 139

Turanskyj, Tajana, 151
Turkey, xii, xiii, 106

Ubu Roi (Jarry), 70
UKIP (UK), xxi, 16–17
Ukraine, xxx
UN, 118, 133n3
UNESCO, 30
United Kingdom, xiii, xviii, xx, xxi,
 xxiii, 10, 16, 23, 80, 132, 140, 144,
 147, 153, 156
United States, xii, xxi, xxx, 8, 13, 31,
 37, 50, 58, 62, 73, 77, 100, 107, 108,
 110–11, 115, 117–18, 120, 129,
 130–32, 136, 140, 144, 180
universalism, 5, 31, 58–59, 72, 77,
 182–83
university, the, xiii, 3, 8, 12–15,
 28–36, 84–85, 96–97, 141, 147–48,
 195
Unresticted Warfare (Qiao Liang and
 Wang Xiangsui), 135

Venezuela, 89, 108–10
Varoufakis, Iannis, xii, xxv, 11, 100,
 124
Vattimo, Gianni, 185
violence, xii, xxx, xxxi, 6, 18, 23, 24,
 26, 39, 79, 176, 178–79, 184–86,
 187n2, 191, 199, 200
virtual, the, 4, 18–21, 23, 25, 27, 42, 195
Vogl, Joseph, xiv, xvii, 61–74

Wall Street, xxvii
Wacquant, Loic, 150
war, xi, xiii, 11, 22, 23, 61, 68–69, 77,
 88, 104–5, 108, 134–40, 142–44
war machine, 136, 138–40, 142
Warren, Elizabeth, 123–24
Wekker, Gloria, 16
welfare system, the, 104, 146, 152, 157,
 199
Westwood, Vivienne, 156
Wilders, Geert, 17, 24, 32, 75
work, 12, 55–56, 57, 83, 91, 92, 94, 95,
 97–98, 105–6, 140–41, 142, 146–47,
 150–53, 157, 186, 198–99;
 automatization of, 94–95; labor
 movement, 49, 51, 76; labor reform,
 146–47, 153; refusal of, 94–95,
 140–41; relocation of, 95
workerism (*operaismo*), 90, 94, 140
World Economic Forum, xxvii
WTO, xxvii

Xenofeminism, 35
Xenophobia, xxi, xxiii, 8, 11, 23–26,
 36, 80, 104–5

Yeltsin, Boris, xx
Yemen, xii, 108

Zimbabwe, 105
Žižek, Slavoj, xxvii, 11, 15, 36, 71, 81
Zoé-egalitarianism, 36, 41